DUST

AND

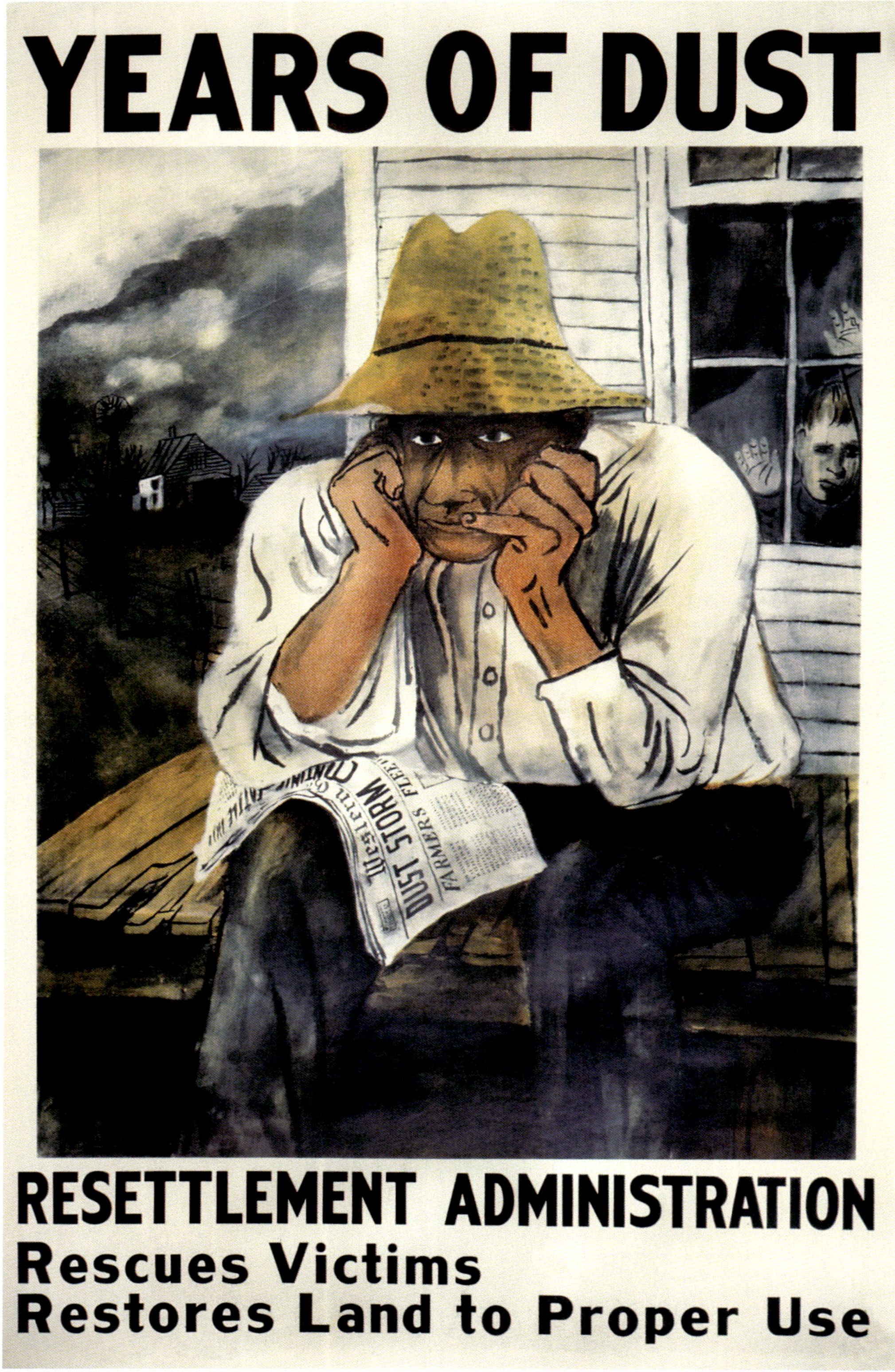
YEARS OF DUST
DUST STORM
RESETTLEMENT ADMINISTRATION
Rescues Victims
Restores Land to Proper Use

COLUMNS

MAIN

Cabinet

181 Wyckoff Street
Brooklyn NY 11217
tel + 1 718 222 8434
fax + 1 718 222 3700
email info@cabinetmagazine.org
www.cabinetmagazine.org

Fall 2009, issue 35

Printed in Belgium by the immaculate staff of Die Keure.

Cabinet (USPS # 020-348, ISSN 1531-1430) is a quarterly magazine published by Immaterial Incorporated, 181 Wyckoff Street, Brooklyn, NY 11217. Periodicals Postage paid at Brooklyn, NY and additional mailing offices.

Postmaster
Please send address changes to Cabinet, 181 Wyckoff Street, Brooklyn, NY 11217.

Subscriptions
1 year (4 issues): US $32, Canada $38, Western Europe $40, Elsewhere $50
2 years (8 issues): US $60, Canada $72, Western Europe $76, Elsewhere $96

Email subscriptions@cabinetmagazine.org or call + 1 718 222 8434.
Subscriptions address: 181 Wyckoff Street, Brooklyn, NY 11217, USA
Please either send a check in US dollars made out to "Cabinet," or mail, fax, or email us your Visa/MC/AmEx/Discover information. Subscriptions are also available online at www.cabinetmagazine.org/subscribe or through Paypal (paypal@cabinetmagazine.org).

Institutional subscriptions are available through EBSCO or Swets, or via our website. Different rates apply.

Advertising
Email advertising@cabinetmagazine.org or call + 1 718 222 8434.

Distribution
Cabinet is available in the US and Canada through Disticor, which distributes both using its own network and through Ingram, Source Interlink, Armadillo News, Ubiquity, Hudson News, Small Changes, Last Gasp, Emma Marian Ltd, Cowley Distribution, Kent News, LMPI, MSolutions, The News Group, Don Olson Distribution, and Chris Stadler Distribution. If you'd like to use one of these distributors, contact Melanie Raucci at Disticor. Tel: + 1 631 587 1160, Email: mraucci@disticor.com.

Cabinet is available in Europe and elsewhere through Central Books, London. Email: orders@centralbooks.com.

A version of Cabinet printed as a book (and sporting an ISBN) is available through D.A.P./ Distributed Art Publishers. To order through DAP, call + 1 212 627 1999 or email dap@dapinc.com.

Email circulation@cabinetmagazine.org or call + 1 718 222 8434 if you need further information.

Submissions
See <www.cabinetmagazine.org/information/submissions.php>. No paper submissions, please.

Cabinet is a non-profit 501 (c) (3) magazine published by Immaterial Incorporated. Our survival is dependent on support from foundations and generous individuals. Please consider supporting us at whatever level you can. Contributions to Cabinet are fully tax-deductible for those who pay taxes to Uncle Sam. All donations are acknowledged online. Donations of $25 or more will be noted in the next possible issue, and those above $100 will be noted for four consecutive issues. Checks should be made out to "Cabinet" and sent to our office address. Please mark the envelope, "Do not let this gather dust."

Cabinet wishes to thank the following visionary foundations and individuals for their support of our activities during 2009. Additionally, we will forever be indebted to the extraordinary contribution of the Flora Family Foundation from 1999 to 2004; without their generous support, this publication would not exist. We would also like to extend our enormous gratitude to the Orphiflamme Foundation for a recent generous donation.

$50,000
The Andy Warhol Foundation for the Visual Arts
The Lambent Foundation

$10,000 - $14,999
The New York City Department of Cultural Affairs
The New York State Council on the Arts
The National Endowment for the Arts
Stina & Herant Katchadourian
The Peter Norton Family Foundation

$5,000 - $9,999
Suzy Coue-Wilson & Edward Wilson
The Danielson Foundation

$2,500 - 3,000
Conor O'Neil
CEC ArtsLink

$1,000
Martha & Thomas G. Armstrong
Elizabeth Arndorfer & Clint Smith

$500 or under
Spencer Finch
Jim Hodges
Deborah Lovely
Paul Ramirez Jonas
James Siena
Debra Singer & Jay Worthington
Kara Vander Weg & Brett Littman
Chris Vroom

$250 or under
Ann & Jim Chamberlain
Fred Clarke
James D. Cox
Jane Crawford
Jeffrey Cunard
Diane Freeman & Bob Wells
Steven Igou
Ben Marcus
Julia Meltzer
Helen Mirra
Jason Olin
Pelli Clarke Pelli Architects
Jocelyn Prince & Lucky Leone
Jonathan Rabinowitz
Jim Shaw
Linnaea Tillett

$100 or under
Mark Allen
Siemon Allen
Eshrat Erfanian
George Ganat
Jeffrey Lependorf
John Muse
Judith Schaechter
Gretchen Schaffner
Mono Schwarz-Kogelnik
Robert Ulbing

Cover: Airport employees sweep the red carpet during a sandstorm in preparation for the arrival of French President Nicolas Sarkozy at Kuwait International Airport, 11 February 2009. Photo Remy de la Mauviniere/AFP/ Getty Images.

Page 4: Ben Shahn, *Years of Dust*, 1937. Beginning in the early 1930s, areas of the US experienced a severe drought that brought huge dust storms to parts of the Midwest and southern plains. In 1935, Franklin D. Roosevelt's government created the Resettlement Administration (later known as the Farm Security Administration) to help alleviate the rural poverty that resulted from the dust storms and the Depression. This poster publicizing the program is believed to be the first designed by the artist. Courtesy Franklin D. Roosevelt Presidential Library and Museum / NARA.

CONTRIBUTORS

Magnus Bärtås, an artist and writer, is professor of fine art at Konstfack in Stockholm. Together with Fredrik Ekman, he has published two books of essays, *Orienterarsjukan och andra berättelser* and *Innanför cirkeln* (Bokförlaget DN, 2001 and 2005, respectively). He has recently participated in group shows at the Zendai Museum of Modern Art in Shanghai, the Museum on the Seam in Jerusalem, the Miroslav Kraljevic Gallery in Zagreb, and the Seoul Photo Fair.

D. Graham Burnett is an editor at *Cabinet* (at whose event space he co-hosts the monthly Poetry Lab) and a member of the faculty at Princeton University (at which he teaches history of science). He is the author of several books, including *Descartes and the Hyperbolic Quest* (American Philosophical Society, 2005), *A Trial By Jury* (Knopf, 2001), and *Masters of All They Surveyed* (Chicago, 2000).

Alexandra Cardia is a graduate student at New York University's Arthur L. Carter Journalism Institute.

Colby Chamberlain is a Jacob K. Javits Fellow in the art history department at Columbia University. A former managing editor of *Cabinet*, he is a senior editor for the online magazine *Triple Canopy*.

Steven Connor is Director of the London Consortium and a critic and broadcaster. He is the author of many books on literary and cultural history, including *Dumbstruck* (2000), *The Book of Skin* (2003) and *Fly* (2006). His *Paraphernalia: A Metaphysics of Unremarkable Things*, is forthcoming from Profile Books. His website at <www.stevenconnor.com> gives access to many of his essays, talks, and broadcasts.

Brian Dillon is UK editor of *Cabinet* and AHRC Research Fellow in the Creative and Performing Arts at the University of Kent. The US edition of his book *Tormented Hope: Nine Hypochondriac Lives* (Penguin, 2009) will be published by Farrar, Straus and Giroux as *The Hypochondriacs* in spring 2010. A novella, *Sanctuary*, will be published by Sternberg Press later in the year. He is the author of a memoir, *In the Dark Room* (Penguin, 2005) and a regular contributor to the *Guardian*, the *London Review of Books*, *Frieze*, *Tate etc.*, and the *Wire*.

Jeff Dolven teaches English at Princeton University. He is the author of *Scenes of Instruction* (University of Chicago Press, 2007), and his poems have been published in the *Paris Review*, the *Times Literary Supplement*, and elsewhere. With D. Graham Burnett, he organizes the Poetry Lab series at *Cabinet*'s event space.

Melissa Dubbin and Aaron S. Davidson are artists based in Brooklyn. Their latest project, *Fallen Books*, was designed by Francesca Grassi and published by onestar press. Their work can be seen at <www.dubbin-davidson.com>.

Jean Duprat is a nuclear astrophysicist at the Centre de la Recherche Scientifique (CSNSM-CNRS) in Orsay, University of Paris XI. He is responsible for the French program of micrometeorite research in Antarctica and is leading a team that studies the chemical and isotopic composition of these particles.

Fredrik Ekman is a writer, librettist, and editor. Together with Magnus Bärtås, he has published two books of essays, *Orienterarsjukan och andra berättelser* and *Innanför cirkeln* (Bokförlaget DN, 2001 and 2005, respectively). With composer Erik Mikael Karlsson, he has produced a number of electro-acoustic pieces and musical radio dramas, notably *Night of Enchantment* and *Die Hoffmann-maschine*.

Raiford Guins is assistant professor of digital cultural studies in the Department of Comparative Literary and Cultural Studies and Consortium for Digital Arts, Culture, and Technology (cDACT) at SUNY Stony Brook. He is a founding principal editor for the *Journal of Visual Culture*, author of *Edited Clean Version: Technology and the Culture of Control* (University of Minnesota Press, 2009), and co-editor of *The Object Reader* (Routledge, 2009) and *Popular Culture: A Reader* (Sage, 2005). He is currently writing a book on video game history and preservation.

Daniel Heller-Roazen teaches at Princeton University. He is the author of *The Inner Touch: Archaeology of a Sensation* (Zone Books, 2007), *Echolalias: On the Forgetting of Language* (Zone Books, 2005), and *Fortune's Faces: The Roman de la Rose and the Poetics of Contingency* (Johns Hopkins University Press, 2003). His essay in this issue is drawn from his new book *The Enemy of All: Piracy and the Law of Nations* (Zone Books, 2009).

Adam Jasper recently completed a dissertation on minor aesthetic categories. He is a contributor to *Frieze*, *Art Review*, and *Art & Australia*, among others.

Rebar is a San Francisco-based studio operating at the intersection of art, design, and activism. In addition to the Cabinet National Library, Rebar is known as the inventor of PARK(ing) Day, an annual, one-day global event where artists, activists, and citizens convert metered parking spaces into temporary public parks. Rebar has lectured and exhibited at venues worldwide, including the 2008 Venice Architecture Biennale and ISEA 2009 in Dublin. For more information, see <www.rebargroup.org>.

Dorion Sagan is a writer based in Toronto and Amherst, Massachusetts. He has co-authored *What is Life?* (University of California Press, 2000) with Lynn Margulis, *Into the Cool* (University of Chicago Press, 2006) with Eric D. Schneider, and *Death & Sex* (Chelsea Green Publishing, 2009) with Tyler Volk.

Arielle Saiber is associate professor of Italian at Bowdoin College. Her publications include essays on Dante, medieval and Renaissance mathematics, Renaissance typography, genre theory, and electronic music; a co-edited volume of primary documents, *Images of Quattrocento Florence* (Yale University Press, 2000); and *Giordano Bruno and the Geometry of Language* (Ashgate, 2005). She is currently writing a book on the dialogue between mathematics and literature in early modern Italy.

Justin E. H. Smith teaches history of philosophy and history of science at Concordia University in Montreal. He is currently writing a satirical novel about Soviet ethnography, entitled *Nâk*. An extensive archive of his writing can be found at <www.jehsmith.com>.

Valerie Smith is the director of visual arts, media, and film at Haus der Kulturen der Welt in Berlin, where she recently curated the exhibition "Rational/Irrational." She is currently working on a project about rage.

Rebecca L. Spang teaches history at Indiana University. Her book *The Invention of the Restaurant* (Harvard University Press, 2000) has appeared in Portuguese, Brazilian, Japanese, Turkish, and Greek editions. She is currently interested in money.

Emily Thompson is a historian of technology at Princeton University. She is the author of *The Soundscape of Modernity: Architectural Acoustics and the Culture of Listening in America, 1900–1933* (The MIT Press, 2002). Her current research explores the transition from silent to sound motion pictures in the American film industry.

Christopher Turner is an editor of *Cabinet*. His book, *Adventures in the Orgasmatron: How the Sexual Revolution Came To America*, is forthcoming from Farrar, Straus and Giroux.

W. J. Walter lives in Paris.

Susanna Whatman (1752–1814), the wife of English papermaker James Whatman, was the mistress of Turkey Court in Kent. In 1777, she began to compile a book to instruct her servants on housekeeping.

COLUMNS

"Ingestion" is a column that explores food within a framework informed by aesthetics, history, and philosophy. / "Inventory" examines or presents a list, catalogue, or register. / "Colors" features a writer's response to a specific color assigned by the editors of Cabinet. / "Leftovers" investigates the cultural significance of detritus.

INGESTION / PULLING A RABBIT OUT OF A CAT

REBECCA L. SPANG

In late May 1838, the Paris press was rife with alarming headlines. "Horrible massacre of the Innocents! Blood, blood, and still more blood!" screamed the often rather stodgy *Constitutionnel*, while the *Gazette des tribunaux* (which reported legal cases) whispered of the mounting terror occasioned by a series of dastardly killings.[1] As these and many other graphic accounts made clear, Paris was once again awash in blood—cat blood, that was, for brave police commissioner Vassal had apprehended a gang of cat butchers who made their living selling cat pelts to furriers and feline filets to the *gargotiers* who operated the city's cheapest restaurants.

This tale—replete with severed heads, melting fat, and fur-strewn floors—was reprinted by at least eight of the major Paris-based dailies, with the notable exceptions of the *Moniteur universel* and the *Journal des débats* (the government's official and quasi-official organs). Why such widespread coverage?

As a historian of restaurants, I was initially inclined to see public fascination with the arrest and trial of Brutus Bezoni's gang as fueled by the strict separation of dining room from kitchen found in most restaurants—a yawning divide traversed only by the waiter. Never meeting, or even glimpsing, the cook, and seeing his or her dinner only in its fully sauced and prepared state, how was the ordinary restaurant customer to discern all of the *plat du jour*'s ingredients?

Gibelotte de lapin, like other stews, posed a particular problem of interpretation: made from a rabbit cut into small, uniform pieces and simmered with bacon, mushrooms, eels, and onions in white wine and bouillon, the *gibelotte* appeared on the customer's plate coated in a flavor-masking sauce.[2] Though the dish's name referred to its primary ingredient (*gibier* means "game," and *lapin*, "rabbit"), the sauce was its exemplary feature. Unable to penetrate the "fiery hell" of the restaurant kitchen, how was the eater to know what mysterious rituals had been performed in the preparation of his or her dinner, which animals sacrificed to what unknown gods? While printed menus bearing the words *gibelotte de lapin* seemed to offer the diner some assurance, guides to Parisian life insisted that in all but the most expensive restaurants, menus more closely resembled works of escapist fiction than accurate renderings of the kitchen's contents. Fish on the menu, but none in the kitchen; rabbits on the menu and cats in the stewpot—such were the hazards to which restaurant dining exposed the unwary eater.[3]

Croquades faites à l'audience du 14 nov.
(Cour d'Assises)

Si, pour reconnaître le monarque dans une caricature, vous n'attendez pas qu'il soit désigné autrement que par la ressemblance, vous tomberez dans l'absurde. Voyez ces croquis informes, auxquels j'aurais peut-être dû borner ma défense :

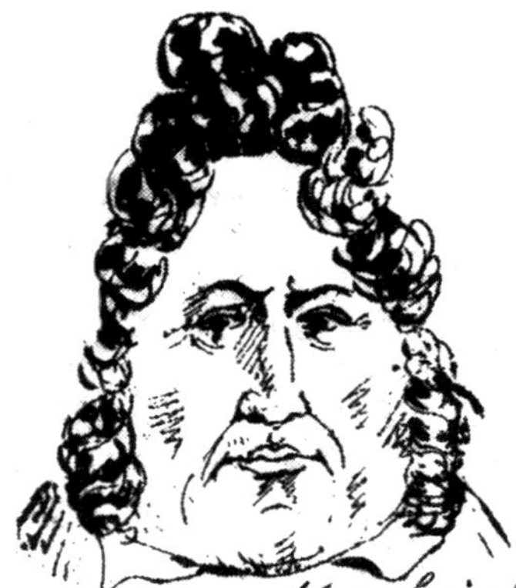

Ce croquis ressemble à Louis Philippe, vous condamnerez donc?

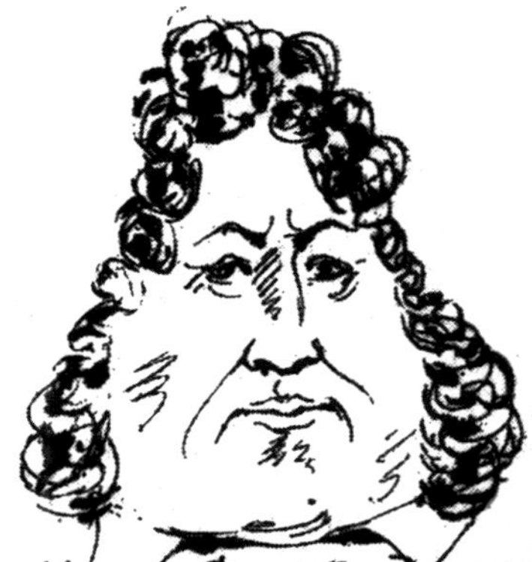

Alors il faudra condamner celui-ci qui ressemble au premier.

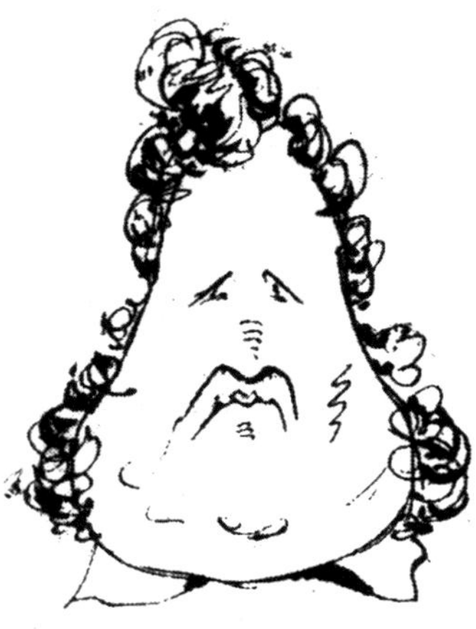

Puis condamner pour cet autre qui ressemble au second...

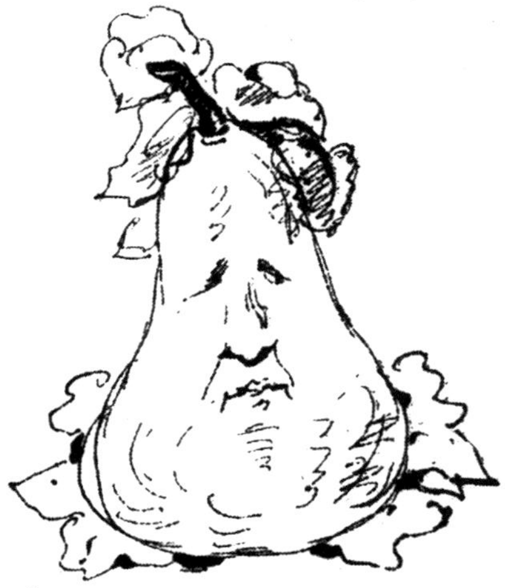

Et enfin, si vous êtes conséquens, vous ne sauriez absoudre cette poire qui ressemble aux croquis précédens.

Ainsi, pour une poire, pour une brioche, et pour toutes les têtes grotesques dans lesquelles le hazard ou la malice aura placé cette triste ressemblance, vous pourrez infliger à l'auteur cinq ans de prison et cinq mille francs d'amende!??

Avouez, Messieurs, que c'est là une singulière liberté de la presse!!

(procès du journal La Caricature) Ch. Philipon

Doubts about restaurateurs' honesty were widespread. Yet something made this one case of fraud a particularly compelling news item in the spring of 1838. If the cat had long been condemned to a rather liminal position in European society,[4] the substitution of cats for rabbits during the reign of Louis Philippe (1830–1848) was a far from marginal subject. Across a host of genres, from Honoré de Balzac's short story, "Peines du coeur d'une chatte anglaise" ("An English Cat's Broken Heart," in which a rakish French tomcat tells a horrified rooftop audience of the suffering inflicted on his friends and relations by unscrupulous restaurateurs) to fashion writing and boulevard dramas, swapping cats for rabbits came near to being a cliché during this period. *Gibelotte de lapin* was, according to many authors, a slightly special dish, but it nonetheless formed the staple diet of *littérateurs*.

The 1838 scandal was hardly the first time that the rumor of cat stew drifted across Paris. Nor was it the last: cat eating would become an emblematic activity of the Prussian siege of 1870–1871, and of the privations endured during the World Wars. In 1872, Pierre Larousse's *Grand dictionnaire universel du XIXe siècle* offered as its sample usage of the word *gibelotte* the truism: "cats lost in Paris are unfailingly consumed in the form of *gibelotte*," while Joseph Favre's *Dictionnaire universel de cuisine pratique* (1883) commented that the rabbit's cleverest trick had been to convince the cat to replace him in the stew pan.[5] But none of this can account for the many columns of print devoted to the felicides of 1838.

In the oft-told tales in which rabbit stew was really cat stew, there existed at least a starkly simple correspondence. The restaurant patron was instructed that *lapin*, in the context of the menu, always meant *chat*—the signifier might seem a bit arbitrary, but it was stable. In the echelon of rabbit qualities established by the emerging nineteenth-century discourses of "taste," however, this potentially reassuring certainty was lost. Within the gastronomic hierarchy, *lapin* actually referred to a whole spectrum of animals with fuzzy tails and floppy ears. Without even getting into the technical terms for newborns, young ones, and adolescents, nineteenth-century rabbits were ranked on a scale of flavor and cost from semi-wild warren rabbits (whose flesh was said to nearly resemble that of hares) to hutch rabbits to those raised in the city in empty barrels, never seeing sun or sky. In this continuum, in this class system ranging from independent country-living aristocrats to an oppressed, tenement-dwelling proletariat, the cat could be seen simply as the very last rung on the rabbit ladder. In the market and in the kitchen, "identity" resulted not from some one-to-one relationship, but from the work of differentiation.[6]

The rabbit hierarchy mimicked the social structure of rabbit eaters. So while an unsophisticated gourmand might contentedly eat a stew made of any sort of rabbit, balking only at cat, the finicky gourmet would rebel at the thought of anything but a semi-wild rabbit, fattened on herbs and aromatic grasses. The line demarcating edible from inedible varied from eater to eater and from context to context—what might seem, in a cheap eatery serving meals for two francs, a reasonably good cut of meat would be immediately rejected in the private dining rooms of an opulent restaurant (where the eater would be lucky to find a single menu item, much less an entire dinner, selling for two francs). "Tell me what you eat, and I shall tell you who you are," Brillat-Savarin had written in 1826, but how to apply that maxim if one did not know what one was eating?[7]

As Sandy Petrey has noted of another famous July Monarchy scandal—the caricature of King Louis Philippe in the shape of a pear—simply saying, "The king is not a pear" made it possible for future speakers to use *pear* to refer, in fact, to the king.[8] In November 1831, editor and artist Charles Philipon was on trial in Paris, charged with having committed "outrages against the person of the king" by depicting Louis Philippe busily obscuring the unfulfilled promises that had brought him to power the previous year.[9] Defending himself, Philipon protested that while the figure he had drawn and published might *look like* the King, resembling that august personage and being him were two very different things indeed. To support his point, Philipon quickly sketched a version of the offending portrait along with three other images. The second drawing looked like the first; a third version resembled the second; and a last like the third—yet who would say that the final one was the King? Instead, as Philipon told the court: "It's a pear!" Since everyone knows that a pear cannot be king, Philipon continued, everyone must also know that the figure in the caricature was not Louis Philippe. Appearances, the cartoonist argued, are deceiving.[10]

Brought together in order to be kept apart, king and pear were henceforth inseparably linked, as connected by the denial of identity as by its assertion. So, too, the gastronomic guide and the rabbit-raiser's handbook brought together all sorts of small quadrupeds in order to tell them apart. But because of the on-going deferral of mammalian identity, and the

opposite: Sketch made by Charles Philipon in court, 14 November 1831.

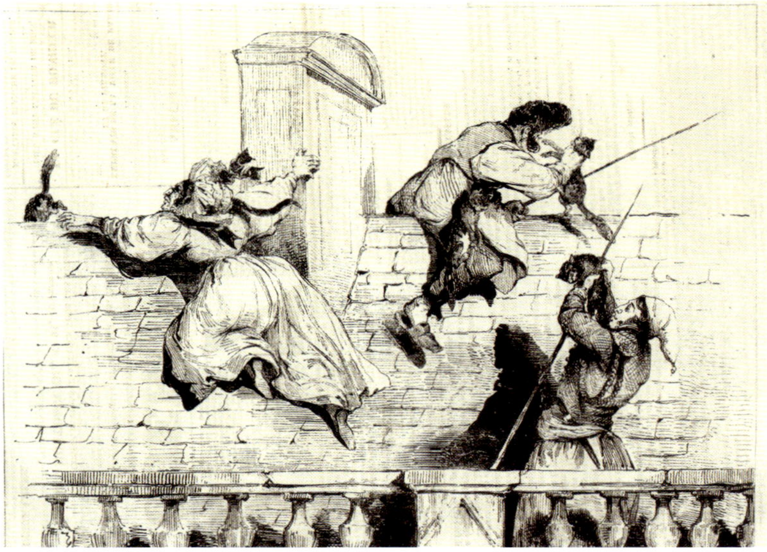

King Louis Philippe and company go hunting. From *Le Charivari*, 1835. Courtesy Houghton Library, Harvard University.

ever-growing specificity of the rabbit-eating market, the rabbit itself was no fixed quantity. Rather, subject to substitution, fraud, and replacement (and to the culinarily sensible practice of using locally available ingredients), the rabbit had a sort of slipperiness rarely considered characteristic of fur-bearing mammals, one that even allowed cats to function as ersatz rabbits.

In the late 1830s, rabbits were just as much in the French news as cats; so much so that one newspaper jested, "It is clear that from now on, the Criminal Court will only consider matters concerning rabbits and pseudo-rabbits," and in January of 1838 (five months before Bezoni's trial), the theatrical journal *Le Corsaire* declared: "Never have rabbits made so much noise."[11] Just what were rabbits doing in the winter of 1838 to make so much noise? It was not so much that the rabbits were being loud, as that a great deal was being said about them and attributed to them. The government's budgets for both 1837 and 1838 had included the not insignificant sum of 70,000 francs to reimburse the Crown for rabbits killed on royal lands during the revolution of 1830. (As they had been during the turmoil of 1789, game animals were among the first victims of the July Revolution.)[12] The Ministry of the Interior had tallied 100,000 rabbits "missing" from the royal forest in 1837, and estimated their value at 14 sous each. While one opposition newspaper quite legitimately inquired how the government had gone about counting "missing" rabbits, the budget item nonetheless remained.[13]

At the same time, the Crown gave only a measly 12,000 francs as its contribution to the relief of the poor of Paris in the horrible winter of 1837–1838.[14] In 1836, the zoologist Geoffroy Saint-Hilaire's tender concern for the living arrangements provided for the newly-arrived orangutan at the Jardin des Plantes had already led more than one republican to quip that Louis Philippe's regime was better for wild animals than it was for people. The discrepancy between the sum to be spent on the Paris poor and that spent on rabbits only reinforced this point. As cats had replaced rabbits in so many stewpans, so rabbits had replaced people in the monarch's heart and budget calculations.

The first substitution, that of cats for rabbits, was technically fraud—the latter, scandal, but one given a particular twist in the pages of the era's best-known illustrated newspaper, Philipon's new satiric daily, *Le Charivari*. Its pages full of "letters from the Crown's rabbits" in 1837, *Le Charivari* was also no stranger to the subject of cat stew. Several years earlier, in the spring and summer of 1835, nearly every week had seen a new mention of *gibelotte de chat*. In its first lengthy exegesis of the cat-rabbit problem, *Le Charivari* used this rumor to political ends, in an article accompanying a lithograph titled "Hunting Hares for the Castle's Table." This image showed three figures—easily recognized by even the most unsophisticated reader as King Louis Philippe, his sister Adelaide, and the cabinet minister Montalivet—on the roof of the Tuileries Palace, hunting cats. Adelaide, in the lower left, grabs at the tail of a fast disappearing tomcat; in the lower right, Montalivet (wearing a chef's bonnet) strangles a luckless feline; at the peak of the roof, Louis Philippe, his belt hung with dead cats, leans comfortably against a chimney as he strangles yet another—the scalp-seeking savages of James Fenimore Cooper had come to life on the palace roof tops. Somebody, the article said, is stealing the cats of Paris; and, as the rumors about vanishing children in the 1750s had suggested that human babies were being sacrificed so that the ailing King Louis XV could bathe in their blood, so now the cats were disappearing to go in the palace's stewpans. By implication, the July Monarchy was so stingy, so eager to drain its people of all they had, that it was even willing to take their cats.

After the passage of the strict censorship laws of September 1835, no more images of the king's cat hunting, per se, appeared. The government's censors, we might conclude, could only protect Louis Philippe by prohibiting depictions of cats, rabbits, and pears as well. Only a week into the new press regime, a proposed caricature on pet keeping in *Le Charivari* was banned, so the editors claimed, because a sitting rabbit, viewed from behind, was said to resemble a pear too closely. The work of satire, like that of the market, depends on substitution and exchange.

When the more "serious" dailies of 1838 reported the cat butcher's trial, it was as if their columns had been invaded by the allegorical animals and satirical stews of *Le Charivari*'s bitter counter-discourse. And yet *Le Charivari*'s explicit political reproach (made before September 1835) was modified and recast. In the widely circulated accounts of cat murder in the rue l'Hôtel de Ville, narrative asides warning readers of the grisly scene behind the as-of-yet-unopened door combined with references to "shadows," "corpses," and "maniacal laughter" to reframe the great kitten fricassee not as satire directed against a political regime, but as a parody of crime reporting, a mockery of murder.

So how then, finally, to understand this episode? Was Brutus Bezoni a real live perpetrator of the criminal acts satirically predicated of the King? Was his trial a referendum on the government? I doubt it. But it seems certain that an image—that of the duplicitous cat-serving cook—that first entered one organ of the daily press (*Le Charivari*) as focused political commentary then re-emerged elsewhere expressing more general social anxiety about the deceptiveness of appearances and the potential duplicity of the marketplace. The image had not been emptied of its political significance; in fact, the widespread attention to the trial and accounts of gastronomic fraud that followed it actually allowed a yet more subtle piece of commentary. In 1843, *Le Charivari* compared Louis Philippe's regime to a 32-sous restaurant—insinuating that the King's was a cat-serving establishment, one where the seeming cornucopia of the printed menu only veiled the corruption in the kitchen.

If the implications of this parallel had been universally agreed upon, if there had been the sort of commonality of understanding that would allow us to say that "Brutus Bezoni symbolized Louis Philippe," or that *lapin* always meant *chat*, then these images and commentaries would have attracted the censor's scissors just as quickly as that poor martyred rabbit whose only crime had been to look a bit pearish. But it was the pear that at this point had become the icon of caricature, the symbol of satire, if you will—so while pears were relentlessly hunted and destroyed, commentary nevertheless survived, striking a tone that often seemed an odd combination of Aesop's fables and *La Cuisinière bourgeoise*.

1 *Le Constitutionnel*, 28 May 1838, p. 3; *Gazette des tribunaux*, 9 April 1838, p. 679, and 27 May 1838, p. 755.

2 This particular recipe is from Alexandre Viart, *Le Cuisinier royal* (Paris: Barba, 1838), p. 237, and is quite similar to those in older books such as *Nouveau traité de la cuisine* (Paris: Saugrain Fils, 1739), vol. 1, p. 363.

3 In one popular play, a group of waiters sing about "fish and fresh vegetables on the menu," until the youngest points out, "but we don't have them in the kitchen!" The owner responds that he had asked if they all had fish and fresh vegetables "on their menus, not in the kitchen." See Xavier and Duvert, *Les Cabinets particuliers* (Paris: Barba, 1832), p. 9. Numerous contemporaneous accounts described the ruses of restaurant life; see my *The Invention of the Restaurant: Paris and Modern Gastronomic Culture* (Cambridge, MA.: Harvard University Press, 2000), chapter 7.

4 Robert Darnton's *The Great Cat Massacre and Other Episodes in French Cultural History* (New York: Vintage, 1985) describes apprentice printers gleefully killing cats in early eighteenth-century France.

5 Pierre Larousse, ed., *Grand dictionnaire universel du XIXe siècle* (Paris: Larousse, 1872), vol. 8, p. 1245; see also the article "Chat," in which he makes an effort to redeem the cat's reputation, vol. 3, pp. 1064–1068, and p. 1245. Joseph Favre, ed., *Dictionnaire universel de cuisine pratique* (Paris: Librairie-Imprimerie des Halles, 1883), p. 1239.

6 A simple semiotic lesson, really. Much as Terry Eagleton tells the readers of his *Literary Theory* that "*cat* is *cat* because it is *not cap* or *bat*," so too a hutch rabbit was a hutch rabbit because it was not a warren rabbit. See Terry Eagleton, *Literary Theory: An Introduction* (Minneapolis: University of Minnesota Press, 1983), p. 127.

7 Jean Anthelme Brillat-Savarin, *Le Physiologie du goût* (Paris: Sautelet, 1826), p. viii.

8 Sandy Petrey, *In the Court of the Pear King* (Ithaca: Cornell University Press, 2005).

9 <www.greatcaricatures.com/articles_galleries/censor/html/1831_0630_replatrage.html>. Accessed 10 August 2009.

10 The court, unpersuaded by this ingenious defense, found Philipon guilty and sentenced him to six months in jail and a stiff fine.

11 *Le Droit*, 8 July 1838, p. 3368; *Le Corsaire*, 27 January 1838, p. 2.

12 Marieke and Pierre Aucante, *Les Braconniers* (Paris: Aubier Montaigne, 1983), pp. 89–95.

13 *La France*, 7 April 1837, p. 2.

14 For comments on the miserliness of the Crown's contribution to the relief of the poor, see *La France*, 29 January 1838, p. 2.

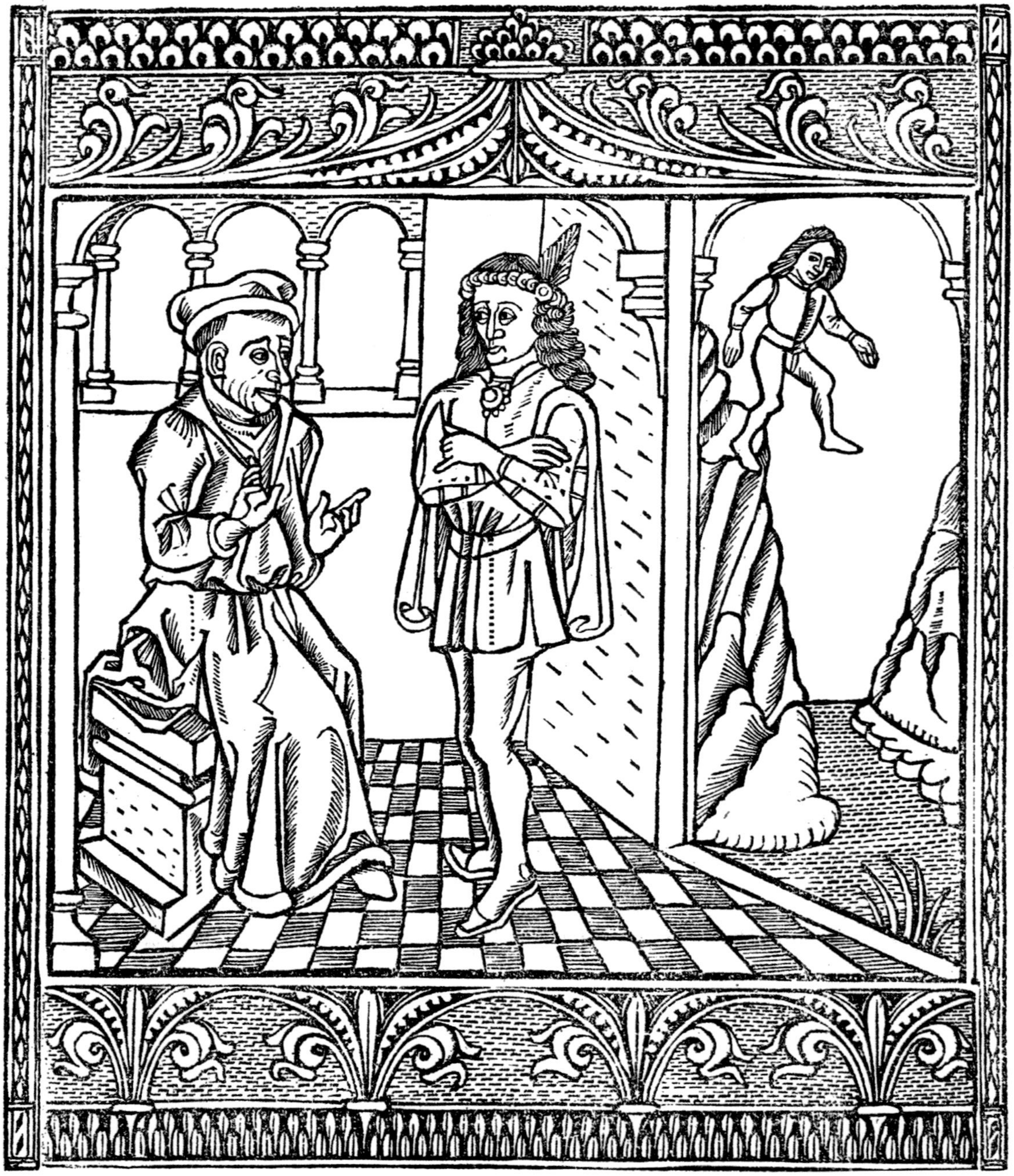

Woodcut illustration accompanying 1485 edition of *Aesopus Moralitus: Vita, Fabulae*. This popular book of moralized tales, most of which involve animals, was among the standard texts used to teach young children to read. In this scene, Aesop is shown attempting to reform his adopted son—who had been caught plotting Aesop's murder—by giving him a series of precepts by which to live. Overcome by guilt, the son throws himself off a steep cliff. Courtesy Metropolitan Museum of Art.

INVENTORY / WHEN IN (RENAISSANCE) ROME...

ARIELLE SAIBER

Nanna (a prostitute): *Suppose there's a nobleman asking for you [to attend a social gathering]. ... You have to know how to talk: answer to the point, don't ramble on. ... Don't sit there looking too gauche or too flirtatious, but carry yourself gracefully. And if there's playing or singing, keep your ears fixed on the music or song, praising the musicians and the singers, even if you don't enjoy it or understand it. And if there's a scholar there, approach him with a cheerful face, showing you appreciate him more—yes, even more—than the master of the house.*

Pippa (Nanna's daughter and an aspiring prostitute): *Why do that?*

Nanna: *Out of respect.*

Pippa: *Oh, come on!*

Nanna: *Why, all you need is for one of those fellows to attack you in writing, and to have the gossip spread everywhere, with those slanderous things they're so good at saying about women.*

Good advice from a fictional prostitute, created by the renowned and feared cultural critic, Pietro Aretino (1492–1556), whose pen could make or break a reputation. Aretino's 1536 text *Il Dialogo*, recently translated as *The School of Whoredom*, is a relentlessly explicit satire of the Renaissance advice book, and the mores of virtually everyone who might seek out such a thing—the aristocracy, landed gentry, commoners, artists, clergy, merchants, military, academics, courtesans, and courtiers.

The Renaissance was a golden age for art and literature, and so too for advice. Before the late fourteenth century, there were some advice manuals but, with the invention of the printing press, the increase in literacy, and the rising importance of vernacular writing, the genre exploded. Across Italy, and especially in cities such as Florence and Venice, the middle- and upper-classes were acquiring a greater sense of personal agency, and discussions of individual "virtuosity" and self-fashioning were often paired with those of moral and civic "virtue." With this came anxiety over the relative merits of high birth and earned status, and in books circulated widely in the newly blossoming print culture, dissimulation came to be openly discussed as a kind of art. The codification of comportment flourished through the dispensation of advice on just about every aspect of body, mind, soul, and property. One wonders how much these advice texts facilitated social reform, and how much they were an instrument of social control; how much they formulated new ideals of doing and being, and how much they reflected what had already evolved.

Advice guides in the Renaissance, while not the money-makers they often are today, came in many formats. Some appeared as small, paperbound print editions, and some as luxury tomes, such as the first edition of Castiglione's *The Courtier*. Some advice books were practical instruction manuals, teaching readers how to do things like mix paint (Cennini), have gorgeous, brilliant children (Marinello, Mercurio), or live long and age well (Zerbi). Some were compilations of rules, like Della Casa's famous *Galateo*, a precursor to Miss Manners, while others drew on advice that had originally appeared in religious sermons, such as those of the famous and frightening Ferrarese monk, Girolamo Savonarola. Some advice appeared in epistolary form intended for a small readership or sole reader, such as Piccolomini's letter for the ten-year-old future King of the Austro-Hungarian Empire. Others—Annibale Guasco's counsel to his daughter, for example, as she embarked on a career as lady-in-waiting to the Infanta, Caterina of Spain—were in fact written with distribution in mind. Advice also took the form of aphorisms (Petrarch's *Remedies*) and preening autobiographies telling "how *I* did it" (Cornaro). Some books, like Giambattista Della Porta's massive compendium of "secrets," were written in Latin and billed as valuable, hard-to-acquire wisdom that should not be spread around, yet were translated immediately into many languages and sold widely. Cookbooks were printed (Maestro Martino, Scappi), as well as many recipe books for beauty products. One famous advice book was written in the hopes of winning back the job of its author, then in exile: Machiavelli's *The Prince*.

Often, advice writing took the form of a dialogue between friends, or between an elder and student or young relative. Less of it was written by women, although they were often subjects (and objects) of the texts, and their avid readers. Much advice pointed to the importance of finding a middle ground or equilibrium. And while biblical references were common, citations from classical authors demonstrating the pedigree of both the advice and the advice-giver were equally frequent. Parodies like Aretino's were not unusual, but the helpful tips listed below were written in all seriousness, despite what reading them in this form might suggest. My advice: *caveat lector*!

If a nobleman asks you for a loan:
I would sooner give him twenty as a gift than a hundred on loan. I would gladly avoid him altogether so as to have to do neither.

—Leon Battista Alberti, *The Family in Renaissance Florence* (ca. 1434–1443)

When choosing what to wear, as a male courtier:
Black is more pleasing in clothing than any other color ... I mean of ordinary attire, for there is no doubt that bright colors are more becoming on armor.

—Baldassare Castiglione, *The Book of the Courtier* (1528)

How to approach, for the first time, a woman you love:
His first words shall test her mind and probe her wish in a manner so ambiguous as to leave her a way of certain escape by making it possible for her to pretend not to see that his talk is actually of love.

—Baldassare Castiglione, *The Book of the Courtier* (1528)

When looking for someone to help you mix ultramarine blue paint:
Beware of elderly women.

—Cennino Cennini, *The Craftsman's Handbook* (fourteenth century)

If you think you might get poisoned at a meal:
Anoint yourself with a special cream or oil around your heart before you go, and once again when you return.

—Isabella Cortese, *Secrets* (1561)

To make a black star appear on the forehead of a white horse:
Get a mole, cook it in water, and beat it finely with an iron tool. Attach the [animal] to the forehead of the horse for a full day and night, and in a few days the hairs below will fall out and black ones will grow in.

—Isabella Cortese, *Secrets* (1561)

After blowing your nose:
You should not open your handkerchief and look inside, as if pearls or rubies might have descended from your brain.

—Giovanni Della Casa, *Galateo* (1558)

How to catch a partridge:
Partridge love deer exceedingly ... thus, if a man put on a deer skin, and the horns upon his head, and come closely to them, they, supposing it is a deer indeed, will entertain him, and draw near to him, and will not fly away, and embrace him as much as one would do a friend come from a long journey. But by this great friendliness, they get nothing but nets and snares.

—Giambattista Della Porta, *Natural Magic* (1589)

How to make a virgin of a deflowered woman:
Make little pills ... of burnt alum and mastic with a little vitriol and orpiment. Make them into very fine powder, that you can scarce feel them ... let them dry, being pressed thin, and lay them on the mouth of the matrix, where it was first broken open. Change it every six hours, always fomenting the place with rain or cistern water. ... [After twenty-four hours] it will here and there make little bladders, which being touched, will bleed much blood, that she can hardly be known from a maid. ... [Alternately,] inject the dried blood of a hare or pigeon, which being moistened by the moisture of the matrix, shows like live, fresh blood.

—Giambattista Della Porta, *Natural Magic* (1589)

To stay young:
Suck the blood of a youth ... an ounce or two from a scarcely opened vein on the left arm ... when the moon is waxing.

—Marsilio Ficino, *Three Books on Life* (1489)

The correct position for the matrimonial act:
The wife must be with her face upwards towards the heavens, and the husband with his face downwards; this will facilitate pregnancy. But how shocking when, by means of diabolical habits and notions, married people do the reverse!

—Frate Cherubino da Siena, *Rules of Married Life* (ca. 1490)

A father, to his daughter, on the current trend:
Don't dye your hair blond.

—Annibale Guasco, *Discourse to Lady Lavinia, His Daughter* (1586)

If you are from Lombardy, but wish to speak well:
Dip a little bit the pencil of your tongue in the fresh and clear color of the Tuscan language, whereby you shadow the stains of our mother tongue, yet so lightly, that your speech is [still] known for the Lombard.

—Stefano Guazzo, *The Art of Conversation* (1574)

Conversing with princes:
[It] should be avoided as much as possible.

—Stefano Guazzo, *The Art of Conversation* (1574)

To be a successful boss:
Injuries must be done all together, so that, being tasted less, they offend less; and benefits should be done little by little so that they may be tasted better.
—Niccolò Machiavelli, *The Prince* (1513)

How to cook octopus:
Octopus is a vile fish of little worth: cook it however you wish.
—Maestro Martino, *The Art of Cooking* (mid-fifteenth century)

To sing more sweetly:
Put a leaden plate on your stomach [as Nero did]. ... Cabbage soup is useful for the same effect.
—Giovanni Camillo Maffei, letter on singing" (1562)

How to know if a woman is pregnant with a boy:
When she has a nosebleed, the blood comes more from the right nostril than from the left one.
—Giovanni Marinello, *Medicine for Women's Infirmities* (1563)

To have beautiful and noble progeny:
According to Hippocrates, and before him Empedocles, one should have excellently done paintings, portraits, or statues of one's relatives, or other illustrious people, in the bedroom [to be recalled, or gazed upon during copulation].
—Girolamo Mercurio, *The Midwife* (1596)

In teaching a young child to read:
Use fruits or pastries cut out in the shapes of different letters.
—Matteo Palmieri, *On Civil Life* (1529)

If you have insomnia:
Stay awake and enjoy it!
—Francesco Petrarca, *On Remedies for Fortune Fair and Foul* (ca. 1366)

When speaking or writing:
Take to heart what Caesar, a man of great talent and wisdom, said in the first book of his *On Analogy*: "Avoid as you would a rocky promontory a strange and unfamiliar word."
—Aeneas Silvius Piccolomini (later Pope Pius II), letter for the future King Ladislas of Bohemia (1450)

To help strengthen your memory:
[If you nap midday, though you shouldn't,] get your sleep with your feet uncovered by any shoes, ... keep your head covered moderately with cloths, ... avoid sleep reclining on the back, ... [when awakening] rub the head with an ivory comb and a rough, coarse rag, ... swallow six raisins and as many juniper berries.
—Jacobus Publicius, *The Art of Memory* (1482)

To keep yourself from the sins of the senses and imagination:
Carry a small figure of death made of bone in your hand.
—Girolamo Savonarola, sermon (1496)

How to cook carp tongue:
Detach the raw tongue from the head allowing part of the throat to remain attached. If one wishes, one can make a potage with *zibibbo* and other raisins, spices, juice of unripe grapes, water, white wine, and minced little herbs. But I find that the best way to cook it is to boil it in water and salt, and then sprinkle it with fennel flowers, grease it with oil, and cook on the grill. Serve with orange juice and pepper—more [pepper] than one would use for other dishes.
—Bartolomeo Scappi, *The Art of Cooking* (1570)

To dye your hair blond:
Get cumin and *requilina* [perhaps the herb horsetail] and boil them with alum ash, and when you wash your hair with this, your hair will become blond and [the color] will last a long time.
—Caterina Sforza, *Recipes for Beauty* (late fifteenth century)

To defend against nervous ailments, paralysis, twisting of the mouth, spasm, and trembling:
[Use] pigeon nests to scent [your] home.
—Gabriele Zerbi, *On the Care of the Aged* (1489)

To prevent spleen problems:
They say, if we can believe it, [put] the right shoe on first.
—Gabriele Zerbi, *On the Care of the Aged* (1489)

Full bibliographic information for the sources cited here is available online at <www.cabinetmagazine.org/issues/35/saiber.php>.

COLORS / VERDIGRIS

JEFF DOLVEN

The Baron Verdigris, despite his name, was black and white. This could hardly be helped in Aubrey Beardsley's pen-and-ink frontispiece to *Baron Verdigris: A Romance of the Reversed Direction*. But the Baron acquires little more color from the prose of Jocelyn Quilp, the possibly pseudonymous (and if not, now forgotten) author. His skin is pale; his moustache is of an "inky blackness."[1] Beardsley omits to ink that signature feature, but its blackness greatly impresses the Lady Meningitis, the Baron's consort. She sings,

Verdigris, oh Verdigris!
My love for thee will never cease.
The night is dark that tempests lash
But not as dark as thy moustache,
My Verdigris![2]

Nor is there much color elsewhere in the book, aside from the blood spilled by the Baron in his gentlemanly rampages. So his surname—which calls to mind a distinctive, half-organic, half-metallic green—is something of a puzzle.

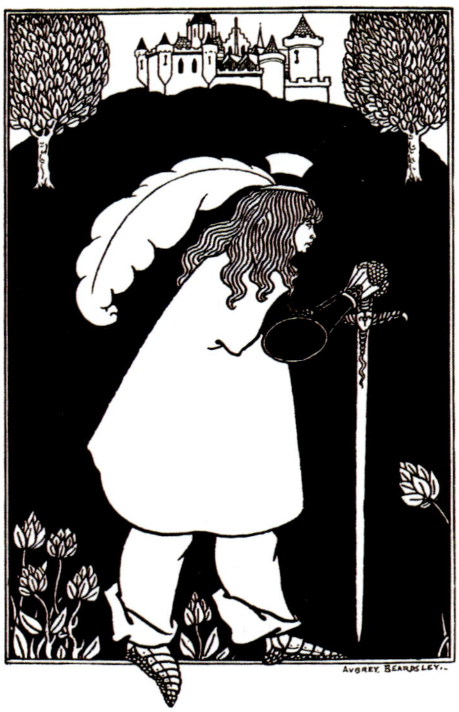

The Baron Verdigris in Aubrey Beardsley's pen-and-ink frontispiece to Jocelyn Quilp's *Baron Verdigris: A Romance of the Reversed Direction* (1894). Courtesy Firestone Library, Princeton University.

It would be a mistake to credit *Baron Verdigris* with the deepest literary guile, but the book, published in 1894, is nothing if not clever, and there may be an answer to the puzzle in its subtitle, *A Romance of the Reversed Direction*. Quilp's conceit is that her hero, an eleventh-century aristocrat, has discovered the secret of time travel without getting very good at figuring out when he is. Having toured the *fin de siècle*, he knows his future as the past, and he is constantly toggling between the dialect of a Victorian toff and a Shakespearean king. It is this dislocation that shows his true color: for verdigris is imbued with temporal paradox. Colloquially, it is the patina that convinces us of the age of bronze statues and copper roofs. In more technical usage, it refers to the blue-green, green-blue, and green copper salts of acetic acid (copper acetates). Either way, it is a peculiarly verdant rust: a sign of age, in the livery of spring.

The name *verdigris* means the green of Greece, *viride graecum*, and by the time Pliny writes of it in his first-century *Naturalis Historia* its use as a pigment was apparently already well established. (As a remedy, too, for ailments ranging from watery eyes to leprosy.) How was it made? Pliny recommends "drilling holes in white copper and hanging it up in casks over strong vinegar"; you can then scrape the green film from the copper (it is mucilaginous in texture at this stage, hence the early anglicization *verdigrease*).[3] By the time European painters began to use it as a pigment, many refinements had been introduced, and the vineyards of Montpellier gradually became the most important and productive sources for the stuff. The Montpellier method—as Jacques Montet described it for Diderot's *Encyclopédie*—was to layer copper strips with fermented grapes in earthenware jugs. Over three or four days, the acid in the grapes would form white crystals on the strips; the strips were then removed from the jugs and laid out on a rack, where they were periodically wet with wine until that valuable green film had formed. Given that the whole process was a kind of accelerated aging, wine would seem to be a fit collaborator. (Interestingly, the production of verdigris in Montpellier was a business largely controlled by women: in this sense, verdigris was ahead of its time.)[4]

If the process was cumbersome, the results were unmatchably lush, a vibrant green that fertilized the painters' foliage and spotlit their drapery. The literature on pigments is filled with complaints about the tendency of verdigris to dull and blacken over time, completing its career as rust.[5] But the process could be halted with varnishes, and in oil paint verdigris was much more stable; indeed, it positively ripened, with the

Recipe 84

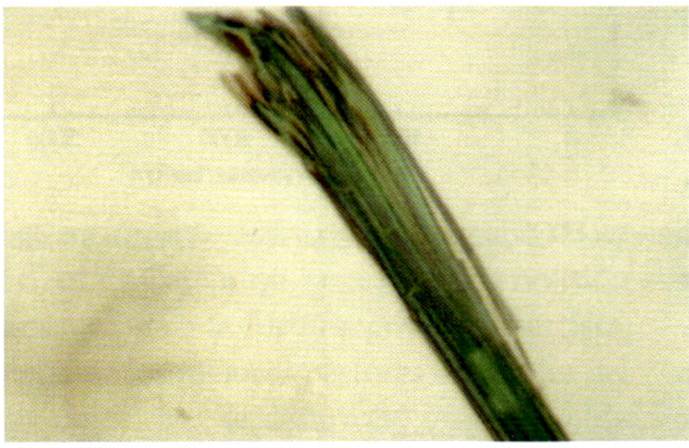

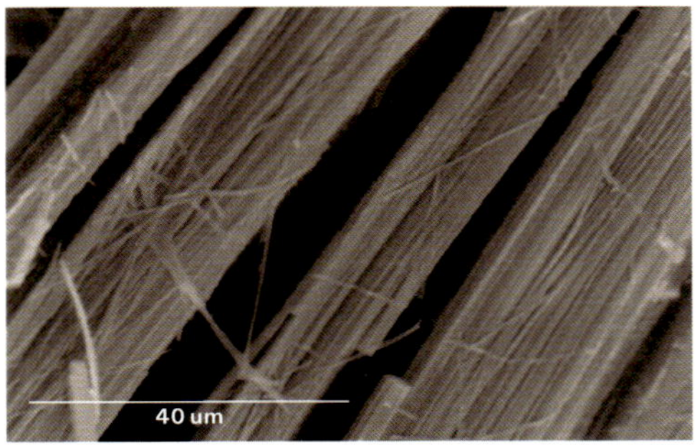

Recipe 101

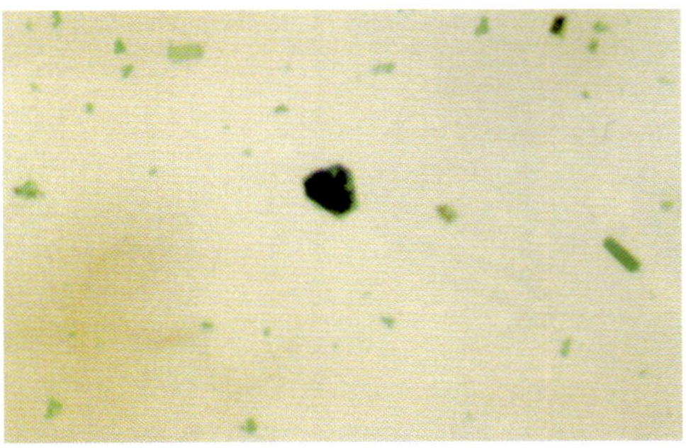

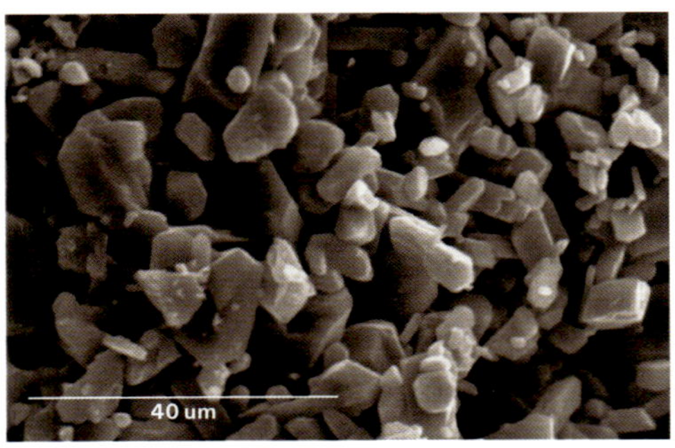

Verdigris according to recipes 84 and 101, originally published in the fifteenth-century "Manoscritto Bolognese," each shown at 200x magnification with optical microscopyand with secondary electron imaging below. Recipe 84 calls for sealing a beaker of red wine vinegar and a copper sheet within a glass vessel for two weeks at 40° Celsius. The acetic acid and water vapors produced by the vinegar corrode the copper sheet, forming the pigment. Recipe 101 begins by grinding the pigment produced by Recipe 84 and placing it in a fired clay bowl. Vinegar is added, and allowed to evaporate, three times. From Stefanos Kroustallis, *Art Technology: Sources and Methods* (2008).

bluish green of its first application becoming, over the first month or so, vivid and pure as a spring leaf.[6] Well into the eighteenth century, its rivals—various mixes of yellows and blues, malachite, or green earth—paled by comparison. One can see it to good effect in the fabrics of Titian's *Vanity of the World* (ca. 1515) or the forests of Abraham Janssens van Nuyssen's *Diana with her Nymphs* (ca. 1610). And we are every day surrounded by its vernacular beauty, spreading over shining metals like lichen on a stone, or sober algae on a bright pool.

Despite his privileged relation, the Baron gives no sign of caring about all this art history, or beauty. He is only out to poison Lady Meningitis, if he can figure out how to do so without anachronism. The one unmistakable green in his romance is the cloth binding, which has held its color for over a century by virtue of the sort of coal-tar synthetic pigment that consigned verdigris to art history (along with its poisonous successor Scheele's Green, which, as a pigment in wallpaper, laced the drawing rooms of nineteenth-century Europe with arsenic).[7] It may be that the illustrator Beardsley had the Baron's greeny name on his mind in making that frontispiece. If the blacks are dark as the Baron's heart, the articulated plate of his armor looks a lot like the leaf-work in the four corners of his composition—a little allegory, if you're searching for one, of the paradoxes of verdigris, vegetable and metal, permanence and transience, chlorophyll and corruption. But for all that, there is a straighter path to the problem in a more familiar source, one with a nobler, if still equivocal, hero. In Book VI of the *Aeneid*, Virgil recounts with grim respect the strength of the ancient ferryman Charon, *deo viridisque senectus*: the old age of the gods is green.[8] What is that green, but verdigris?

1 Jocelyn Quilp, *Baron Verdigris: A Romance of the Reversed Direction* (London: Henry and Co., 1894), p. 19.

2 Ibid., p. 68.

3 Pliny, *Naturalis Historia*, trans. H. Rackham (Cambridge, MA: Harvard University Press, 1940), vol. 9, p. 209.

4 Reed Benhamou, "The Verdigris Industry in Eighteenth-Century Languedoc: Women's Work, Women's Art," *French Historical Studies*, vol. 16, no. 3 (1990), pp. 562–566.

5 Margriet van Eikema Hommes, *Changing Pictures: Discoloration in 15th-17th-Century Oil Paintings* (London: Archetype, 2004), pp. 59–62.

6 Hermann Kuhn, "Verdigris and Copper Resinate," *Studies in Conservation*, vol. 15, no. 1 (1970), p. 16.

7 Victoria Finlay, *Color: A Natural History of the Palette* (New York: Ballantine, 2002), pp. 263–266.

8 Virgil, *Eclogues, Georgics, Aeneid*, trans. H. Rushton Fairclough (Cambridge, MA: Harvard University Press, 1999), pp. 526–527.

LEFTOVERS / LEIBNIZ'S SYRUP OF IPECAC

JUSTIN E. H. SMITH

There was once a prominent mid-twentieth century British philosopher, bearing the auspicious family name "Wisdom," who at a certain point in his career—pehaps in a spell of depression, when logical analysis came to seem empty to him—discovered psychoanalysis. Professor Wisdom wrote a book about the eighteenth-century philosopher George Berkeley, a psychobiography of sorts, in which he made the case that the Irish idealist's rejection of matter is best understood as a vestige of his passage through the anal phase, a sort of delayed grappling with the "non-being" of that dark mass that came out of him in the form of feces.

Now this is just the sort of theory one is trained as an academic philosopher not to propose. It is the sort of theory, one is given to know, that will swiftly land one on one's ear outside any respectable philosophy department in the English-speaking world. The French, in contrast, are rather more permissive of this sort of unfalsifiable belle-lettrification of the genesis of the dead masters' ideas. Putting the finishing touches on my book on G. W. Leibniz, on a topic for which most of the secondary literature is, for better or worse, in French, I was delighted recently to come across this gem of Francophone scholarship, which I translate verbatim:

By invoking Leibniz's meticulousness, his scrupulous character, his tiny handwriting, his taste for endless accumulation of information and of other more tangible goods and, finally, his certain sexual frigidity, an orthodox psychoanalyst would without doubt have made the diagnosis of a fixation or a regression of the libido with the anal phase predominating.

The author adds that "the retrospective psychoanalysis of a person who has been dead for so long amounts to an extremely hazardous enterprise," but this disclaimer is not enough to prevent the picture the imagined psychoanalyst paints from sticking in our heads. Leibniz, the picture suggests, was in his own way perverted, as is anyone who ever accomplishes anything of note.

I am professionally obligated to erase that picture. Yet the longer I dwell with Leibniz, the more his cramped, obsessive handwriting enters into my dreams, the more my wife has to insist on quotas for the number of times per day I'm permitted to mention his name, the more I find myself entertaining psychogenetic theories of my own. Much of Leibniz's philosophy, I have come to believe, is motivated by a preoccupation with the simultaneous instability and inescapability of the body, or, more to the point, of his body. His body is in constant flux, like a river or a fountain, yet he has no choice but to flow along with it.

Some will recognize in the image of the river an allusion to Leibniz's metaphysics of corporeal substance: every monad is the active, perceiving center of an infinitely complex organic body, and no monad can be entirely disembodied, since embodiment is in metaphysical rigor nothing but the phenomenal consequence of the monad's confused perception. No monad, moreover, can ever come into or go out of existence except by God's miraculous intervention since, though always embodied, in itself it is perfectly simple, and therefore logically insusceptible to dismantling. So monads exist eternally in a bodily form, yet not, as certain mystical traditions had supposed, eternally attached to some particular chunk of matter. Rather, they change their matter constantly, just as a wave traveling over the surface of the ocean is constantly in the process of changing the water that constitutes it. The monad that is the soul is always embodied, yet its body is always slipping away from it. Leibniz's soul is embodied, yet he doesn't have the comfort of having a body.

Even those familiar with Leibniz, however, will probably not know that throughout his career he shows a particular interest in discovering new methods of probing into the inner workings of men and dogs and frogs. "We need to find ways to penetrate ever further into the innermost part of a living being," he writes in an unpublished manuscript of 1671. One way of doing this, he proposes, is by further developing the science of anesthesia: "We must find a way to put a person into a deep sleep, in order not to harm him, to the extent that he would feel nothing, and could be easily awakened from this state." Should this not be possible, there are fortunately also animals, on which experiments can be made without concern for their pain. "We must conduct innumerable anatomical studies on animals, living as well as dead," Leibniz writes, complaining that veterinary science has been principally based on equine diseases, since the cure of these is of immediate economic relevance. We can learn not just about anatomy from animals, but also about pathology and the stages of development of diseases, since with animals, unlike humans, "we can cut them open and examine them when and how we please."

Autopsy on human beings is also useful for penetrating into the body, even if we do not have the convenience of being permitted to perform it while they are still alive. Leibniz further hopes that

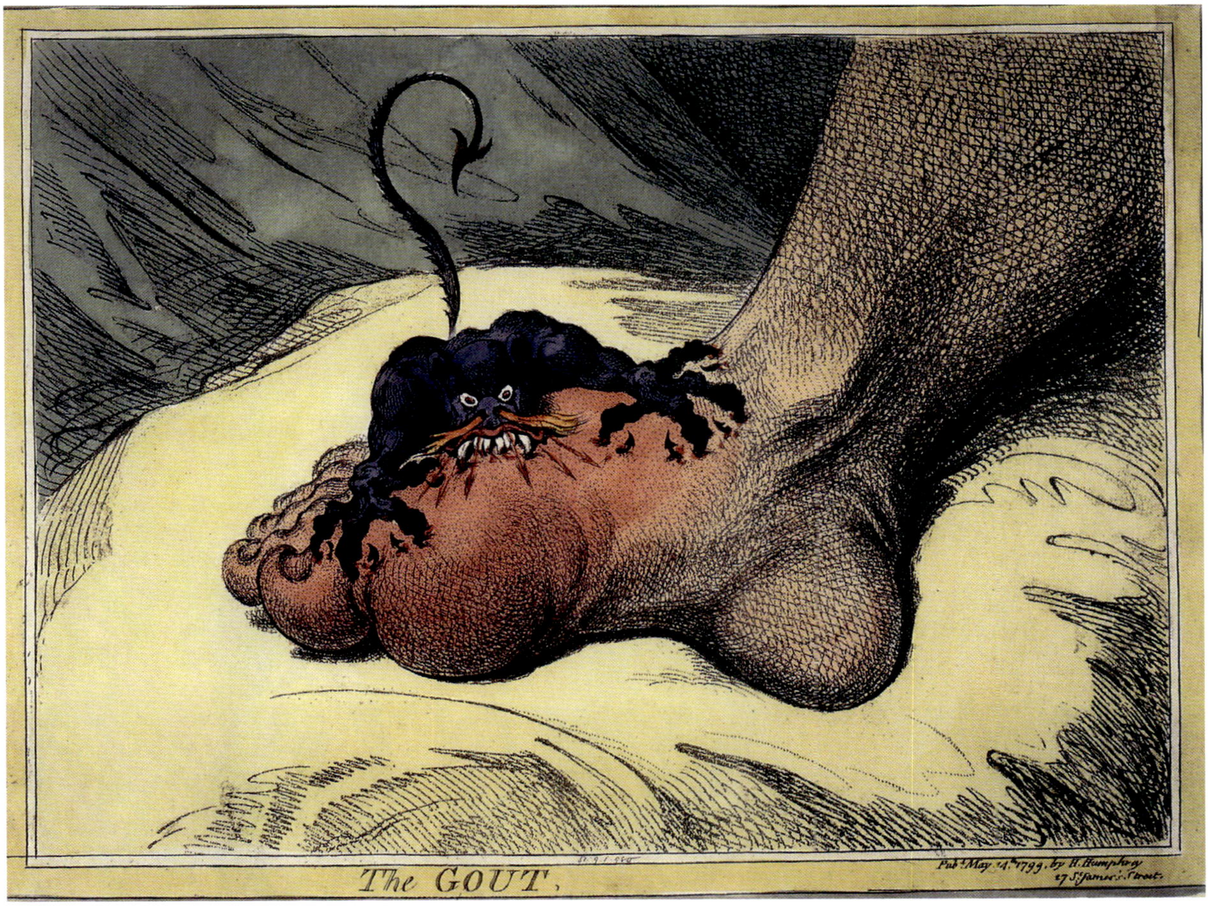

James Gillray, *The Gout*, 1799.

a flesh-eating liquid might soon be discovered that would leave the veins and arteries intact, the better to study them. What is desired is greater knowledge of the living human being, but the only two paths toward it are the living animal or the dead human, and the hope is that these two together might enable us to converge upon an adequately clear picture of the true subject of interest. To this end, all opportunities should be taken to study bodily excrescences such as sweat, blood, urine, saliva, and even breath, which might, Leibniz thinks, be best examined when reduced to a solid state.

Leibniz's persistent aim is to know the inner through the outer: "We must namely find, by the use of reason, the communications of the external members with the internal viscera, so that it will be possible to do a great deal already through external treatments." He believes, for example, that the condition of the hair, its texture and color, can tell us a good deal about a person's constitution and health. Traditional forms of reading from external signs, such as the shape of the cranium or the nose, are of course rejected, as it is only what truly emerges from within—what is pushed out from the invisible part of the body and becomes visible—that is diagnostically useful. In contrast, physiognomy as traditionally practiced can tell us nothing about the current, changeable state of a person, since the features that it studies are permanent and coeval with that person: "From the figure of the hair of a man all sorts of useful conclusions may be drawn with certainty. Of the nose and other parts I do not wish to say."

One would not expect to learn much about a philosopher's broader concerns from his preoccupation with vomit, yet here, as elsewhere, Leibniz surprises us. Emetics are a longstanding interest for him, and in a 1695 text written for the German Leopoldine Academy, Leibniz lays claim to the discovery that the Brazilian ipecacuanha root, which we know better today in the form of "syrup of ipecac," works not just as a remedy for dysentery (in France, Helvetius had used it to cure the Sun King's bad case of the runs twenty years earlier), but also as an emetic, a diuretic, and a diaphoretic. In the early 1670s, Leibniz had dreamed of discovering new ways of bringing the inside of the body out at will, and a quarter of a century later he finds the very potion to make this dream come true.

Leibniz promotes not only experimentation on living animals and dead humans, but also on the self. He believes that bloodletting can be beneficial in some cases, but "it is much more often bad and damaging." He adds: "I only had my own blood let one time, and this just out of curiosity when I was in very good health." And he advocates not just self-experimentation and self-diagnosis, but also self-treatment. He writes in 1676, at the age of thirty, that "when one begins to be seized by gout, or to detect it, one must make incisions or scarifications at every new moon, as close to the true time of the new moon as possible, on the pad of the toe above where one begins to feel or to detect the affliction." Forty years later, in 1716, Leibniz would die of complications from the self-treatment of gout, having built a wooden clamp to cut off circulation to an afflicted foot. It is not known whether at that time he was practicing incisions as well.

Two years prior, in his famous *Monadology*, a sort of précis of his mature philosophical system, Leibniz wrote: "All bodies are in a perpetual flux like rivers, and parts are entering into them and passing out of them continually." It is precisely this capacity to endure throughout the flux that wins for the human being, together with his body, the status of true substance as opposed to mere aggregate. The corporeal substance is what is in constant communication with its environment, what has its being only through its environment, to the extent that it takes in material from its environment and transforms that material into itself. Leibniz has saved the body from the mere contingent association with the immortal soul that Descartes had reserved for it, by showing that the impermanence of its parts need not amount to the unreality of the whole. The leeches sucking his blood, the incisions in his toes, confirmed as much.

Richard Wollheim, who more than anyone made me, when I was young, want to become a philosopher, wrote in his memoir, *Germs*, of his early childhood experience learning to use toilet paper: "It is what I think of when I hear moral philosophers discuss responsibility." If the particular mechanisms and stages of psychoanalysis have by now been discredited, this does not mean that it is no longer true that human beings, including moral philosophers, first come to gain their most basic orientation in the world through their experience of their bodies, and that the abstractions they manage to arrive at much later, in adulthood, are not replacements for these primary experiences, but only late-coming outcroppings of them. Wollheim's genius consisted in his mastery of the abstract language of adult philosophy, together with his ability to translate this language back to bear on the sort of entities—embodied, desiring, eating, and excreting ones—that philosophy is in fact about (whatever else it might pretend to be about, e.g., angels, God, disembodied minds, or minds only contingently wrapped up with bodies).

I once had a precocious and overconfident student, who preferred Levinas and Derrida and other mystifiers of youth, and who, when presented with a summary of Daniel Dennett's austere explanation of consciousness, exclaimed: "He's just, like, working out his issues." She may have been right, but I wouldn't claim to have any knowledge of what those issues might be simply from the content of the theory. No, one needs to go the other way, from the explicit elaboration of the personal issues to the content of the theory. Thanks to Leibniz's severe graphomania, this is to some extent possible, once one has deciphered his cramped and anal handwriting.

What about his frigidity? Did Leibniz really fill up every square millimeter of his manuscripts with dense text only to compensate for the great absence of any "love life"? Of course, no decent seventeenth-century philosopher was married. The preferred form of love for a man who had chosen the contemplative life was seraphic: clearly erotic, and clearly heterosexual, but not defined by consummation. This is what Henry More enjoyed with the married Lady Anne Conway, and what sustained John Locke in his decades-long cohabitation at a country estate with the married Lady Damaris Masham, whose husband was an absent and indifferent Member of Parliament in London. And it is what characterizes the deepest love Leibniz experienced in his life, with the very married Queen Sophie Charlotte of Prussia. As with our effort to understand the medieval institution of same-sex marriage between "blood brothers," who often requested that after death they be buried in the same grave in an eternal embrace, the question "Yes, but were they, you know, doing it?" does not really get to the heart of the matter. Whether they were or not, the era of accounting for our erotic impulses in terms of our orifices had not yet begun, so it is not at all surprising that what drips from the pages of the correspondences between these men and women is just love, and not the fluids thought in our strangely Galenic era to be charged with it.

No, Leibniz saved his reflections on fluids for his more private, less courtly, less charming writings, for his auto-diagnoses and his correspondences with medical men. In 1715, Leibniz boasts to his friend Schelhammer that, while Louis XIV might have given Helvetius monopoly rights for the use of ipecacuanha to stop diarrhea, it was he, the great Leibniz, who discovered that it could be used not just to stop a king up, but also to keep his juices flowing. Leibniz is old when he writes this, twenty years after the initial discovery, and by now he knows he is not long for this world. But he draws comfort from this claim to a legacy. He has discovered the perfect emetic. The psychobiographical temptation would have a Leibniz scholar trying to trace the metaphysical innovation of the flux of corporeal substance back to his pharmaceutical preoccupation with coaxing out, as Henry Miller would later say, "everything that flows." And from there the scholar might go further still, back to the sort of thing Wollheim used to think about whenever he heard moral philosophers talk about responsibility. But I certainly am not going to try. I am a philosopher, and not at all qualified.

Bibliography:

Mirko Grmek, *La première révolution biologique* (Paris: Payot-Rivages, 1990).

Justin E. H. Smith, *Divine Machines: Leibniz's Philosophy of Biology* (Princeton: Princeton University Press forthcoming, 2009).

John O. Wisdom, *The Unconscious Origins of Berkeley's Philosophy* (London: The Hogarth Press and the Institute of Psycho-Analysis, 1953).

Richard Wollheim, *Germs: A Memoir of Childhood* (London: Waywiser Press, 2004).

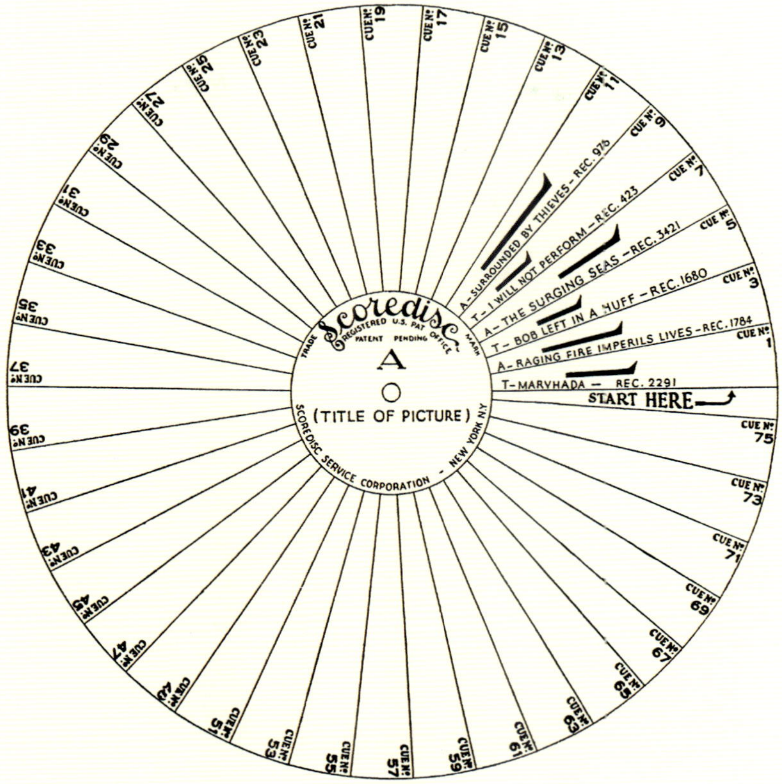

Scoredisc non-sync record cueing disc, ca. 1929.

REMIX REDUX

EMILY THOMPSON

A photograph of a simply handcrafted wooden box constitutes the frontispiece to Bill Brewster and Frank Broughton's history of the DJ, *Last Night a DJ Saved My Life*. The box, looking like the long-lost Ark of the Covenant, contains not two stone tablets but two turntables. It is identified by the authors as a "custom-made double turntable built in 1955 by Edward P. Casey of the Bronx, New York." The humble box encapsulates the now well-known history of the DJ's art of remixing recorded sounds. From its post-war origins in the Caribbean musical culture of sound systems, the practice migrated to and was transformed within the West Indian immigrant communities of New York's outer boroughs. It developed in the hands of African-American and Latino DJs, culminating in a celebratory embrace of the hip hop aesthetic of cut-n-mix by mainstream pop culture across America and around the world.

This story, told and retold in countless histories of the DJ, is complicated, however, by the existence of another box which appeared decades earlier. In 1929, RCA—and numerous other companies—manufactured a dual turntable unit that was the functional equivalent of the modern DJ's kit. This box was deployed not in dance halls but in motion picture theaters, where it played a vital, if brief, role in the transition from silent to sound motion pictures. It subsequently disappeared into history's long-forgotten and silent corners, but by bringing it back to light we can recover not only an important episode in film history but also a curious pre-history to the remix aesthetic that resounds today.

While attempts to sync cinematic images to phonographic sound had occurred regularly ever since motion pictures were first invented in the 1890s, virtually all such attempts had failed. They failed to maintain mechanical synchronization between sound and image, and they failed to produce sound sufficiently loud for everyone in a theater to hear. The acoustical phonograph of the early twentieth century, whose only source of power was the sonic energy writ into the undulating

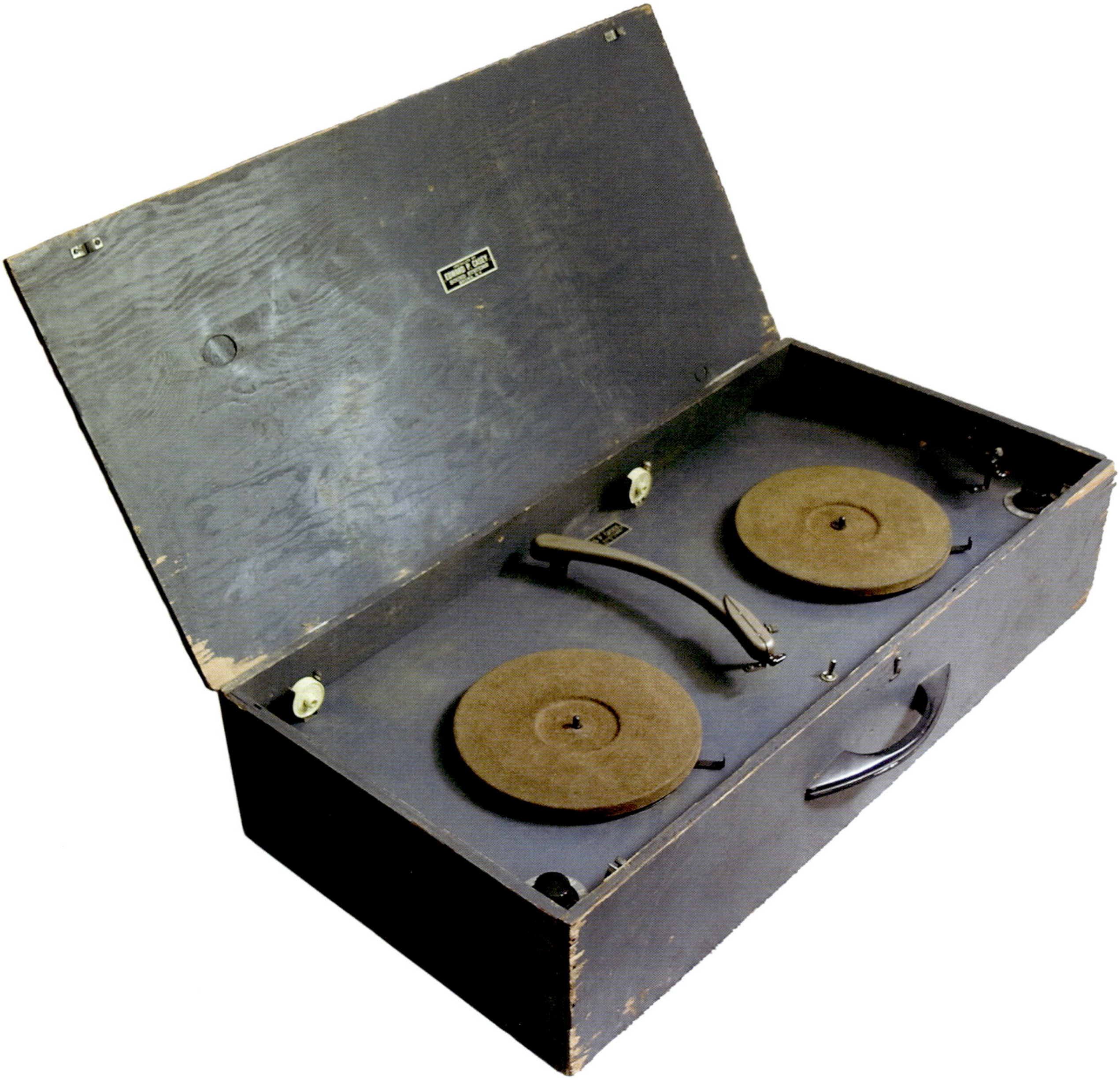

groove of the record, was loud enough to fill the front parlor of a home with music, but not a nickelodeon theater that might seat several hundred or more movie-goers.

During World War I, the phone company AT&T expanded its interest in sonic technology beyond the bounds of the telephone system. Engineers at its manufacturing subsidiary, Western Electric, developed an electrically based system for sound recording and reproduction which utilized vacuum-tube amplifiers to achieve a much greater volume of sound. After the war, the technology was applied to the phonograph, and the flowery horn of the old Victrola was replaced by the bass-thumping loudspeaker of the new, electrically powered Orthophonic, or "right-sounding," phonograph. Western Electric engineers also devised a way to link their new phonographs electrically with motion-picture cameras and projectors, and they redesigned the records to hold the approximately ten minutes of programming that made up a standard reel of film.[1] The result was the synchronized and amplified sound that had long been sought for sound-motion pictures.

The Western engineers went west to pitch their new product to Los Angeles's movie moguls, but the film industry's biggest players were uniformly uninterested, convinced by years of hard experience that sound pictures were doomed to fail. Only Warner Bros.—a second-tier studio with ambitions to move up in the Hollywood hierarchy—agreed to gamble on the new technology. The first Vitaphone pictures, as the new sound movies were called, began to appear in specially equipped theatres in 1926.

Vitaphone programs typically opened with a series of shorts, one-reel musical performances by famous vaudevillians which replaced the series of live acts—singers, comedians, acrobats—that preceded feature films in most silent cinemas. While these shorts were filled with dialogue as well as music, the early Vitaphone feature films that followed were not talking movies, but rather traditional silent fare, now accompanied by a recorded musical score instead of a live performance by theater musicians. Warner Bros.' goal was not to revolutionize cinema by giving it a voice, but simply to improve it by controlling and standardizing its musical aspects. Studio-generated recorded musical scores would replace the theater-specific performances with a sonic product that would be the same for every movie-goer in every town.

Of course, talking pictures would soon revolutionize the film industry in ways that the Warner brothers had never imagined. But from 1926 into 1929, as the transition to sound pictures took place, talking feature films were not the norm. What movie-goers saw on screen was no different from what they were used to seeing. What they heard was similar or perhaps better. In big-city picture palaces, the orchestral score now poured forth from loudspeaker horns rather than from live musicians performing in the pit; in small towns, memories of the often-mediocre musical accompaniments of the local pianist and drummer were washed away by the recorded swells of seventy-piece studio orchestras.

While theater musicians lost their livelihood, projectionists took on new tasks and responsibilities. Not only did they have to continue choreographing invisible transitions from one projector to another during reel-changes, but they now had to wrangle records as well as reels. Of course, records sometimes skip, and when a Vitaphone record jumped its groove, the manufacturers assumed that synchronization was irreparably lost. Operating manuals instructed projectionists to cut their losses and immediately start up the next reel and record, simply omitting any material remaining on the disc and reel that had fallen out of sync. But projectionists chose not to accept defeat in this way, and they grew adept at restoring sync on discs that had skipped. They did this by transgressing the long-standing First Commandment of phonography: "Thou shalt not touch the record."

Vitaphone records almost always skipped forward, moving the sound ahead of the image. The loss of synchronization was immediately evident during dialogue sequences, but for non-talking films an incongruous juxtaposition of image and music could be just as noticeably out of sync, and audiences were quick to make their displeasure known. To enable the image to catch up with the sound, "the trick," as one sound man recalled, "was to look at the screen and then close your eyes and hold the disc and let it slide on the turntable, and then take your hand off real quick and look at the screen. And you got quite expert. Some of the projectionists would look at it and say, 'A-a-a, it's jumped two grooves,' and hold it down and take it off, and be pretty close to being in sync. In the meantime, of course, the audience is applauding, yelling and whistling, if you were out of sync."[2]

By breaking the rules and grabbing the record, motion-picture projectionists began to construct a new relationship between phonograph records and the people who played them. No longer simply cueing the

opposite: Edward P. Casey's 1955 custom-built double turntable for DJ'ing. Photo Richard Espinosa.

needle and letting the records play themselves, these men began to engage with the discs and intervene in their playback. And this was just the beginning.

After a theater had installed a new sound system, the management necessarily continued to show silent films as well as sound pictures, since there weren't initially enough of the latter being produced to fill the bill seven days a week. In theaters that had fired their musicians, some projectionists began to deploy the sometimes-idle sound system to create their own sonic programs to accompany those silent films. Kenneth Graham, for example, a projectionist at the Fox Golden Gate Theatre in San Francisco, installed a microphone in his booth to provide "voice-over" narration during silent trailers for upcoming films. He did it so well that the audience didn't realize these weren't "talking trailers."

In 1927, Henri Tussenbrook of the Majestic Theatre in Hartford, Connecticut, connected a standard electric turntable to the theater's new Vitaphone sound system and played standard Victor records to accompany the theater's silent films. Tussenbrook's playlist matched the music on record to the moods and actions on screen. For the Fox film *The Loves of Carmen*, his score included *Pupilos Brujas* by Jose Bohr y su Orquesta Tipica (Victor #79724); Toscanini's *Carmen* (Victor #839); *Dream Tango* by the International Novelty Orchestra (Victor #20454) and twenty-five other discs. "The effect," judged one listener, "was very good and it was hard to realize that the music had not been especially written and recorded for the picture."[3]

Perhaps following the lead of enterprising men like Tussenbrook, different equipment manufacturers, including Western Electric, began to market special turntable units to provide recorded music and sound effects to accompany silent films. These devices were called "non-synchronous" units to acknowledge that, while the music would be chosen and timed to fit the mood and action on screen, the practice of cueing records in sequence could not match the precise level of synchronization between sound and image achieved through the Vitaphone process.

Non-sync systems, with mellifluous names like Orchestraphone and Theatrephone, Mell-O-Tone and Bell-O-Tone, generally consisted of a multi-turntable unit with a rotary control to fade the output from one turntable to the other. Advertisements described models with as many as six turntables available for simultaneous or sequential cueing, but two platters was clearly the standard. If the theater was already wired for sound, the output of the unit would be tied into the extant amplifiers and loudspeakers. If there was no synchronous

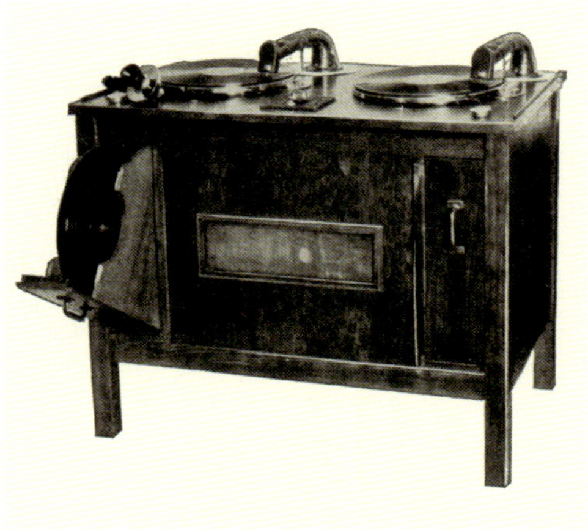

Motio-Tone Non-Sync Turntable Unit in wooden desk cabinet, ca. 1929.

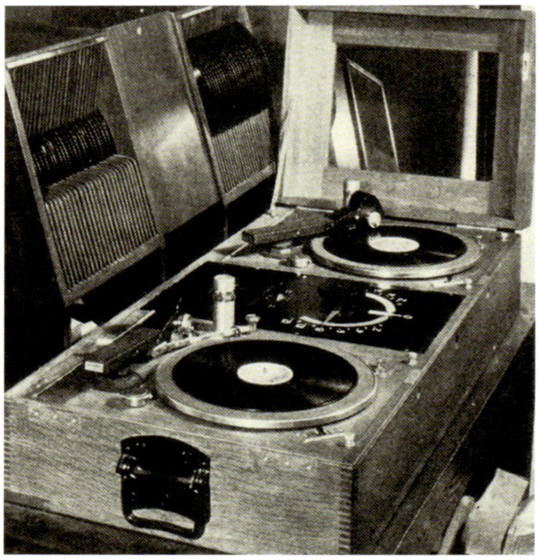

Western Electric Non-Sync Turntable Unit, ca. 1929.

sound system in place, the theater owner would have to purchase and install an amplifier and speakers, but the cost was still far less than that of a full synchronous-sound outfit. Whereas Western Electric's Vitaphone system cost thousands of dollars up front in addition to hundreds more each month in leasing fees, the Good-All Orchestrola non-sync system could be had complete for just 495 dollars. Good-All claimed to be delivering 250 such units per month in 1929, and 48 other manufacturers of non-sync units were listed in that year's *Film Daily Year Book*.

Who manned all these turntables? Apparently, it was not always men, as is clear from the occasional appearance of feminine pronouns in descriptions of non-sync operation. Many units were placed in projection booths where they were presumably operated by

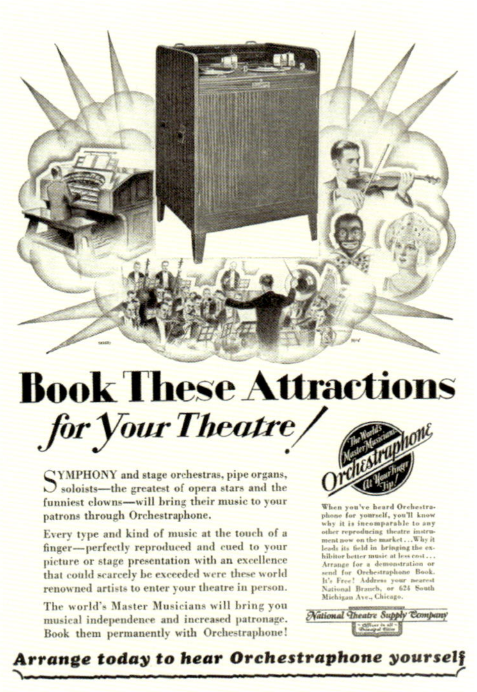

Advertisement for Orchestraphone in September 1928 issue of *Motion Picture Projectionist.*

projectionists, an almost exclusively male group given the strenuous, dangerous, and unionized nature of the profession. But some models were offered in attractive wood cabinets, which suggests they were intended not for the projection booth (where fire codes generally prohibited wooden furniture), but for the main house, perhaps even for the now-empty orchestra pit. It is likely that, in some theaters, the former accompanist was put in charge of the non-sync unit, possibly "performing" in front of the audience as before, but this time playing records instead of a piano or violin. In small-town silent cinemas, these musicians had often been women, and these women had long been the target of criticism by industry professionals for their perceived lack of talent. Advertisements for non-sync systems seized on this dissatisfaction with the performers in the small-town venues, emphasizing the benefit of the devices, which could now, through the technology of recorded sound, offer "The World's Master Musicians—At Your Finger Tips!"

The non-sync units were not, in fact, the first attempt to construct a technological solution to the problem of inferior live music in movie houses. As film historian Rick Altman has described, a range of music-generating devices was designed and installed in silent cinemas.[4] Most notable were the photoplayer pianos, automatic or player pianos that were modified to meet the needs of motion-picture theaters. Whereas standard player pianos played only a single perforated-paper roll at a time, photoplayers could hold a battery of rolls, each containing the code for different songs or styles of music. Individual rolls within the battery could be cued instantaneously by the machine's operator, causing the piano to shift suddenly from a sentimental melody during a love scene, to the martial strains of military marches, to whatever else the drama on screen required. Segues must have been non-existent, but if a theater lacked a living pianist capable of performing this kind of thematically varying accompaniment himself or herself, a less talented person would have been capable of cueing a photoplayer to similar, if not as seamless, effect.

Even the live performance of silent movie music, whether by lone pianists or full orchestras, had typically possessed a similarly mechanical aspect. Most musicians compiled their accompaniments—in advance if they had lead time, off the cuff if not—by cutting and pasting popular songs and classical themes into a pastiche that was ultimately more "assembled" than "composed." Orchestra directors at the big city picture palaces drew upon expansive music libraries to compile their scores. Solitary pianists in more modest establishments used "cheat books" put out by music publishers, with which they could quickly and easily call up music that would change the mood from romantic to threatening with just the flip of a page. Recognizing the enormous market for sheet music that theater musicians constituted, music publishers distributed cue-sheets for specific silent films in circulation, indicating how to deploy their tunes to compile a professional-sounding score. The earliest Vitaphone scores, while recorded in the studio and reproduced in the theaters on disc, followed these compositional patterns and drew upon the same standard songs and themes that had served silent cinema for years. Not for another decade would the Hollywood Composer emerge as an auteur in his own right.

Following the practice of music publishers, record companies—as well as some manufacturers of non-sync systems—began to sell special libraries of discs, compilations of thematically organized music and sound effects from which operators could construct their scores. Victor labeled its non-sync offerings as "Pict-Ur-Music." For an additional fee, some outfits, including Victor, offered cueing services for feature films, providing a cue sheet indicating which discs to deploy during each scene to create a truly "professional" sounding score. One company, Scoredisc, even offered an ingeniously simple technology that ensured appropriate and accurate selecting and cueing.

Scoredisc offered its clients a library of over a thousand discs of indexed music and sound effects. For each feature film in circulation, the company compiled an appropriate score out of the music and effects on these records. In order to enable theater personnel to generate that score in their house, Scoredisc sent along not a cue sheet, but a pair of cardboard discs, one for each turntable on the non-sync unit. Each disc was inscribed with a series of cuts radiating out from its center, with each cut constituting a cue. One disc contained all the odd-numbered cues, the other all the even-numbered ones, and the operator would set up and play back these cues in sequence, alternating turntables, to create a continuous score. For each cue, a record identification number was printed next to the cut, telling the operator which Score-Disc record to place on the turntable. The cardboard disc was then placed on top of the record, and the cut indicated precisely where, on that record's surface, the needle was to be cued to provide the specified sound. The record spun underneath the stationary cue-disc, with the needle accessing the record from above through the cut. The length of the cut controlled how long each cue would play, as the needle would be stopped in its progression by the cardboard when the end of the cut was reached. Just prior to that moment, however, the operator would fade to the other turntable's output, where the next cue would be set up and ready to go. To assist with the transitions, the disc also included for each cue a brief printed description of the image on screen, or the text of a screen title, to indicate the precise moment for the sonic change-over. By following these cardboard templates, the operator could recreate the score that Scoredisc had compiled. The turntable tender was simply a pair of hands following instructions in order to generate a pre-determined sound product.

Non-sync turntables could have allowed a new kind of sonic artistry to develop in 1929; they could have enabled a new musical creativity to be expressed through the personal selection and juxtaposition of recorded sounds. But within an industry and musical culture where standardization was the goal, the creative potential of this technology would not be fulfilled at this time. The musical possibilities of two turntables would remain latent for decades, awaiting a culture less captivated by top-down directives, an audience less enamored of master narratives.

Theater musicians assumed that audiences would soon grow tired of the "mechanical music" of sound movies and call them back to the pit for an encore, demanding a return to live musical performances. They were mistaken. Informal polls as well as box office receipts indicated that people prefered recorded and standardized sound accompanying their movies. Sporadic attempts by musicians to picket motion picture theaters and demand a return to work quickly failed, and those jobs were lost forever.

Projectionists initially enjoyed increased pay and status when turntables entered their booths, but this moment was brief. By 1930, the disc-based Vitaphone system was superceded by systems in which the sound was recorded optically onto the film itself, integrating sound and image even more tightly, with no room for creative manipulation at the site of reproduction. The year 1930 was also when silent film production essentially ceased. The non-sync units were no longer needed, as most theaters now screened all-sound movies, all the time. The transition was complete, and projectionists went back to threading projectors at their old levels of pay. The non-sync turntables were presumably discarded, and definitely forgotten.

There is no apparent connection between the non-sync units of 1929 and the turntable kits that emerged many years later to become new musical instruments in the hands of hip hop performers. While the technology is virtually identical, its cultural context was not. DJs in the 1970s deployed their turntables to effect a musical transition explicitly in opposition to what had come before. By spinning their discs, these artists rejected claims of studio expertise and the ideal of a standardized master narrative in favor of a new aesthetic of DIY and re-contextualization. What they spun, however, was structurally similar to the live performances of silent cinema musicians, the original cut-n-mix performers. Perhaps history itself is ultimately a remix, a reworking of old ideas in new contexts, a constantly changing juxtaposition of old and new. DJs now spin turntables forward and backward, but the record still goes 'round in circles.

1 Standard records, which spun at 78 rpm, played for just a few minutes. To increase play time to ten minutes, Vitaphone records spun at 33 1/3 rpm, and their size was increased from the standard ten-inch diameter to sixteen inches.
2 New York Times Oral History Program, The American Film Institute/Louis B. Mayer Oral History Collection, Part 1, no. 22: James G. Stewart, "Development in Sound Techniques," p. 50.
3 William Schlasman to R. M. Hatfield, 27 October 1929, Western Electric Collection Box 430, Location 100-09-01, AT&T Archives.
4 Rick Altman, *Silent Film Sound* (New York: Columbia University Press, 2004).

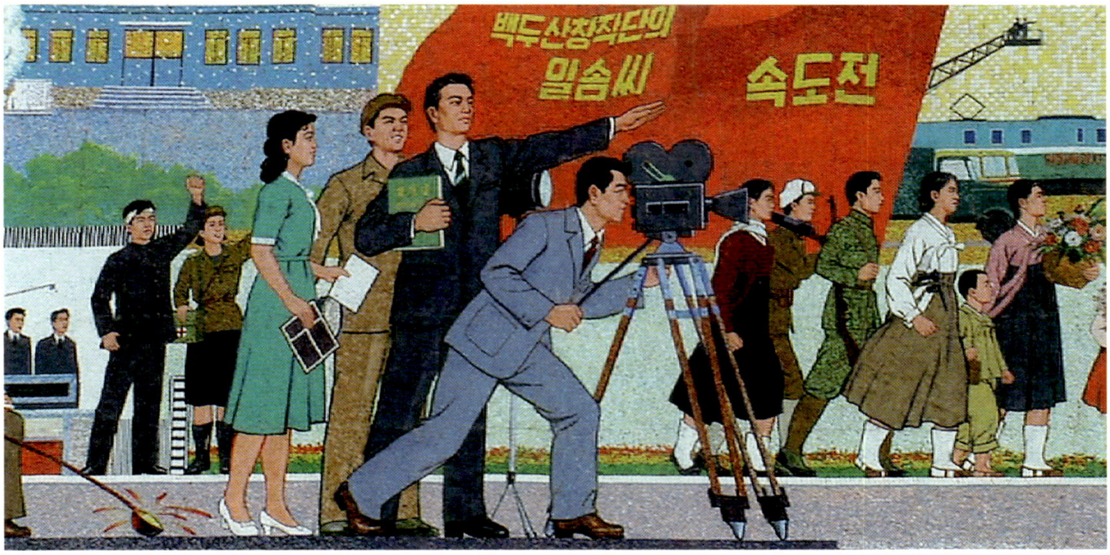

Mural at the studio complex built by Kim Jong Il outside Pyongyang. The red banner extols the value of speed in the nation's economic development. Photo Magnus Bärtås.

ALL MONSTERS MUST DIE

MAGNUS BÄRTÅS & FREDRIK EKMAN

After crying himself to sleep, the little prince wakes up the next morning with a heavy heart. His father—the king—is dead, poisoned by the power-hungry black knight El El. Before dying, the king had managed to pass along a valuable gift to his son, a little stone sculpture of a strange creature he called Galgameth. The prince's streaming tears fall on the sculpture, and later, while the prince sleeps, the figure comes to life in a little cloud of stardust.

In the morning light, the prince discovers that something is moving under the blanket; a small lizard-like creature is looking at him with round, mocking eyes. Amazed, the prince stares back at the little monster. The creature leaps, lands on the chandelier, and immediately begins to feast on the metal candelabra. The monster clearly has an appetite for iron, which it chomps without the slightest resistance. It does not take long before the creature grows many times larger; no swords or lances can penetrate its armored body. Galgameth becomes the prince's ally in the battle to uphold his father's honor.

Galgameth is an American fantasy film from 1996 which passed quietly into the anonymous rows of VHS boxes in the children's section of video stores. But for those who know the film's genesis, it holds special significance. *Galgameth* is the last part of a monster genealogy that reflects political intrigues and raises questions about how the cute operates in the realms of art and power.

Galgameth can be traced to three earlier generations of monsters. The first is Godzilla—or Gojira, which is the original Japanese name—the mother of all film monsters. The first Gojira film from 1954 is a dark, melancholy elegy characterized by sophisticated visual language and sound design. There is nothing kitsch or ironic about it, even if the special effects can no longer impress a public that has grown up with digital imaging. The monster Gojira was a product of the atomic age; the film begins with scenes of a fishing boat that is hit by a devastating light, alluding directly to the American test in March of that year of a 1.5 megaton hydrogen bomb in the Bikini Atoll in the Pacific Ocean. The Japanese tuna-fishing boat, *Lucky Dragon No. 5*, found itself in the vicinity of the test site and was enveloped by the radioactive fallout. The crew fell ill with radiation sickness and the incident triggered an international crisis. In Japan, fear of radioactivity once again took hold—the so-called "tuna fish horror."

In the film's story, Gojira emerges during the Jurassic period and survives at the bottom of the ocean only to have his habitat destroyed by the American test. After absorbing the radiation, the now homeless monster begins to wander. The Japanese fleet lays down depth charges and the military erects a high-voltage line to protect the coast, but nothing can stop Gojira. The scales on his back glow and a beam of radioactivity, transmitted from the monster's jaw, makes buildings and houses melt.

The images from the film recalled the recent past for the Japanese nation. The smoking ruins of Tokyo the day after Gojira's attack were a reminder of the devastating bombing of the city at the end of the war. The images of burned children being examined with Geiger counters at a hospital evoked the still-vivid memories of Hiroshima and Nagasaki.

The person responsible for designing the Gojira figure was Eiji Tsuburaya (1901–1970), the legendary special effects creator at the Toho Studios in Tokyo. Tsuburaya's figures—such as Gamera (a jet-propelled giant turtle), Rodan (a flying dinosaur), Mothra (an enormous moth), Booska (a forerunner of the Teletubbies), and Ultraman (a humanoid alien in an attractive red and silver costume)—are still beloved by the Japanese public and have been reprised again and again in films, video games, comic books, TV series, and toys. But none of these figures rival Gojira—"Japan's best-known international film star"—a national monument whose statue stands in Ginza in Tokyo. The Gojira series is one of the most enduring in all of film history, spanning over fifty years and twenty-nine movies.

Gojira's success in Japan created a new genre, the *kaiju* film, which quickly spread to neighboring countries. In 1962, the South Korean filmmaker Kim Myeong-jae contributed to the genre with a film titled *Pulgasari*. The film itself has been lost, but two film posters found in recent years serve as proof of its existence. According to the Korean national film archive, the story, which takes place during the Koryo Dynasty (918–1392), is based on a Korean folk story: a martial arts master is murdered but reborn in the form of an iron-eating monster named Pulgasari who takes revenge on his murderers.

Like *Galgameth*, this film would also be a footnote in film catalogues were it not for a series of extraordinary events that unfolded at the end of the 1970s. South Korea was at that time a dictatorship under General Park Chung-hee. In schools, students learned that North Korea's leader, Kim Il Sung, was a devil who literally had horns on his head. The censorship rules within the South Korean film industry were very strict, even though General Park himself was an enormous film fan. In 1961, he had fallen in love with a melodrama called *Sangnoksu* ("The Evergreen Tree"), a film that he came to regard as the cinematic national anthem of South Korea. The film was made by a young director, Shin Sang-ok, and the main role of the young self-sacrificing woman teacher at a village school was played by his wife Choi Eun-hee. In the 1950s, the married couple had established Shin Films following the Hollywood studio model. By the 1960s, the operation had grown to dominate the entire South Korean film industry, producing everything from period films, melodramas, horror films, and war films to musicals and "Wild East" movies, the so-called Manchurian Westerns.

Choi Eun-hee, known by film lovers as Madame Choi, was Korea's greatest star. She had begun her career as a theater actress in productions of Shakespeare and Molière during the Japanese occupation (1910–1945), and was forced to perform for Japanese troops. Shortly after the Korean War broke out in 1950, she was kidnapped and brought to North Korea where she was compelled to appear in propaganda plays for the Communist troops. In 1953, she finally managed to escape and return to Seoul, where, instead of being welcomed, she was branded a traitor and brought to trial. The case was dismissed on one condition: that she entertain South Korean troops. Choi, considered to have the first "Western" face in Korean film (large eyes, strong eyebrows, and a pronounced nose), is said to be the most photographed figure in South Korean film history. She also broke many taboos: her 1958 on-screen kiss was the first in Korean history. In the 1960s, she took on an enormously diverse set of roles in Shin's films: chaste widow, housewife, princess, and flirtatious prostitute in films centered on life around the American army bases. She was also the director of three films.

General Park was so eager to see Shin and Choi's films that he demanded newly developed reels be brought directly to the presidential palace. The couple became constant guests of the dictator, who enjoyed playing cards with Shin, whose signature look at the time consisted of tinted pilot glasses and a black silk cravat with white polka dots. But the card games with the dictator came to an abrupt end in 1975 when Park got the idea that the director was conspiring against him and banned Shin from working in film. His studio was closed and his staff was dismissed. Around the same time, Shin and Choi divorced.

Shin died in April 2006. In July of the same year, we traveled to South Korea to meet with Choi Eun-hee. After long negotiations, she had agreed to meet us at the Marriott Hotel in central Seoul. We had prepared for our meeting with sessions at the national film archives, newly moved into laboratory-like premises in a building made of glass and polished stone. We had seen as many of her films as possible, but now we wanted to hear her version of the bizarre events that began in 1978.

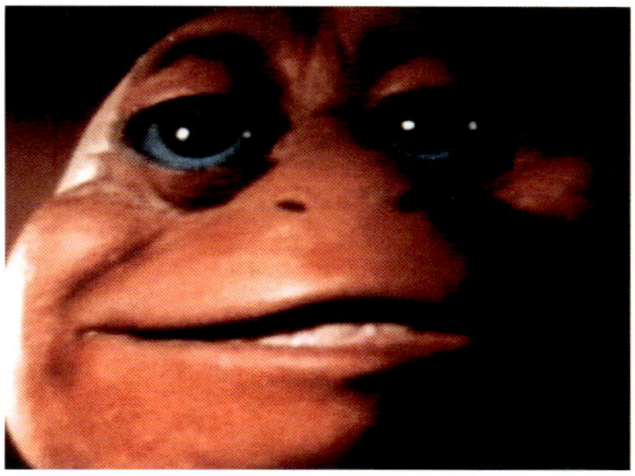

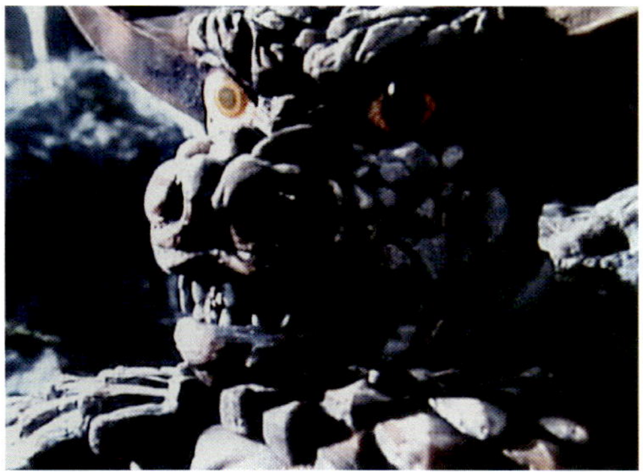

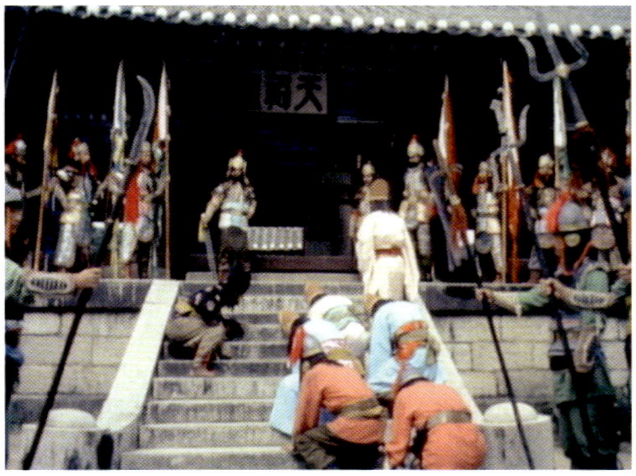

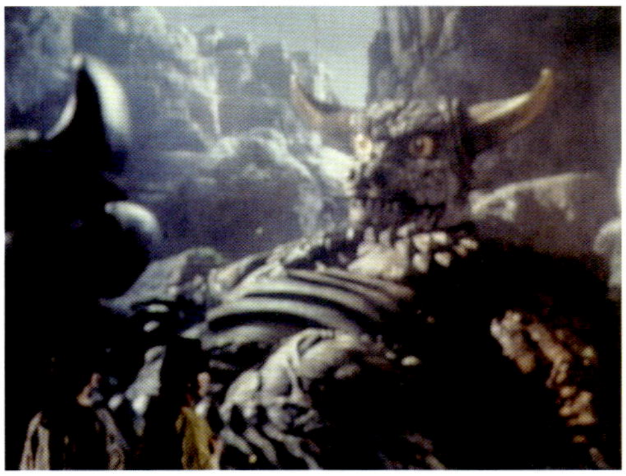

Film still from *Galgameth*, 1996 (top); three stills from *Pulgasari*, 1985.

The seventy-nine-year-old Choi arrived fully dressed in black. She had improbably smooth skin, full lips, tinted sunglasses, and a black onyx cross around her neck. Madame Choi told the story of her life methodically and chronologically. She became immersed in her own narrative, losing track of time; the hour we had been promised turned to five, extending to lunch at a *bulgogi* restaurant and *soju* drinking.

In 1978, Choi recalled, she was in Hong Kong on a business trip. On her way to a meeting, she was attacked; a sack was pulled over her head and she was taken to the harbor where she was placed aboard a small boat and injected with sedatives. After eight days, the boat docked at the North Korean harbor of Nampo. Waiting for her on the dock was a short man with a strange haircut. He greeted her with a smile: "Thank you for being here, Madame Choi. I am Kim Jong Il."

Shortly after her arrival, Choi was dressed in traditional Korean clothes and photographed. Kim Jong Il proudly displayed the pictures to his father, Kim Il Sung, at the time the dictator of North Korea, who announced that Madame was still beautiful, especially dressed in *hanbok*.

Thereafter, Choi was invited to the Friday parties at Kim Jong Il's personal palace, where she was expected to appear as if stepping out of one of her films. The parties would always include a film screening, followed by backgammon and mah-jong, punctuated by enormous glasses of cognac which had to be drunk standing on one foot. There was dancing to an all-female combo band, which played jazz and disco. In the small hours of the morning, Kim Jong Il would climb onstage and direct the band.

Kim Jong Il had an enormous archive of 35mm films, probably over 15,000, and was eager to discuss film with Choi. He could not emphasize enough the importance of film as a propagator of national identity and community. The archive was only accessible to the "royal family," but Kim considered her part of the family. He seemed to forget that she was there against her will.

Outside of the weekly parties, it was an idle life for Choi in captivity. There was no certainty about her future and her days dragged on. Eating, she recalled, was "like consuming sand." The years went by and she filled her days with gardening. She sculpted small clay cranes and placed them in the garden, their beaks pointing south.

Five years went by. For the last three, Choi had fallen out of favor and was no longer invited to the Friday parties at the palace. But then on 6 March 1983, an invitation arrived. It was a huge banquet with magnificent flower arrangements. Choi was seated as the guest

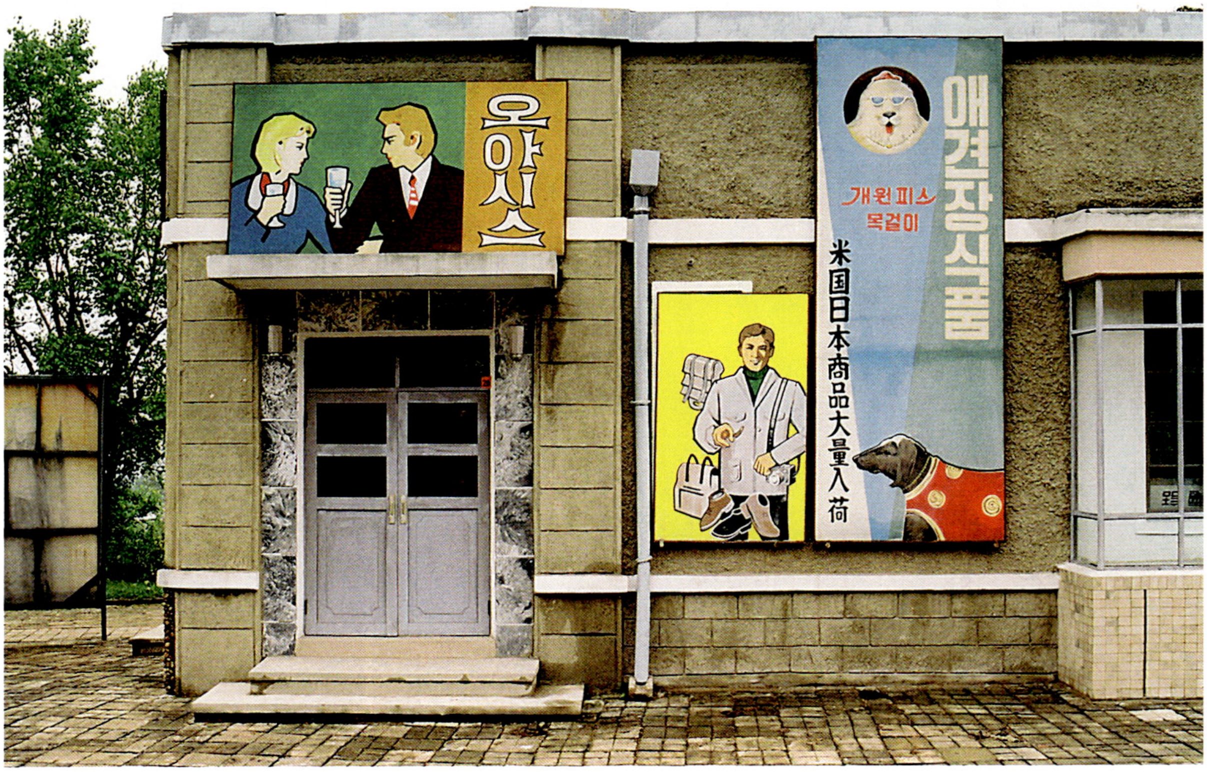
오아시스
애견장식품
개원피스
목걸이
米国日本商品大量入荷

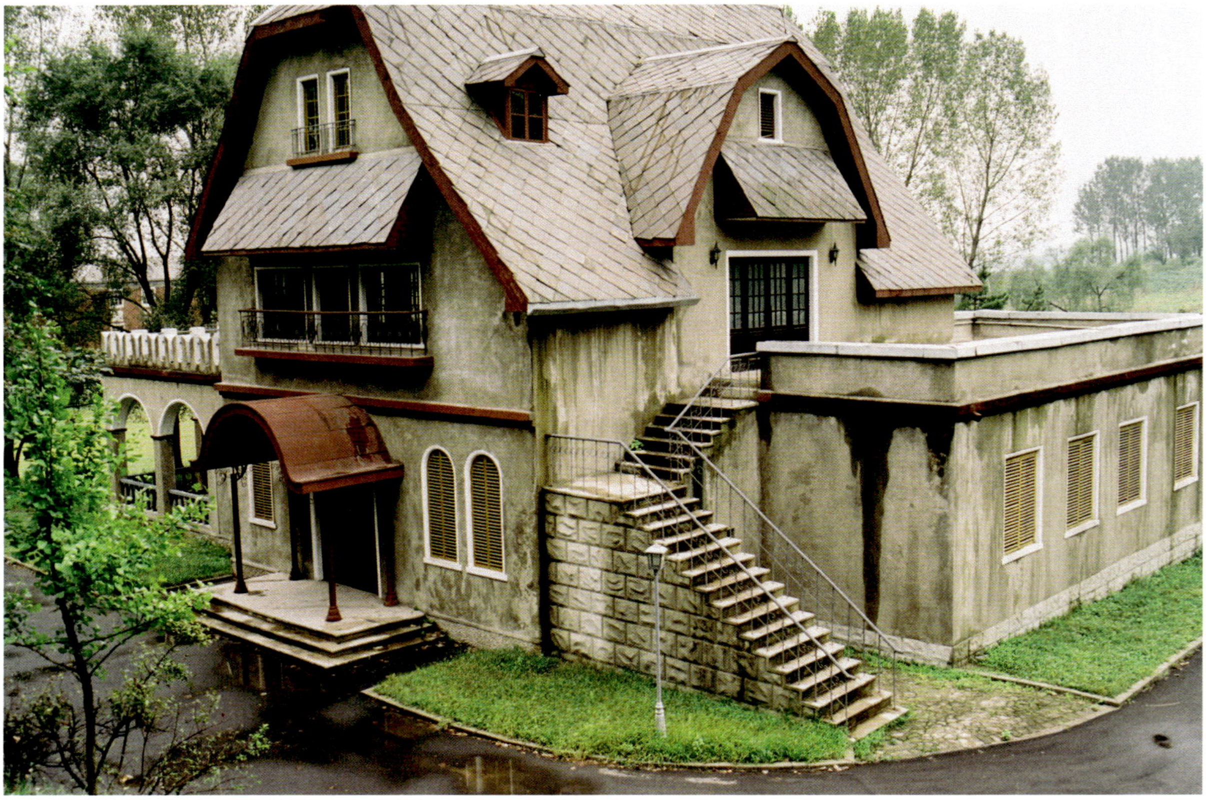

of honor and Kim Jong Il was unusually excited. He made a speech in which he appointed her the mother of North Korea, the mother of *Chosun*. He talked about how Korea consists of one people, with a shared history and culture. And then the unbelievable happened: surrounded by dignitaries, Shin Sang-ok arrived. Dumbfounded, Choi stared at his emaciated face. Finally Kim Jong Il exclaimed, "Why are you just standing there? Come on, hug each other."

It turned out that soon after Choi's capture, Shin himself had been kidnapped. A failed attempt to escape his kidnappers landed him in a forced-labor camp, where for four years he survived by eating salt, grass, and bark. Now, Kim Jong Il wanted to crown them king and queen of the North Korean film industry—and declare them husband and wife. They had no choice but to accept. And so it was that Shin Films miraculously reemerged in North Korea, with Shin and Choi once again a married couple. They were given an enormous budget and a newly constructed film lot outside Pyongyang; they had access to as many extras as they needed.

Choi Eun-hee and Shin Sang-ok directed seven films in North Korea and assisted on ten others before they managed to escape. In 1986, Choi and Shin were invited to serve as jurors at the Vienna International Film Festival, but soon after their authorized arrival in Austria, they slipped away from their bodyguards and fled by taxi to the American Embassy.

The last film that Shin worked on in captivity, though he never managed to finish it, was called *Pulgasari*, like its South Korean precursor. The film was Kim Jong Il's idea; the dictator had many opinions about cinema and was deeply involved in the country's filmmaking industry. In an interview, Shin recalled that Kim Jong Il preferred action films, porn films, and horror films—his favorites were *Friday the 13th*, *Rambo*, and James Bond. According to Shin, Kim Jong Il believed that events portrayed on film were largely real: "I had to explain to him that most American films are fictitious." But despite this confusion, Kim Jong Il perhaps intuited something deeper about the relationship between film and politics, a relationship illuminated by the neo-liberal concept of "soft power." Soft power, a term coined by the American sociologist Joseph Nye, refers to a country's ascendancy not through military or economic might but as a result of the enticements of its popular culture. Through soft power, popular culture disseminates latent political messages. Film humanizes people and places them in history; it mythologizes a country and its communities. Every shrewd politician with a feeling for soft power sees the potential of film to propagate narratives that tell how "our people" are human beings who suffer, love, and prevail.

Like the original version, the later *Pulgasari*, which helped establish the *kaiju* genre in North Korea, is based on a folk tale, but one now reworked according to revolutionary ideals. A blacksmith has been imprisoned for concealing his collection of metal tools, which are being forcibly seized across the land by a local warlord seeking raw materials to transform into weapons. Before he dies, the blacksmith makes a little figurine out of a grain of rice. His daughter, the heroine of the film, discovers it in his discarded clothes and takes it home as a memento.

In the evening, the heroine sits with her needlework; preoccupied by her sorrow, she happens to prick her finger. When a drop of blood falls on the rice figurine, a little blue halo of light appears above it without her noticing. When the figurine wakes up the next morning, it immediately grabs one of the needles in her sewing kit, puts it in its mouth, and bites it in two. Gorging itself until there are no more needles, it then leaps into the girl's arms to nibble at the needle she holds between her fingers.

Pulgasari quickly bulks up on this iron diet, and joins the villagers in their uprising against the feudal overlord, which culminates in an attack on the imperial palace. But the monster is ultimately too demanding, as its enormous appetite for iron makes it increasingly difficult to feed. The heroine finally martyrs herself in order to destroy Pulgasari's rapacity: just as her blood fosters its initial hunger for iron, so it ends it. That *Gojira* is the forerunner to *Pulgasari* is exemplified by the fact that Choi and Shin hired Toho Studios, the special effects team from Tokyo, to work on the film. It was Kempachiro Satsuma, a longtime portrayer of Gojira, who was given the task of bringing the Pulgasari rubber costume to life.

All North Korean films are made for domestic consumption, and so every film has to be seen as a message to the nation's own inhabitants. One might interpret *Pulgasari* as a critique of the dictator's power over the people, the emperor symbolizing the despot Kim Il Sung who lives luxuriously while his people suffer hardships. But such a critical perspective is, of course, officially impossible in North Korea: the oppressors must be capitalists from South Korea, Japan, or the US. It is against them that weapons must be directed. The weapons in *Pulgasari* are created from within, from soil, rice, and

opposite: Two slices of pseudo-reality from the North Korean studio complex. In a set depicting Seoul (top), the banner on the right, promoting a variety of dog-related products, proclaims, "American and Japanese products imported in quantity!" The complex also boasts Bavarian homes (bottom) made of military-grade cement. Photos Magnus Bärtås.

blood. The food—iron—is uranium, enriched in the blacksmith's forge. The weapon is transformed and refined into an increasingly diabolical force. In the end, it is only the spirit of the people that can disarm the weapon. As it happens, the North Korean nuclear weapons program had secretly commenced by that time, and the national mentality needed to be prepared for this step.

In addition to the nuclear weapons motif, something else connects *Gojira* and *Pulgasari*: ambiguity in the face of horror. In both films, the monsters are expected to be terrifying. They come bearing destruction, they run amok, and they have the power to wipe out the entire human race. But at the same time, these monsters have mitigating qualities. In *Pulgasari*, this equivocation becomes clear in certain scenes that show the monster as a playful, even cute character. A similar ambivalence was only very weakly suggested in the original Gojira film, but the later films show a more conciliatory attitude toward the monster. In the 1968 film *Kaiju Soushingeki* ("Destroy All Monsters"), Gojira is even represented as the overindulgent parent of the cuddly Minilla.

In other spheres of Japanese popular culture, this movement back and forth between the beastly and the cuddly has always been very clear. During the last few decades, the influence of the cute has expanded enormously at the expense of the terrifying. The concept of *kawaii* has become pedestrian in popular culture, and manifests itself everywhere in a city such as Tokyo: in advertising, apparel, costumes, trinkets, posters, cars, and even the architecture. *Kawaii* has become the most important source of soft power.

That Shin, who received asylum in the United States along with Choi, should ultimately go on to make *Galgameth*, a new, ultra-cute version of *Pulgasari*, parallels this trajectory of power camouflaging itself as cuteness. China is rapidly adopting a similar course: street signs prohibiting certain behavior now feature pictures of large-eyed, doll-like policemen who smile as they raise a warning finger. There is even a name for this development in China: "panda politics."

Under the pseudonym Simon Sheen, Shin took Kim Jong Il's idea to Hollywood, or rather, to a castle in Romania, where *Galgameth* was filmed. Many scenes—for example, the one in which the monster first appears—are borrowed directly from *Pulgasari*. From a psychological perspective, it is incomprehensible that the director, after years of working in a labor camp and being forced to make films in North Korea, would choose to do a re-make of his captor's artistic vision after finally escaping to the US. Was it a case of traumatic repetition-compulsion? Exorcism? Or simply greed? When we contacted the Gojira actor Kempachiro Satsuma's agent in Tokyo, we learned that Shin had made inquiries about whether Satsuma would consider acting the role of Galgameth (Satsuma declined). Perhaps Shin had a vision: the same actor in three different monster costumes, representing three different political systems.

By September 2008, when we visited the studio complex outside Pyongyang where *Pulgasari* was filmed twenty-three years earlier, the huge buildings erected for Shin and Choi stand as isolated monuments. The golden age of North Korean film is over. We can now walk through the muddy streets where film crews erected a vision of Seoul under Japanese occupation. Among the other sets we find a decadent bar district in Tokyo; naïve backdrops for narratives about immoral living in contemporary Seoul; buildings from the *Chosun* era; and even a Bavarian village—a convincing illusion at a distance, though closer inspection reveals that the houses are made of military-grade cement. Ordinary North Korean citizens' ideas about the world outside the country have shaped these sets. Our guide tells us that Kim Jong Il comes here from time to time to provide "on-the spot guidance."

It was different in Choi and Shin's era. Madame Choi tells us that Kim Jong Il had full faith in their film-making, and that while he was entirely engaged in it, he never imposed himself. We are astonished by her forgiving attitude toward the dictator; she even seems to have a slightly guilty conscience overt the fact that they managed to escape from captivity, leaving the North Korean propaganda factory to its fate.

ARTIST PROJECT: FALLEN BOOKS

MELISSA DUBBIN & AARON S. DAVIDSON

Our project "Fallen Books" is a collection of images of toppled books from libraries located in seismically active areas. The photographs are often taken by librarians and depict the aftermath of earthquakes. The images presented here, part of a larger book project, are identified by the library, the name of the given earthquake, the country, and the date, and are organized according to the relative intensity as measured by the Modified Mercalli Intensity Scale. A descriptive and graphic alternative to the Richter Scale, the Mercalli system primarily quantifies the observed effects of earthquakes on humans and man-made objects on a scale of I through XII. Topographic maps of earthquake areas use the scale's color code to indicate how far away from the epicenter the earthquake was felt and at what degree of intensity. Copies of *Fallen Books* are now in the collections of each of the featured libraries. This project is both an archive and a forecast.

THE MODIFIED MERCALLI SCALE

I. Instrumental
Not felt except by a very few under especially favorable conditions.

II. Feeble
Felt only by a few persons at rest, especially on upper floors of buildings. Delicately suspended objects may swing.

III. Slight
Felt quite noticeably by people indoors. Many do not recognize it as an earthquake. Vibration similar to the passing of a truck.

IV. Moderate
Felt indoors by many, outdoors by few during the day. At night some awakened. Walls make cracking sounds. Dishes and windows rattle alarmingly.

V. Rather Strong
Felt by nearly everyone; many awakened. Some dishes and windows broken. Unstable objects overturned. Clocks may stop.

VI. Strong
Felt by all. Windows, dishes, glassware broken; books fall off shelves; some heavy furniture moved or overturned. Damage slight.

VII. Very Strong
Difficult to stand; furniture broken; considerable damage in poorly built or badly designed structures.

VIII. Destructive
Damage slight only in specially designed structures. Fall of chimneys, factory stacks, columns, monuments, walls. Heavy furniture moved.

IX. Ruinous
General panic. Damage great in substantial buildings, with partial collapse. Buildings shifted off foundations.

X. Disastrous
Some well-built wooden structures destroyed; most masonry and frame structures destroyed with foundations. Rails bent.

XI. Very Disastrous
Most buildings collapse. Bridges are destroyed. Large cracks appear in the ground. Underground pipelines are destroyed. Rails badly bent.

XII. Catastrophic
Total damage. Almost everything is destroyed. The ground moves in waves or ripples. Large amounts of rock may move.

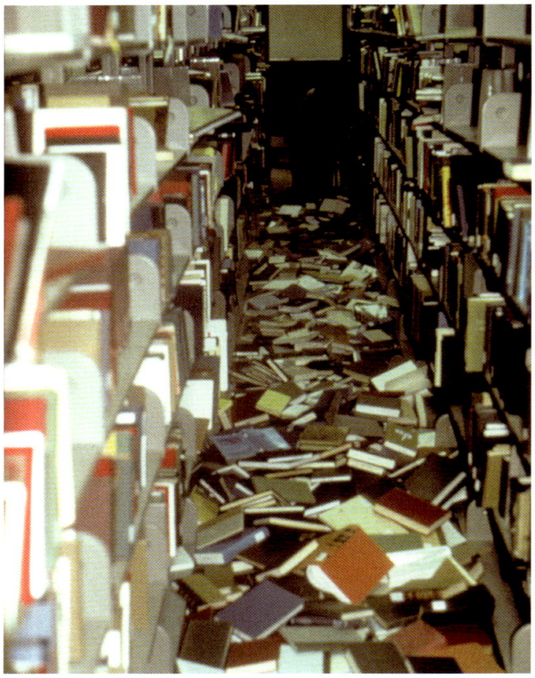

University of California Santa Barbara Library; Santa Barbara / Goleta; USA; 13 August 1978.

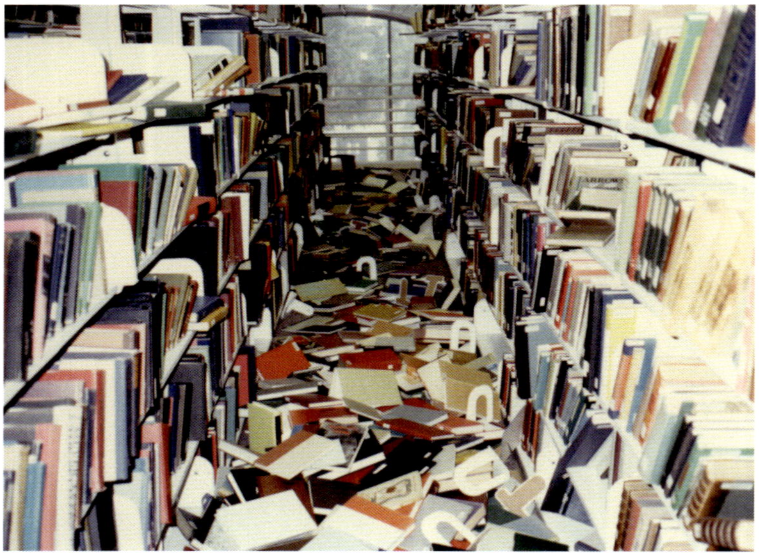

Claremont Colleges Honnold / Mudd Library; Upland; USA; 28 February 1990.

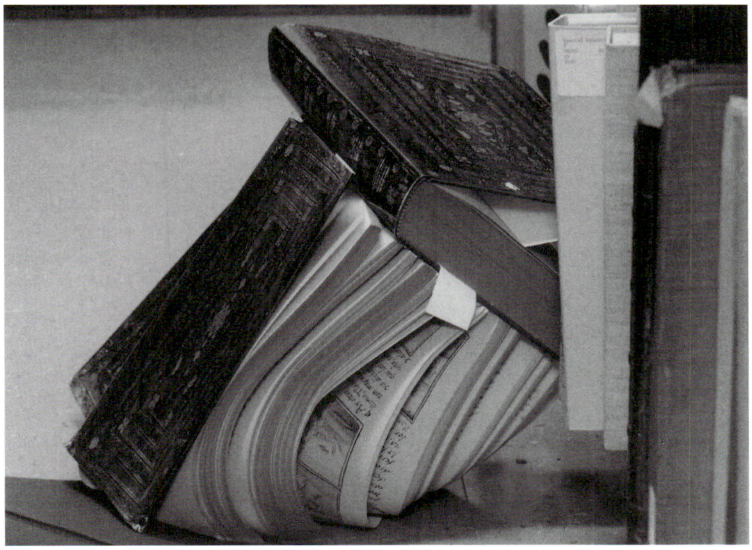

University of California Riverside Library; Big Bear; USA; 28 June 1992.

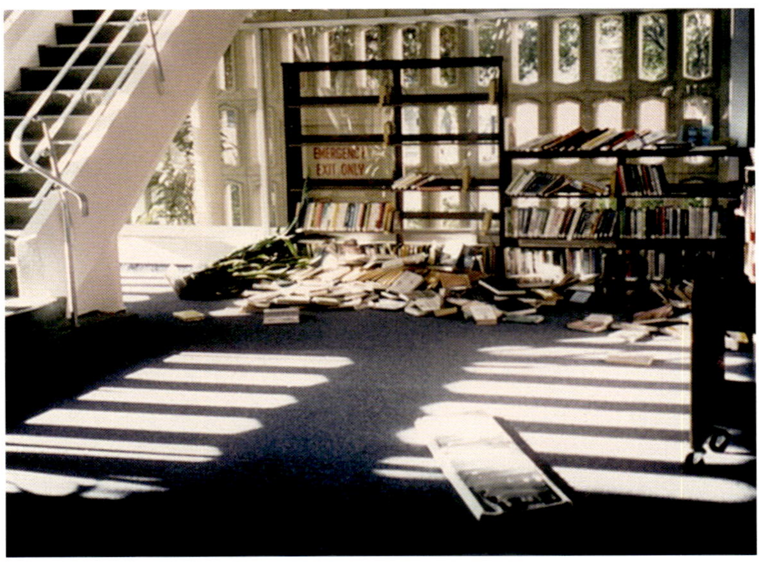

Santa Monica Public Library; Northridge; USA; 17 January 1994.

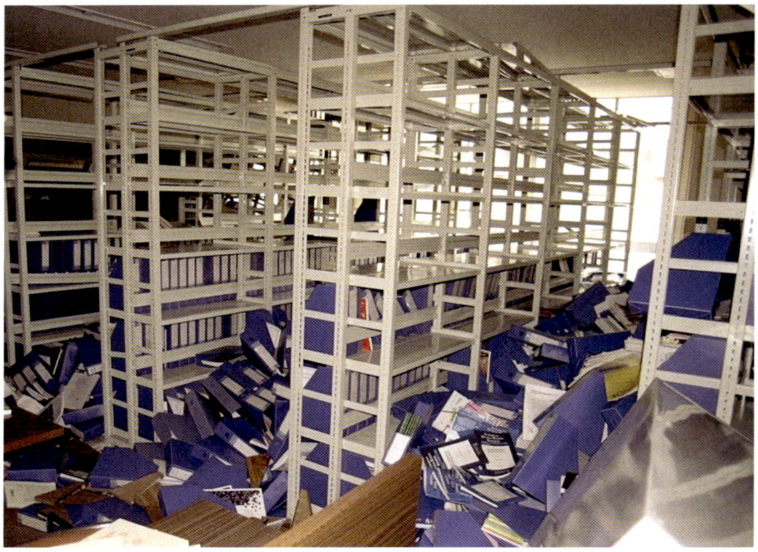

Kobe University Library; Hanshin-Awaji; Japan; 17 January 1995.

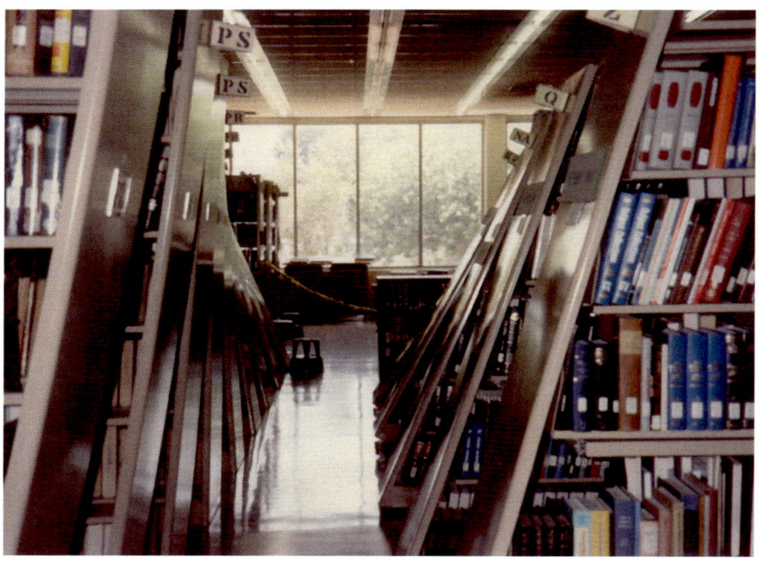

San Bernardino Valley College Library; Landers; USA; 28 June 1992.

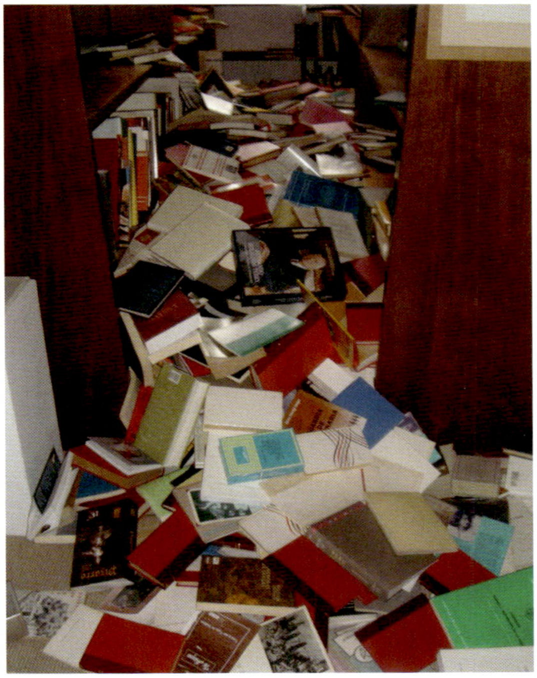

Private Library; Central Coast; Peru; 15 August 2007.

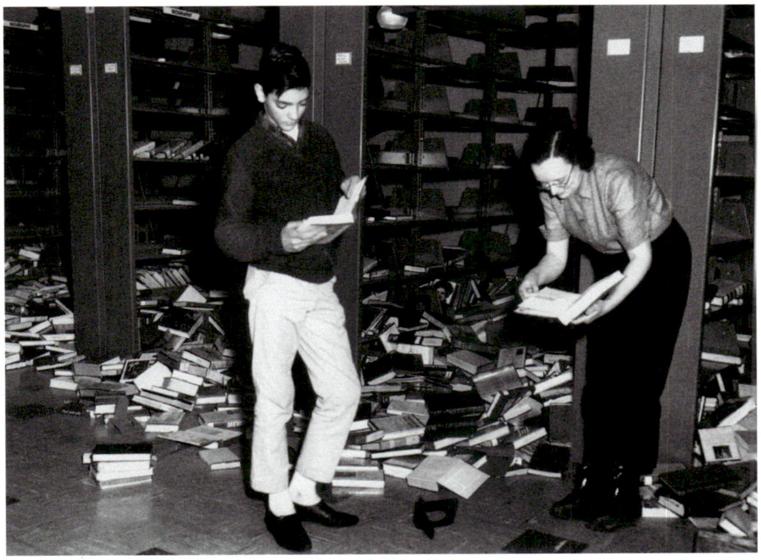

Anchorage Community College Library; Good Friday / Alaska; USA; 27 March 1964.

READING TO THE ENDGAME

D. GRAHAM BURNETT & W. J. WALTER

THE PROBLEM

In his brief essay "Gli scacchisti irritabili" ("The Irritable Chess Players") of 1985, Primo Levi elaborates a set of symmetries between the act of literary creation and the playing of a game of chess. Both a work of literature and the royal game, he suggests, unfold in time within strictures that inexorably invoke "life and the struggle for life." There is, as he puts it, a "symbolic shadow" that lengthens over a chess board, since the way to the end is the way to a death, "a death for which you yourself are guilty." The novel, of course, is the literary form that has evolved precisely to afford language the means of erecting and choreographing such a metaphorical life space. And thus it is no surprise that the novel, too, is haunted by a long shadow: all plots, as Don DeLillo memorably put it, end in death. Moreover, en route to their respective endgames, both chess and the novel offer powerful arenas in which to investigate the question of questions: the ever-vexatious issue of the relationship between fate and agency, between necessity and freedom. Every move is our own, except when it's not. Either way, the board thins, the sheaf of paper in the right hand dwindles, sifting left as if blown by an inexorable wind—though of course, we turn every page. Chess, in this sense, is the opposite of dice, just as the novel is the opposite of Scripture (the exact difference between chance and providence has never been clear, but they share an antithesis in deliberative subjectivity, and this may be a clue).

Stimulated by Levi's juxtaposition, and motivated by the possibilities of extending an Oulipian sensibility into the sphere of literary criticism (OuCriPo?), the authors set out to develop a means by which a given novel could express itself as a game of chess. Initial success here led to expanded ambition, since there was nothing to stop us from elaborating our modest analytic protocol into a full-fledged "engine" that would permit works of literature to confront one another on the chess board. We have advanced this project to what we think of as a workable tool for a certain sort of ludic literary investigation, and we present it here for the first time, together with some preliminary results drawn from several thousand games we have run to date. The current version of the program is playable on the *Cabinet* website, and we would be delighted if it proved useful to those wishing to pursue this or related lines of inquiry.

FROM CHARACTERS TO MOVES

A chessboard consists of sixty-four squares commonly designated by alphanumeric coordinates (a-h across the x-axis and 1-8 up the y-axis). If one were to replace the numerical assignations with a continuation of the alphabet (running, for instance, i-p up the y-axis), each square would be designated uniquely by a two-letter coordinate that we will call a "tuple." Now imagine setting up a simple computer program that knows the rules of chess—nothing more. It knows, for instance, all the moves that are makeable by a given piece, and it can keep track of a chessboard (updating what pieces are on which squares as moves are made). Suppose further that this program takes directions for making moves in the form of a pair of "tuples"—namely, one letter-pair designating the coordinates of a square occupied by a movable piece, and then a second letter-pair designating the coordinates of a square to which that piece can be legitimately moved (including squares where it would capture an opposing piece).

We now have everything in place to convert two texts into a game of chess: we simply feed the program the two novels, asking it to play one text as "white" and the other as "black"; the program searches through the white text until it finds the first tuple corresponding to a movable piece (in the case of an opening move, either a pawn or a knight), and then, having settled on the piece that will open, continues searching through the text until it encounters a tuple designating a square to which that piece can be moved. When it has done so, the computer executes that move for white, and then goes to the other text to find, in the same way, an opening move for black. And so it goes: white, black, white, black, until—quite by accident, of course, since we must suppose that the novels know nothing of chess *strategy* (and our program cannot help them, since it knows only the *rules* of the game)—one king is mated.

Such a set up would be close (there turn out to be interesting differences, but put that aside for now) to permitting two monkeys to play chess against each other by giving each a keyboard and permitting them to jump about on them: send the resulting string of letters to our program, and it scans this string of gobbledygook for tuples that constitute legitimate moves, makes them, and *voilà*, monkey chess.

We experimented with something along these lines (no monkeys, as it happens, but a similar sort of stochasticity) before setting to work building into the basic application a greater sensitivity to the specific qualities of the string of characters upon which it was set to work. Our aim was to produce an algorithm that could, in some modest way, "read" literary works for their distinctive "voice" or "style" and then convert that linguistic particularity into something approaching a style of play.

STYLOMETRICS

In this undertaking, we took our inspiration from the bastard semi-discipline known as "stylometrics." While assigning numerical values to letters and words is an ancient practice (the Greeks even had a word for this activity, *isopsephy*, which they linked to divination), the use of quantitative methods to characterize stylistic features of a given work or author is a surprisingly recent technique of literary analysis. There were some quirky feints in this direction by German biblical scholars in the early nineteenth century (including Schleiermacher, who counted up the instances of exceptional phrases in one of the Epistles by way of calling into question Pauline authorship). Shortly thereafter, classical philologists also began to mobilize simple statistical arguments about word usage as part of various arguments about the chronology and authenticity of canonical works by Plato and others. It was not until the 1970s, however, that the widening availability of programmable computers opened the way to computationally intensive forms of stylistic analysis, and by the mid-1980s these techniques had achieved modest notoriety as a result of apparent victories in several public controversies (in the United States, much attention focused on determining authorship of *The Federalist Papers*, which has become a kind of lab-rat for new stylometric techniques; in Europe, Mikhail Sholokov's *And Quiet Flows the Don* was prominently sliced and diced by a brace of mathematically sophisticated Russian scholars with baroque political axes to grind).[1]

It is the premise of stylometry that writers necessarily, albeit unintentionally, imprint their texts with distinctive statistical signatures, which can be identified by means of close attention to sentence length, word and letter frequency, and other quantitative attributes of their prose. Thus a chess program sensitive to the stylometric parameters of a given text should in principle afford a mechanism for translating authorial voice into a way of playing the game.

THE ALGORITHM

Our working model of such a system is, we freely admit, somewhat primitive and more than a little arbitrary, especially given the imaginable possibilities. But we find it suggestive nevertheless. Let us say that we wish to pit Jules Verne's pre-Freudian chthonic womb-fantasy *Voyage au Centre de la Terre* against Jane Austen's paradigmatic quasi-romance *Sense and Sensibility*. Presented with these texts, our program sets to work on a basic stylometric analysis of the opponents, compiling a list of the sixty-four most commonly used tuples in each text by rank of their frequency. The machine then assigns these tuples, from most common to least, to the sixty-four squares of the board, proceeding in a spiral from the four central positions.

White Spiral

	a	b	c	d	e	f	g	h
8	50	51	52	53	54	55	56	57
7	49	26	27	28	29	30	31	58
6	48	25	10	11	12	13	32	59
5	47	24	9	2	3	14	33	60
4	46	23	8	1	4	15	34	61
3	45	22	7	6	5	16	35	62
2	44	21	20	19	18	17	36	63
1	43	42	41	40	39	38	37	64

Black Spiral

	a	b	c	d	e	f	g	h
8	64	37	38	39	40	41	42	43
7	63	36	17	18	19	20	21	44
6	62	35	16	5	6	7	22	45
5	61	34	15	4	1	8	23	46
4	60	33	14	3	2	9	24	47
3	59	32	13	12	11	10	25	48
2	58	31	30	29	28	27	26	49
1	57	56	55	54	53	52	51	50

Assigning Tuples by Frequency: The sixty-four most frequent letter pairs are assigned to the squares of a chessboard starting from 1 (most frequent) to 64 (least).

The tuples of highest frequency (in Verne's novel, *es, en, le, on*; in the Austen, *he, th, er, in*) thus control the strategic center of the board. Instead of the old, arbitrary tuple coordinates based on a-h and i-p, the squares on the board are now "called" by tuples that have a patterned and systematic relationship with the work in question. And note that these positions are assigned separately for each novel, so each text will play on a coordinate field determined by its own linguistic parameters.

We are now ready to begin play, with the program seeking an opening move for white by scanning, as already outlined, first for a tuple corresponding to a movable piece, and then, having made that determination, for a subsequent tuple corresponding to a legitimate move. In this case, white finds the unconventional-but-storied "Grob attack" or "Spike opening" in its very title (after a heady debate we decided to treat the title and author, though not the publisher or place of publication, as "part" of the analyzable text): the "au" of *Voyage au Centre* having been assigned in this case to g2, and thus to white's g-pawn; and the "tr" of *Centre* designating, again on the basis of the initial tuple frequency analysis, the board position g4. Black, seemingly wobbled by this irregular attack, answers with a hesitant Rook-pawn to h6, on the basis of the "li" in *Sensibility* and the "fo" in the telling opening phrase "for many generations." The contest is joined.

It plays out as depicted below, with white uncorking a fatal King-pawn to d4 on the basis of the palindromic tuples "se" and "es" as they appear in the following sentence:

Mais de faire entendre raison au plus irascible des professeurs, c'est ce que mon caractère un peu indécis ne me permettait pas. (But to make the most irascible of professors hear reason, this my somewhat hesitant character did not allow.)

	White	Black
1.	g2–g4	h7–h6
2.	e2–e4	f7–f6
3.	e4–e5	e7–e6
4.	e5xf6	g7–g5
5.	g1–f3	e8–f7
6.	d1–e2	b8–a6
7.	f1–h3	a8–b8
8.	f3–e5+	f7xf6
9.	c2–c4	h8–h7
10.	h1–f1	h6–h5
11.	b1–c3	c7–c6
12.	f1–g1	f6–g7
13.	e2–e4	b8–a8
14.	c4–c5	b7–b5
15.	c3–e2	g7–f6
16.	e2–c3	b5–b4
17.	a2–a4	b4xc3
18.	g1–g2	c8–b7
19.	e4–f3+	f6xe5
20.	e1–e2	d7–d6
21.	e2–d3	a6xc5+
22.	d3xc3	h5–h4
23.	c3–c4	c5–e4
24.	g2–g1	g8–f6
25.	d2–d4#	
	1–0	

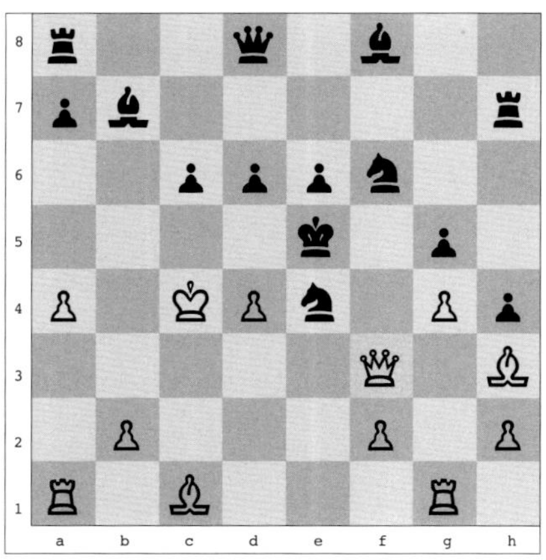

Voyage au Centre de La Terre **(white) traps *Sense and Sensibility* after two careless Knight moves hem in black King at e5.**

PRELIMINARY RESULTS AND DISCUSSION

Over the last several months we have experimented with fifty-five works in five languages (English, German, French, Italian, and Spanish), representing seven national literary traditions (distinguishing American and English writers, and Spaniards from Mexicans), and tending to emphasize classic novels of the nineteenth century. (We are currently working on a version of the program that can handle Cyrillic characters, since we have felt the absence of Russian sources, particularly when running international tournaments). Using batch processing and many machine-hours, we have logged complete records of several thousand games, and have analyzed this data set a number of different ways. Some general observations will give the reader a feel for these results.

For starters, a relatively brief, "tight" game like *Voyage au Centre de la Terre* vs. *Sense and Sensibility* is more the exception than the rule: overall about 30% of our games end in checkmate, and the rest wind up as draws (of which a little less than 30% are stalemates).[2] Of the games that end with a victor, the average number of moves to mate is seventy-one, and in many of these pawn-promotion plays a significant role (pawns reaching the opponent's home row can be "promoted" to Queen, and several "Queens" of the same color can thus occupy the board at the same time).[3] Our longest contest to date is the marathon showdown between Herman Melville's tricky *The Confidence-Man* (1857) and the novel often accorded foundational status in the history of *el realismo* in Spain, *La Gaviota* (*The Seagull*, 1849), authored by the cosmopolitan aristocrat Cecelia Böhl von Faber (writing under the pseudonym Fernán Caballero). This *tête-à-tête* sees von Faber's celebrated *naturalismo* grind Melville's Manichean insouciance to the humiliating configuration shown here after no fewer than 159 moves.

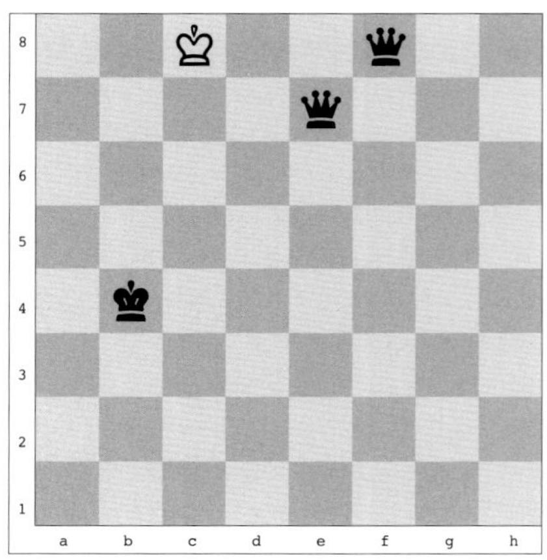

The Confidence-Man **finally cornered by the picaresque *La Gaviota* after a lengthy chase, which concluded black Queen e7-e6+, white King a6-b7; black's other Queen c2-f2, b7-b8; e6-e7, b8-c8; followed by the deep strike f2-f8#.**

Nearly as exhausting is the 141-move slugfest between Benjamin Constant's lapidary tale of ennui and seduction, *Adolphe* (1816), and *La Bodega* (1905), Vicente Blasco Ibáñez's crusading proto-prohibitionist indictment of wine-drenched backwardness in Andalucía—a game that culminates in yet another triumph for Iberian social realism. These contests stand in marked contrast to the Teutonic lightning-strike by which Theodor Fontane's *Effi Briest* (1894)—a favorite of Thomas Mann's—undoes Rafael Delgado's slightly over-ripe late exercise in Mexican sentimentality, *Angelina* (1947): an eleven-move frontal *Blitzkrieg* that ends as follows:

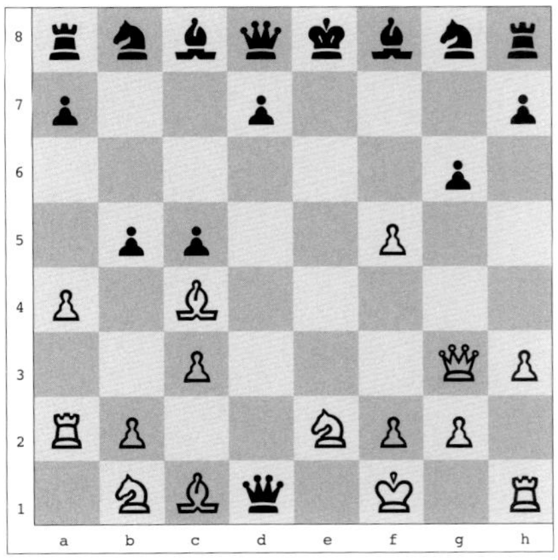

A variation of the "Prussian Pawn": *Effi Briest* (playing black) goes straight up the gut against an inattentive *Angelina*, the crucial move being black King-pawn e3xd2 at move eight, on the basis of *"grün quadrierten"* and *"und dann über diesen hinaus."*

We were prepared to believe, reviewing the transcripts of many considerably more meandering games, that what we were looking at was really—in the end, putting aside the vague charm of thinking of the opponents as works of literature—indistinguishable from the sort of aleatory "monkey chess" alluded to above. But a control seems to prove otherwise: we built a small test module of our program that did indeed choose moves for black and white on a random basis, and discovered to our surprise that this device posted a significantly *higher* rate of checkmate games than actual novel chess (slightly over 40%). We have an intuition as to why this should be so, but it is tentative, and we reserve it at present, welcoming in the meantime suggestions from those interested in taking the question up.

Other peculiarities remain. In something akin to match play, we find French novels in general, and *Adolphe* in particular, to be the toughest competition. This would doubtless delight François Le Lionnais, the chemical engineer who initiated the Oulipo group and authored half a dozen books of chess problems, but we are at present without an explanation as to why it should be so. In our last "world cup," a five-novel French team (led by Alexandre Dumas) trounced the competition, defeating the second-place English team by a 20% margin (the UK was hurt by poor performance from Disraeli's *The Infernal Marriage* of 1834), and leaving the also-ran Italians looking rather like novices. Sample sizes for this tournament were not enormous (on the order of 900 games, resulting in some 300 checkmates), and we are continuing to explore just how statistically robust this apparent anomaly actually is. We are inclined to think that differences in "national styles"—if firmly established—will be explained by reference to the striking, and seemingly consistent, divergence of tuple frequencies across different language groups, divergences particularly pronounced at the high end of the frequency range. Grossly speaking, the four most common tuples in a given French text tend to be relatively close in their overall rate of appearance. By contrast German, for instance, sees a sharper decrease in frequency across this same range (interestingly, English, which on average falls somewhere in-between, shows a much higher degree of *variability* in this metric). How exactly these sorts of statistical characteristics affect game performance under our algorithm we cannot yet say.

As to why Constant's thinly veiled exposé of the intricate erotic politics surrounding Madame de Staël should prove so formidable an adversary, that is a perfect mystery (though it should be noted that both *Frankenstein*, in the second edition of 1831, and Goethe's epochal 1774 *Die Leiden des Jungen Werther*, playing black, successfully fight off forceful opening gambits and record victories against this opponent). For those who remember without fondness the distinctively suffocating adolescent solipsism of *Adolphe*, there is a perverse satisfaction to be had watching *Adolphe* (playing black) fall to *Adolphe* (playing white) in fifty-nine shambolic moves that involve much fruitless horseplay. An appetite for such forms of poetic justice is not, however, consistently sated by our software, as one certainly does not expect *Huckleberry Finn* (1884, playing white) to be picked apart in passive resignation by Kafka's *Die Verwandlung* (*The Metamorphosis*, 1915), and it is difficult to look on with suitably clinical detachment. In particular, a too-little, too-late counterpunch of (promoted) Queen b8-e5 must be said to painfully darken the miasma of futility that hangs over this confrontation from the first move (Huck's defensive "Anderssen" opening, the paralytic a2-a3).

In closing, it is perhaps worth addressing the possibility of *composing* novels specifically calibrated to win chess tournaments convened by our application. The prospect of a "grand-master," a kind of all-purpose novel-killing novel, while alluring, strikes us as beyond reach—indeed as probably a formal impossibility. But a novel written to defeat some other specific novel would appear to be an attainable objective, though a little thought suggests this would be by no means a trivial undertaking. While "encoding" tuples that would defeat a given opponent would in principle be quite easy, the real problem is doing so in the context of a work that must generate, on the basis of stylometric analysis of overall tuple frequencies, the very coordinate plane upon which those moves will be made. This would seem to give the problem a recursive character of some complexity.[4] More work is needed.

1 For an overview of the state of the field in this formative period, see Anthony Kenny, *The Computation of Style* (Oxford: Pergamon Press, 1982). For a brief history of the development of the analytic techniques themselves, consider: David I. Holmes, "The Evolution of Stylometry in Humanities Scholarship," *Literary and Linguistic Computing*, vol. 13, no. 3 (1998), pp. 111–117.
2 Our program treats both three repetitions of the same board position and fifty moves without capture or pawn move as "automatic" draws; this is a slight tweak of chess rules, which require in each case that the draw be formally claimed by a player.
3 Serious chess players will want it noted that a pawn reaching the opponent's home row *may* be promoted to any board piece (except a King) and *may not* remain a pawn. In practice, our program promotes only to Queen. In human play, promotions to other pieces are very rare.
4 A saving grace here may lie in the fact that many of our games play out without making use of more than a small fraction of one or both of the novels at issue. This would seem to open the way to drafting a novel, analyzing its tuple frequency, building the board coordinates (using the spiral configuration outlined above), and then "editing" the opening chapter to plot the moves necessary to defeat a given opponent, *but doing so while maintaining tuple-frequency neutrality* (probably by off-sets elsewhere in the text).

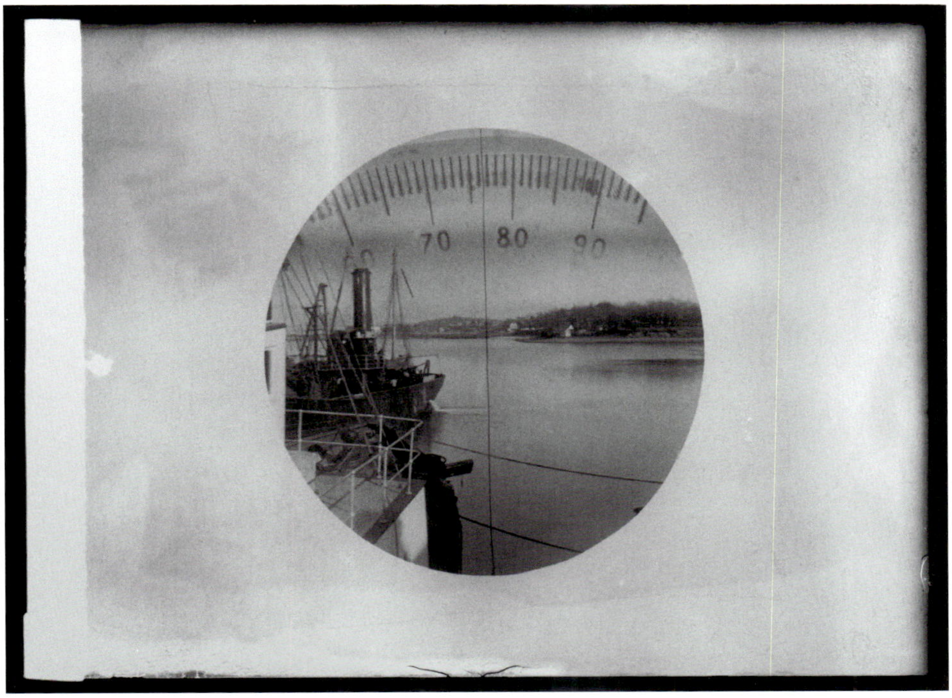

View through submarine periscope, origin unknown, between 1908 and 1919. Courtesy Library of Congress.

PIRATES OF THE DEEP

DANIEL HELLER-ROAZEN

Sovereign powers have long wished to dominate the depths as well as the surfaces of the seas. The first among them may well have been Alexander the Great. The Hellenistic *Alexander Romance* records how, having once come across a crab of monstrous proportions inside whose shell there lay seven pearls the likes of which no man had ever seen, the Macedonian monarch concluded that "they must originate in the inaccessible depths of the sea." That thought immediately led him to another. "Then," Alexander proudly recalled in an informative, if lengthy, letter to his mother, "I made a large iron cage, and inside the cage I placed a large glass jar, two feet wide, and I ordered a hole to be made in the bottom of the jar, big enough for a man's hand to go through. My idea was to descend and find out what was on the floor of this sea."[1] The classical and medieval traditions offer multiple accounts of Alexander's voyages beneath the waters.[2] In Greek literary sources, he observes "all kinds of fish," including one enormous swimming beast that dares to pull the sovereign's own cage through the sea, before wrecking it against the shore, spilling the king on the sand.[3] Medieval Latin and Romance versions of the tale find the sovereign in a glass jar, absorbed in contemplation of the strange spectacles before him: "He saw fish looking very much like men and women, walking on their feet on the seabed and feeding on other fish, just as men in this world feed on animals."[4] The Old French adaptation attributed to Alexander of Paris has the king commenting on the ways of belligerent fish in battle.[5] That rendition also suggests that Alexander's wish to fashion the marvelous jar may not have been altogether unrelated to his infamous imperial ambitions. "My lords," the weary monarch declares in the verse romance, before proposing his novel plan, "I have conquered widely. The inhabitants of Jerusalem do exactly as I will. I have destroyed the people of Tyre on account of their great cruelty. Because of me, Darius, King of Persia, has been put to death by his own people. Now I will tell you what I have thought: I have come and gone about the earth enough. I wish to know the truth concerning the people of the seas."[6]

"Cage" or "jar," the vessel Alexander invented to obtain that truth bears more than a passing resemblance to the sturdy and armed devices of underwater travel now commonly called "submarines." It was not till the first half of the twentieth century, however, that common monarchs had at their disposal tools like

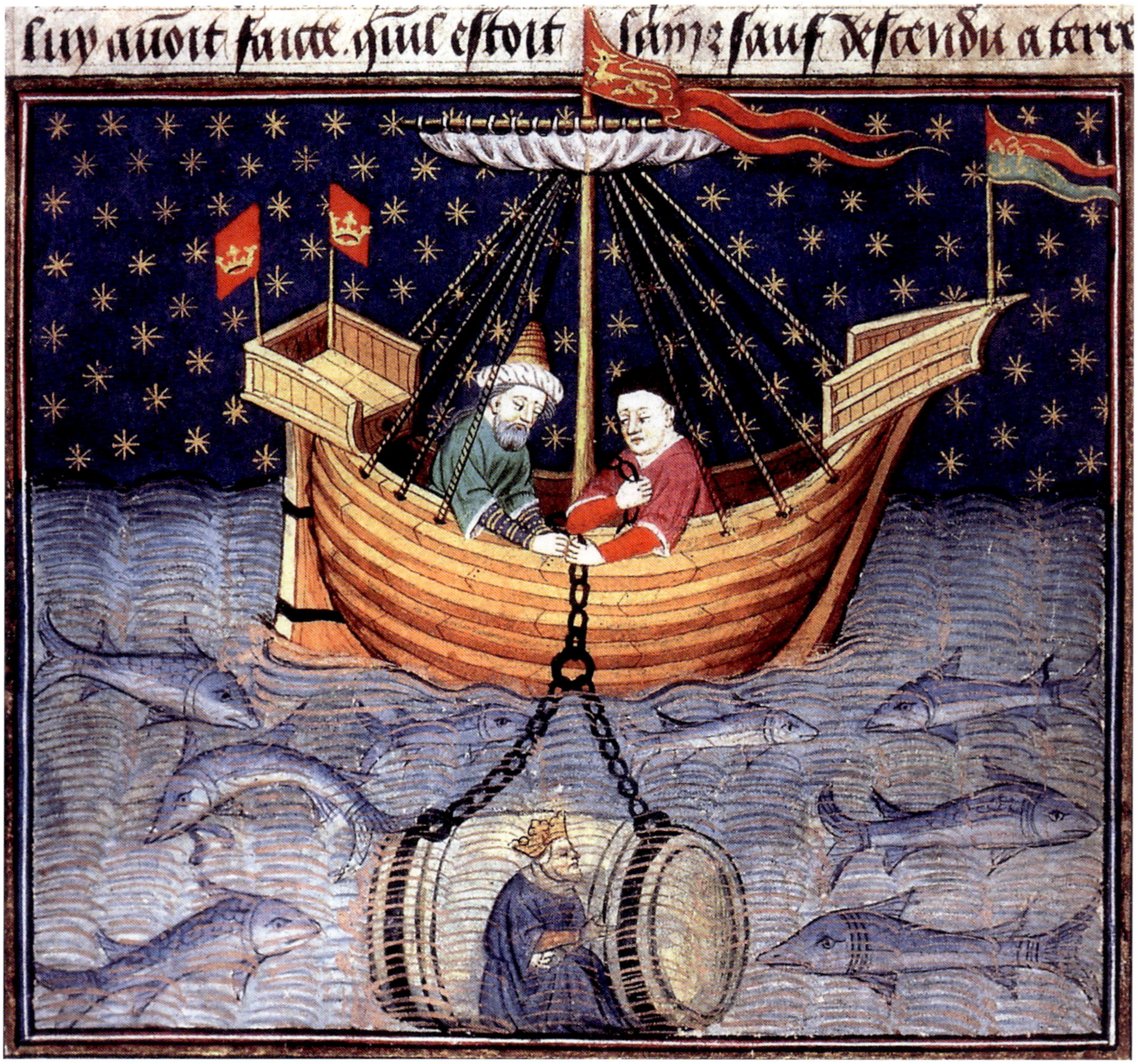

Illuminated manuscript, fifteenth century. Alexander the Great surveys the ocean submerged in a glass diving bell.

Alexander's, and that the unlikely ships began to contribute significantly to the naval forces of sovereign states. The new vessels emerged, so to speak, most notably during World War I, when the German Empire employed them with considerable success against its enemies. Those who witnessed the appearance of the new technology of war naturally noted its remarkable stealth and destructive power, but they also saw immediately that this was a ship unlike those used in traditional combat between belligerents. The submarine marked a departure for the international principles of war. Although the underwater vessel could be, and indeed was, employed against ships of state, by its very form it resisted adherence to the rules established by the law. The modern doctrine of war stipulated that to be lawful, state vessels were to comply with certain principles. They were required, for instance, to affiliate themselves visibly with their state, usually by means of a flag—if not permanently, at least always in the moments prior to attacking. When they waged war, they were to discriminate, at least in principle, between a neutral and an enemy vessel. They also had to be willing to receive on board for safety the crew of the opposing vessel, and if they took captives, they were to do so in accordance with the jurisdiction of the prize court.

By its design, however, the submarine could respect no such imperatives.[7] Its action was secretive by definition; it possessed no technology, at least at its inception, by which to distinguish under water between enemy and neutral ships; finally, its construction did not furnish it with any certain means for taking aboard captives, and its own crew, in any case, was too exiguous to afford personnel for staffing prize vessels and visiting and searching passing ships. The new underwater craft was no more, and no less, than a sealed and swimming weapon for sinking enemy vessels. In the late nineteenth century, some jurists, such as the members of the *jeune école* in France, defended the new war vessels for this very reason, claiming that they were less of the form of a ship than that of a boat. They were particularly close in kind to the novel torpedo-boat; therefore "the existing rules relating to visit and search should not apply to them."[8] But their judgments were "promptly countered," as Colombos recalls, "by those of other sailors, especially by Admiral Bourgeois in 1886: 'the advent of the torpedo, whatever its influence on naval material, has in no way changed international treaties, the law of nations or the moral laws which govern the world. It has not given the belligerent the right of life and death over the peaceful citizens of the enemy State or of neutral States.'"[9] That judgment left little room for doubt. But the juridical status of the seafarers of the new vessels in those years was still far from certain, as interested observers were well aware. With uncanny prescience, Jules Verne famously remarked upon the fact in his 1869 novel, *Twenty Thousand Leagues Under the Sea*. When Captain Nemo and the underwater crew of the *Nautilus* abduct Dr. Pierre Aronnax and his companions, the astute and learned, if understandably bewildered, protagonist exclaims: "With whom were we dealing? Perhaps with some pirates of a new variety, who exploit the sea in their own fashion?"[10]

The question became most acute with the outbreak of World War I. One episode in particular attracted the attention of international lawyers everywhere. It was the sinking, on 7 May 1915, of a large and famous British transatlantic liner, the *Lusitania*, as it made its way from the shores of the United States to England. While expressing its "deepest sympathy" for the death of some two thousand people on board, who were almost all noncombatants, the German authorities publicly justified the act with reference to the maritime blockade the British had imposed on Germany. The English act of war, they claimed, was starving the German civilian population and had, therefore, effectively obliged the well-meaning representatives of their state "to resort to retaliatory measures."[11] The legal authorities of Germany appear largely to have seconded that judgment. They argued that, in any case, it was senseless to demand that underwater vessels conform to the old laws of naval warfare. "New situations," Max Fleischmann of the University of Königsberg explained, with reference to "the case of the *Lusitania*," "necessitate new rules."[12] Ernst Zitelmann, from the University of Bonn, was more explicit. "Legal rules that are inapplicable to new conditions," he wrote, "must give way to new regulations. 'As the reason for the law ceases, so, too, must the law itself cease' (*Cessante ratione legis cessat lex ipsa*). Technical science and polity may create new conditions which of necessity destroy the framework of the old rules of international law. Who would have thought at the time the old rules governing maritime warfare were formed, of the possibilities of submarine warfare? Had the use of submarines been anticipated, special rules governing their employment would have been devised."[13]

Anglo-Saxon jurists of the period tended to find such claims unconvincing. Past practices in war, they recalled, set clear standards that need not be lowered. "Even Semmes," J. W. Garner commented in *International Law of the World War*, "who was variously described as a 'freebooter,' 'corsair,' and 'pirate,' never destroyed an enemy vessel without taking off

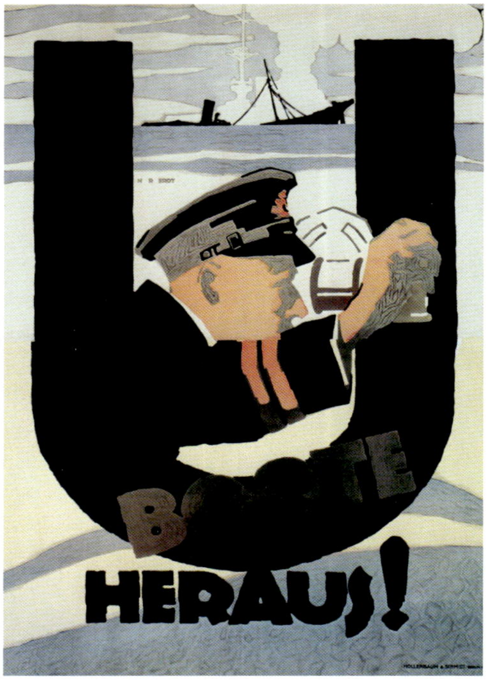

U Boote Heraus! (U-Boats, Launch!). World War I German propaganda poster.

the crew and passengers."[14] When the Confederate Admiral described his treatment of Northern captives in *Memories of Service Afloat During the War Between the States*, he had proudly declared: "We were making war upon the enemy's commerce, not upon his unarmed seamen. It gave me as much pleasure to treat these with humanity as it did to destroy his ships."[15] During the Great War, the President of the United States also pronounced himself on the question, stating that armies that availed themselves of submarines could make no such clear distinction. Responding to the torpedoing of the *Lusitania* in 1915, Woodrow Wilson stressed the "practical impossibility of employing submarines in the destruction of commerce without disregarding those rules of fairness, reason, justice and humanity which all modern opinion regards as imperative."[16] A year later, he went further, declaring the submarine, by virtue of its methods of activity, essentially "incompatible with the principles of humanity, the long-established and incontrovertible rights of neutrals and the sacred immunities of non-combatants."[17] A naval treaty proposed by the United States in 1922 aimed to establish that judgment in the law of nations forever. "It is practically impossible," the opening article of the Washington Conference read, "to utilize submarines without violating the generally recognized principles of international law."[18] The Conference was not ratified, but it was followed, eight years later, by the London Treaty on the Limitation and Reduction of Naval Armament, signed by Great Britain, France, Italy, the United States, and Japan, which aimed to submit the underwater vessels to the same legal principles that held for ships of war. "Submarines," the Treaty declared, "must conform to the rules of international law to which surface vessels are subject."[19]

That restriction of underwater vessels came to be incorporated into the so-called London Protocol of 6 November 1936, which was signed by many sovereign states, Germany not least. Within months, however, the troubled question of the legal status of the submarine once more emerged. The Spanish Civil War had brought new insecurities to the Mediterranean seas. Although the military conflict was one of notable importance, the major powers chose not to intervene and, claiming complete neutrality in the conflict, they formally refused the rights of belligerency. Almost as soon as the Civil War erupted, however, the waters surrounding Spain were affected. Submarines as well as airplanes began targeting maritime vessels bearing goods to and from the Iberian Peninsula, with little regard for their legal status in the conflict. The perpetrators did not publicly identify themselves, but it could hardly be doubted that those acts of maritime destruction would entail consequences for the Civil War. As one contemporary observer recalled, "the attacks were obviously of strategic importance in cutting the flow of supplies from Soviet Russia to the Spanish Government, as both those governments violently denounced the attacks and openly accused Italy of being responsible for them."[20] Soon the range of targets grew wider; not only merchant ships but also war vessels belonging to neutral powers were struck.
To offer a united response to such maritime assaults on non-belligerent vessels, the British and French authorities summoned an international conference at Nyon in September 1937. Nine Mediterranean states, including Bulgaria, Romania, and the Soviet Union, but excluding both Italy and Germany, met to discuss the urgent issue of "attacks ... repeatedly committed in the Mediterranean by submarines against merchant ships not belonging to either of the conflicting Spanish parties." Referring to the London Naval Treaty of 1930, the authors of the Nyon Arrangements judged the recent acts to be "violations of the rules of international law." But then they went one step further. The assaults committed by submarines, they subsequently proclaimed, "constitute acts contrary to the most elementary dictates of humanity, which should be justly treated as piracy."[21]

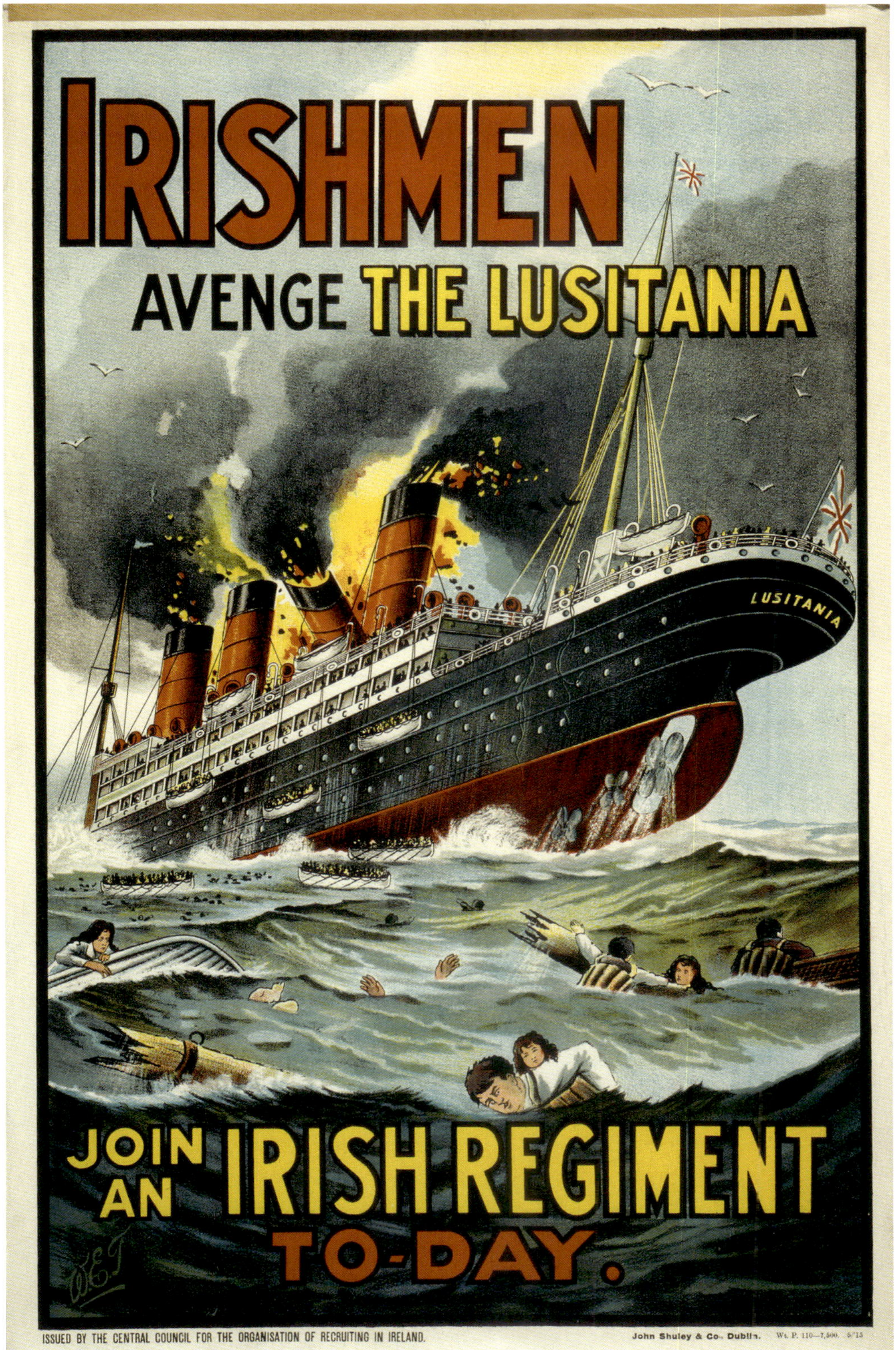

Lusitania poster produced by the Central Council for the Organisation of Recruiting in Ireland, 1915.

That declaration introduced a new term into the discussion of submarines. Admittedly, the choice of diction was by 1937 not entirely without precedent. Commenting on the Nyon Agreement's wording, an unidentified contributor to the *British Yearbook for International Law* recalled in 1938 that two decades earlier, "great indignation was caused by the sinking by German submarines during the Great War, contrary to the rules of maritime warfare with regard to the exercise of belligerent rights at sea, of the merchant vessels of belligerent and neutral powers, and by the loss of non-combatant and neutral lives and property involved. This action was often described popularly as piracy."[22] But the author took pains to specify that this was a resolutely non-technical usage, which had been without significance for the practice of the law: "no captured submarine officers, who had acted in accordance with the orders of the government, were tried as pirates."[23]

There were good legal reasons for that fact, as commentators soon observed. Prominent British and French legal scholars agreed that such a use of the term "piracy" could not be technically exact.[24] But the most vehement responses to the Nyon Agreement came from jurists in Italy and Germany. The most eminent among them was Carl Schmitt, who published a characteristically pithy and polemical essay on the international accord the month it was signed.[25] Discussing the essay in a letter to his friend Ernst Jünger, Schmitt recalled several weeks later, on 14 November 1937, how this particular contribution to the law of nations had arisen from a moment of rare passion. "The essay on 'The Concept of Piracy,'" Schmitt confessed, "emerged from the affect provoked in me when I see how cold-bloodedly the Anglo-Saxons are pursuing the World War, and how they seem to have succeeded at Nyon in achieving the very thing that, throughout the war, we sought to avoid—namely, the renunciation of the honor of the *U-Boot* weapon."[26]

Despite the unusual emotion that elicited it, however, Schmitt's essay was in its argument largely conventional. It aimed to establish the inapplicability of the title of "piracy" to political agents, demonstrating the irreducibility, so to speak, of the "concept of the piratical" to the "concept of the political." Schmitt's most original contribution lay in his analysis of the political meaning of the Allied invocation of "piracy." He argued that the terms of the 1937 agreement belonged "to the great domain of attempts at a new and genuine inter-state European order." This was one new "order" that Schmitt enjoined his readers to oppose, since it implied the confusion of a distinction fundamental to the modern law of nations: namely, that between principles of international relations and principles of domestic jurisdiction; between categories of war and categories of crime; between "politics," in short, and "police."[27] Because "pirates," he recalled, are not in any classical sense legitimate belligerents, the military operation undertaken against them cannot be defined in traditional terms as "war." "The action taken against pirates is therefore equally non-political. It is not war; instead it is either criminal justice, according to the English conception, or, according to the continental system, a measure of international maritime police."[28]

That Schmitt believed he could uphold "the honor of the *U-Boot* weapon" by invoking the hallowed principles of the European law of nations is one startling fact. The same jurist who had famously explained in an article of 1934 how exactly "the Führer protects the law"[29] now strenuously warned his readers that the English notion of piracy would forever disturb the classic order of European public law. "Should the English conception of submarine piracy be established as a general concept of the law of nations," Schmitt wrote, "the concept of piracy will have changed its place in the system of international law. It will have been displaced from the empty space of non-political action into the space of intermediary concepts between war and peace, which is typical of the after-war period."[30] One might certainly respond that a scholar of the law who had publicly revealed the reasons why "the *Führer* has the right, as well as the force, to found a new state and a new order" and who had been willing to assent, not least, to the National Socialist doctrine of the biological substance of race, could not credibly implore others to rise in defense of the traditional legal principles of war and peace.[31] One might doubtless allege that Schmitt's position was incoherent, even hypocritical. But such considerations do not alter one insight he expressed in this brief tract. By 1937, the legal status of warfare had undergone one irrevocable change: state vessels were no longer impervious to charges of criminality. In addition to the classic conception of war as the lawful conflict of sovereign nations, a new model of confrontation had emerged. It pitted not one public figure against its symmetrical antagonist but one collective term against its lesser, infamous opponents, setting the representatives of a universal code of law against the stateless criminals who sought to transgress it.

Schmitt understood that the sole noun that would lend legitimacy to this new confrontation was one the jurists of the tradition had rarely employed: "humanity." Only if war could be defined with respect to such an abstract and general notion as the common species would it become possible to treat the conflict of sovereign states as "either criminal justice, according to the English conception, or, according to the continental system, a measure of international ... police." Only then could enemies be cast as criminals. In his vain and lucid attempt to recall the traditional doctrine of public law he had done so much to supplant with his legal theories of the National Socialist régime, Schmitt also intuited that one figure alone would be sufficient to summon such a generic collectivity: the figure of its archaic foe, "the enemy of the human species." "Against the pirate as 'the enemy of the human species,'" Schmitt remarked, "all humanity—which is otherwise so disheveled—suddenly appears as if united on a single front."[32] Hence the intensity with which the erstwhile "crown jurist" militated against references to piracy in war. Committed by "affect" no less than interest to defending the legitimacy of the German and Italian belligerents, he implored his contemporaries not to conjure, through the magic name of "the common enemy of all," the humanity he hoped might still continue to remain "otherwise so disheveled." But by 1937 it was already too late. The modern submarine was neither the iron cage of the ancient and medieval fables nor the state ship of war of modern times, whose movements across the surface of the seas, while threatening, could still be safely restricted by the old principles of law. The *U-Boot*, a creature of unsettled and unsettling times, penetrated a new dimension. Its destructive operations beneath the surface of the world's waters announced the age in which piracy would inevitably "change its place," and in which it would soon be quite impossible to keep that obscure presupposition of the law of the nations, humanity, from coming into view.

1 See Richard Stoneman, trans., *The Greek Alexander Romance* (London: Penguin Books, 1991), p. 118.

2 On the literary and iconographical traditions of Alexander beneath the seas, see David J. Ross, "Alexander and the Faithless Lady," in *Studies in the Alexander Romance* (London: Pindar Press, 1985), pp. 382–403.

3 Stoneman, *The Greek Alexander Romance*, pp. 118–119.

4 See the Latin and Old French texts in Alfons Hilka, *Der altfranzösische Prosa-Alexander-Roman* (Halle: Max Niemeyer, 1920), § 116, pp. 231–232.

5 Alexander of Paris, *Le Roman d'Alexandre*, eds. E. C. Armstrong et al., trans. Laurence Harf-Lancner (Paris: Le Livre de Poche, 1994), pp. 320–321.

6 Ibid., pp. 316–317.

7 See Judge Atherley-Jones, "The Deutschland," in *Problems of the War: Papers Read before the Grotius Society in the Year 1917*, vol. 3 (1917), p. 39.

8 See John C. Colombos, *The International Law of the Sea*, 6th ed. (New York: David McKay Company Inc., 1967), p. 511. On the *jeune école*'s theories of the submarine, see Arne Røksund, *The Jeune École: The Strategy of the Weak* (Leiden: Brill, 2007), pp. 177–244.

9 Colombos, *International Law of the Sea*, p. 511.

10 Jules Verne, *Vingt mille lieues sous les mers*, ed. Jacques Noiray (Paris: Folio Gallimard, 2005), p. 118.

11 James Wilford Garner, *International Law and the World War*, vol. 1 (London: Longmans, Green and Co., 1920), p. 357.

12 See Max Fleischmann, ed., "Der Lusitania Fall im Urteile von deutschen Gelehrten," in *Zeitschrift für Völkerrecht*, no. 9 (1916), p. 159. Garner refers to this phrase in *International Law and the World War*, vol. 1, p. 375.

13 Ernst Zitelmann, "The War and International Law," trans. William Wallace Whitelock, in *Modern Germany in Relation to the Great War, by Various German Writers* (New York: Mitchell Kennerly, 1916), p. 609.

14 Garner, *International Law and the World War*, vol. 1, p. 370.

15 Raphael Semmes, *Memories of Service Afloat During the War Between the States* (Baltimore, MD: Kelly, Piet & Co., 1869), p. 131.

16 Cited in Garner, *International Law and the World War*, vol. 1, pp. 373–374.

17 ibid., p. 374.

18 On the Washington Conference, see Ronald Roxburgh, "Submarines at the Washington Conference," in *British Yearbook of International Law*, no. 3 (1922–1923), pp. 150–158; H. W. Malkin, "The Washington Conference (November 12, 1921 – February 6, 1922)," in *British Yearbook of International Law*, no. 3 (1922–1923), pp. 179–182.

19 See text of the London Naval Treaty in Dietrich Schindler and Jiří Toman, *The Laws of Armed Conflicts: A Collection of Conventions, Resolutions, and Other Documents*, 3rd ed. (Dordrecht: Nijhoff, 2004), pp. 881–882. That restriction of underwater warfare subsequently came to be incorporated into the London Protocol of 6 November 1936. See the *procès-verbal* relating to the rules of submarine warfare in Schindler and Toman, *The Laws of Armed Conflicts*, pp. 883–884.

20 George A. Finch, "Piracy in the Mediterranean," in *The American Journal of International Law*, vol. 31, no. 4 (1937), p. 659.

21 From the preamble of the Nyon Arrangement drafted at the Nyon Conference on the Prevention of Piratical Acts in the Mediterranean and Turkey. For the full text of the agreement, see Schindler and Toman, *The Laws of Armed Conflicts*, pp. 887–889.

22 Anonymous, "The Nyon Arrangements: Piracy by Treaty?" in *British Yearbook of International Law*, no. 19 (1938), p. 199. Finch observes, moreover, that seeds of the full-fledged formula may be found in Woodrow Wilson's statement before the US Congress on 2 April 1917, that "the present German submarine warfare is a warfare against mankind. It is a war against all nations." Finch, "Piracy in the Mediterranean," p. 665.

23 Anonymous, "The Nyon Arrangements," p. 199.

24 In addition to "The Nyon Arrangements," see Finch, "Piracy in the Mediterranean"; Raoul Genet, "The Charge of Piracy in the Spanish Civil War," *The American Journal of International Law*, vol. 32, no. 2 (1938), pp. 253–263; and "La qualification de 'pirates' et le dilemme de la guerre civile," *Revue internationale française du droit des gens*, no. 3 (1937), pp. 13–25.

25 Schmitt's paper, "Der Begriffe der Piraterie," appeared first in *Völkerbund und Völkerrecht*, vol. 4 (September–October 1937), pp. 351–354. It is reprinted in Schmitt, *Frieden oder Pazifismus? Arbeiten zum Völkerrecht und zur Internationalen Politik, 1924–1978*, ed. Günther Maschke (Berlin: Duncker & Humblot, 2005), pp. 509–511. After the war, Schmitt once again considered the historical significance of the submarine; see *Der Nomos der Erde im Völkerrecht des Jus Publicum Europaeum*, 4th ed. (Berlin: Duncker & Humblot, 1997), pp. 290–293.

26 Schmitt, "Letter to Jünger, November 14, 1937," in Helmuth Kiesel, ed., *Briefe 1930–1983: Ernst Jünger, Carl Schmitt* (Stuttgart: Klett-Cotta, 1999), pp. 69–70. As Masckhe's notes to Schmitt's article indicate, Schmitt promptly mailed a copy of his essay to the *Oberkommando* of the German Marine, whose office duly responded with appreciation. See Schmitt, *Frieden oder Pazifismus*, p. 517.

27 Schmitt, *Frieden oder Pazifismus*, p. 517.

28 Ibid., p. 508.

29 Schmitt, "Der Führer schützt das Recht – zur Reichstagsrede Adolf Hitlers vom 13. Juli, 1934," first published in *Deutsche Juristen-Zeitung*, vol. 39, no. 15 (1934), pp. 945–950. It is reprinted in Schmitt, *Positionen und Begriffe im Kampf mit Weimar-Genf-Versailles 1923–1939* (Berlin: Duncker & Humblot, 1994), pp. 199–203.

30 Schmitt, *Frieden oder Pazifismus?*, p. 508.

31 Schmitt, *Positionen und Begriffe*, p. 200. Numerous texts bearing witness to Schmitt's sympathy with and deference to National Socialist doctrines of race could be cited. One document of particular importance is the report on the conference he organized on 3–4 October 1936, dedicated to "German Juridical Science in Combat with the Jewish Spirit." See "Die Deutsche Rechtswissenschaft im Kampf gegen den Jüdischen Geist," in *Deutsche Juristen-Zeitung*, vol. 41, no. 20 (1936), pp. 1193–1199.

32 Schmitt, *Frieden oder Pazifismus?*, p. 509.

CABINETLANDIA: UPDATE NO. 4

REBAR

The construction of the Cabinet National Library in 2004 was the formative project for Rebar, our San Francisco-based art and design studio. Then, as now, we were self-styled idealistic conceptualists—foolhardy speculators, installation tricksters, land art humorists, remixers and remakers of the everyday landscape. Our ongoing exploration of fragmented landscapes, ambiguously defined sites, liminal territories, niche spaces, loopholes in the code, and eddies in the flow of regulation—an exploration that forms Rebar's principal conceptual program—began in the desolation of Cabinetlandia, a few miles outside Deming, New Mexico.

Yet—as is the case with many outlandish dreams made manifest—the years had not been altogether charitable to the Cabinet National Library. As periodically reported in the pages of this magazine, the desert itself intervened in our intervention. After five years of steady environmental critique from the wind and weather—not to mention visits from creatures hailing from several phyla, the occasional vandal, an intermittent thief, and a valiant (but failed) attempt at a *coup d'état*—the Library had been reduced to ruins. The bottom drawer of the cabinet (originally the snack bar) was partially caked in mud and stuck shut. The Library's collection had dwindled to a single copy of *Cabinet* no. 22 ("Insecurity"), which had hardened into a sturdy adobe brick. That issue—with its cover image of soap opera actor Larry Hagman flashing a spectacular smile now slowly fading into nothingness—seemed an apt metaphor for the entire history of the Library project.

So it was that we decided to commemorate the fifth anniversary of the opening of the Library—to the day—by returning with a grand plan not only to re-secure and renovate the Library, but to carry out a new capital improvement project: the Library Exhibition Annex ("LEA"), a 220-square-inch gallery that boasts more than 380 square inches of white-wall space and will be available for exhibitions, performances, lectures, and other cultural projects. During our four-day adventure (excluding the sixteen-hour drive each way from San Francisco to Cabinetlandia), we encountered many of the same forces that had decimated the Library. Savagely indifferent thunderstorms left us stranded in the mud on three separate occasions. Once, we were forced to abandon the van and all our equipment overnight and literally run for our lives. During the days working at Cabinetlandia, we slogged through rain, heat, mud, dust, more mud, and then lightning storms, though we were also treated to the occasional rainbow.

In the end, the adventure was successful. We rebuilt the Library and re-stocked it with the entire corpus of *Cabinet*. We elevated the Library structure two feet above the desert floor, rebuilt the structural wall with an additional two hundred pounds of mud and cement, added a swale to improve drainage, and cleaned and weatherproofed the cabinet. When we had finished, we celebrated by attending the Cabinetlandia Senior Prom (theme: "Into the Bush"). Everyone had a grand time, though the prom was interrupted by a pitched war for territory between two colonies of fire ants. It turns out that the bite of a fire ant is extremely painful—especially on prom night. And, as we were packing up and preparing to leave Cabinetlandia, we encountered in the desert the very thoughts of the Library itself, spectral images encoded in dust and wind. Loosed from its earthly bounds, it was as though the Library was contemplating its own future potentialities, expressing its internalized delusions of grandeur. We arrived back in civilization with a nagging question: will the dreams of the Library ever be realized, or will the structure succumb to the seemingly inexorable forces of ruin? Is the Cabinet National Library destined to become a durable monument to the fantasies of everyday office furniture, or a mound of defeated dust? Time alone will tell.

The Cabinet National Library 2009 team comprised Matthew Passmore, John Bela, Teresa Aguilera, Masha Slavnova, and Jed Olson. We are also endebted to Cordelia Rose and her crew for a mission-critical tow out of the mud.

For more on the history of Cabinetlandia, see <www. cabinetmagazine.org/information/cabinetlandia.php>

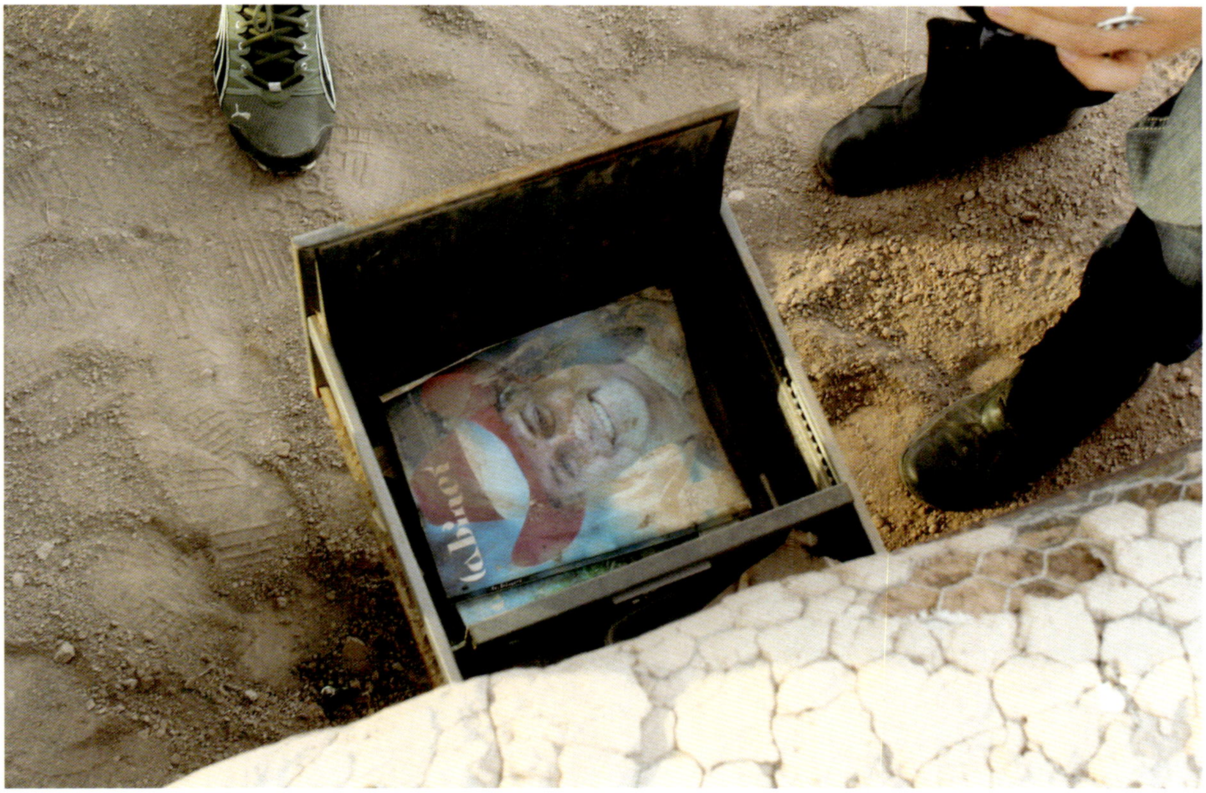

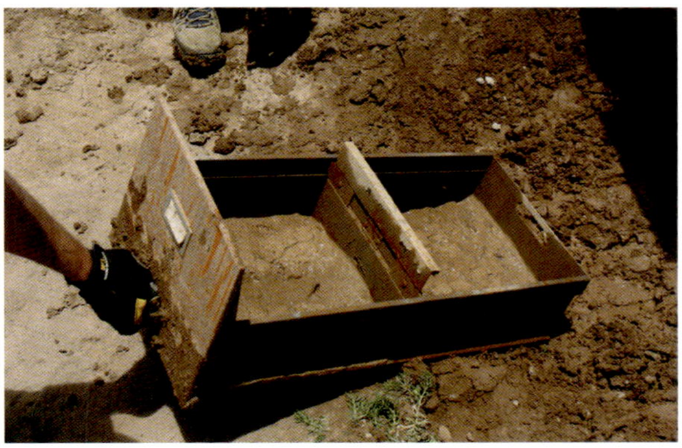

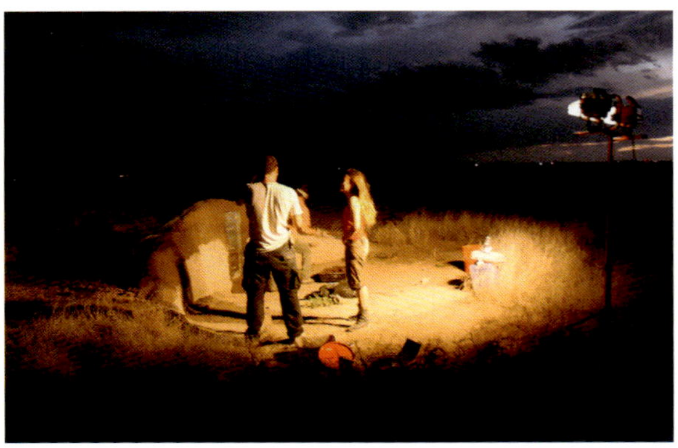

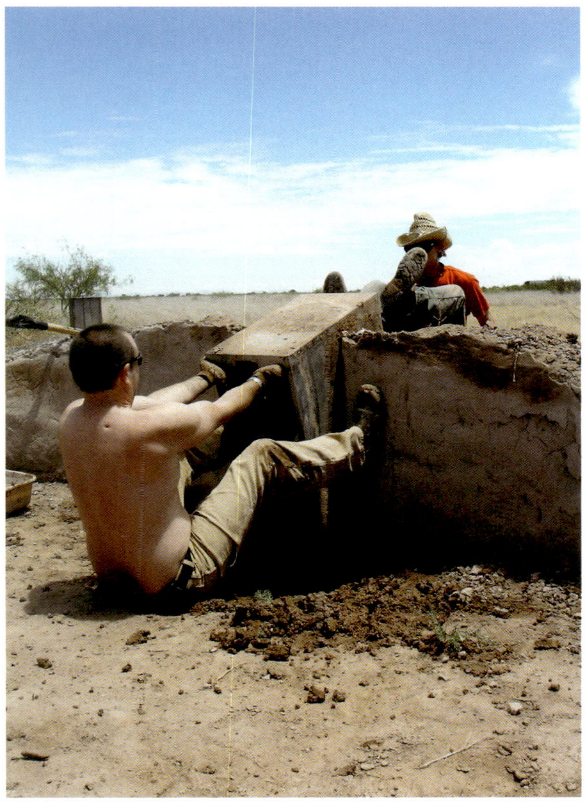

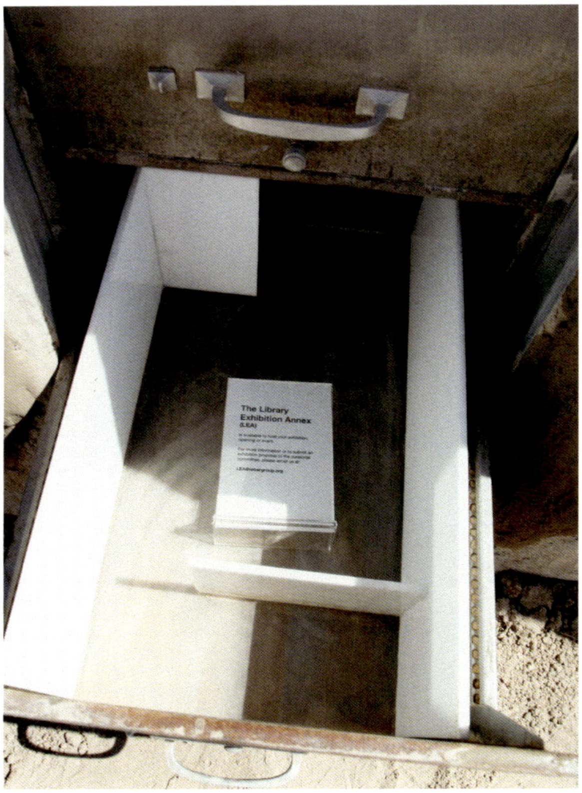
The Library
Exhibition Annex
(LEA)

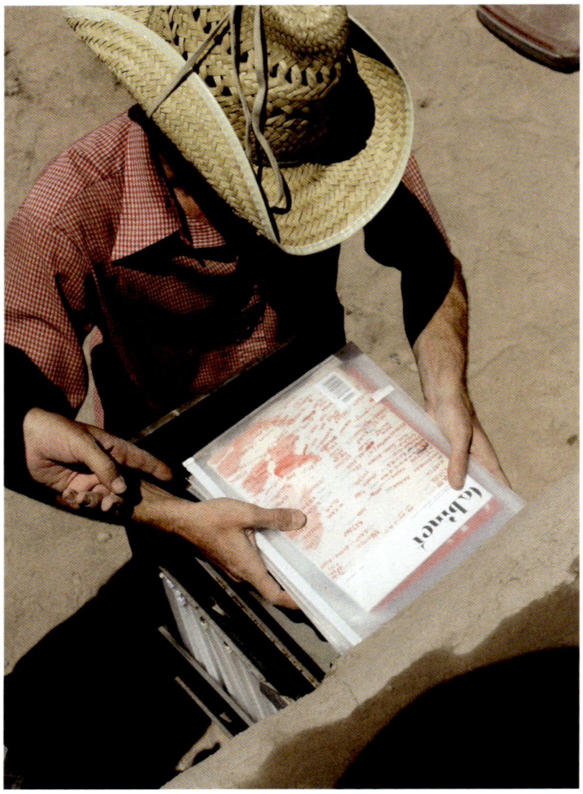
Cabinet

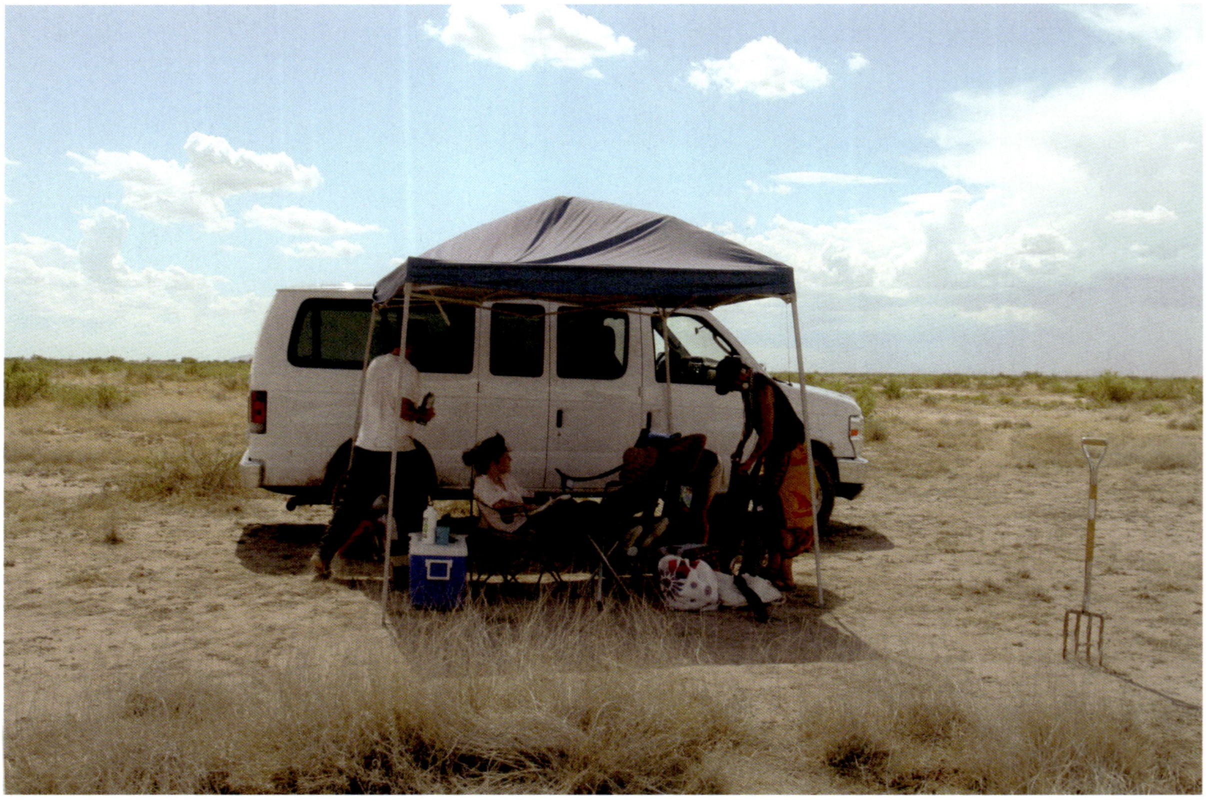

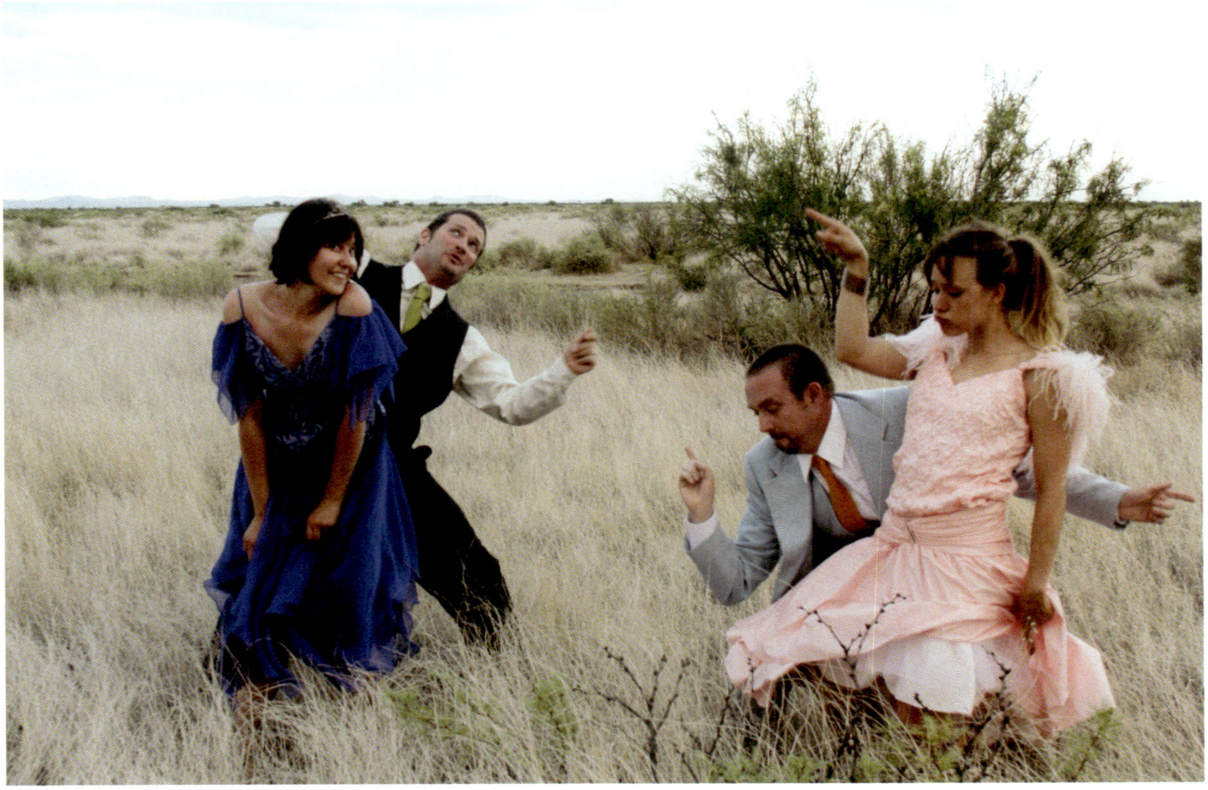

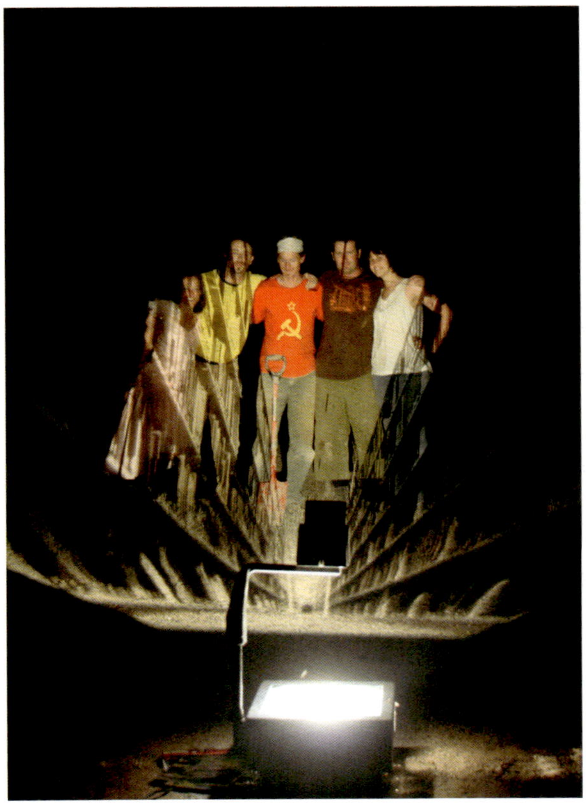

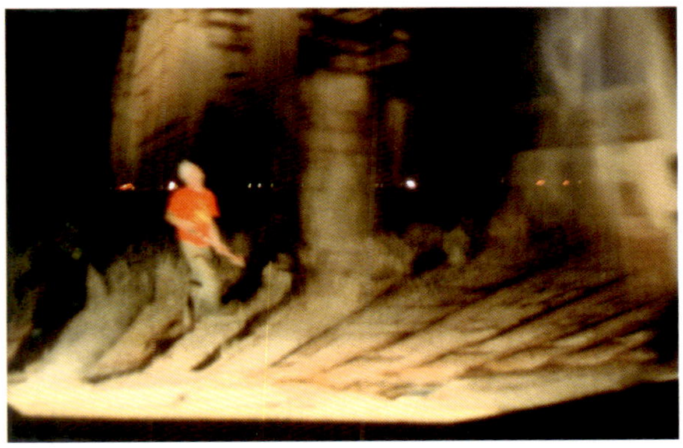

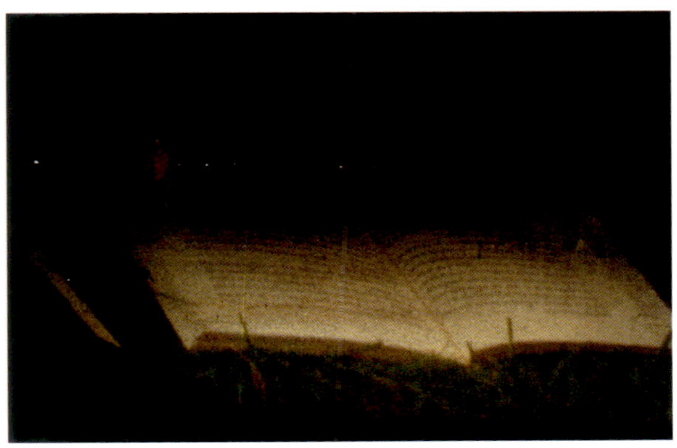

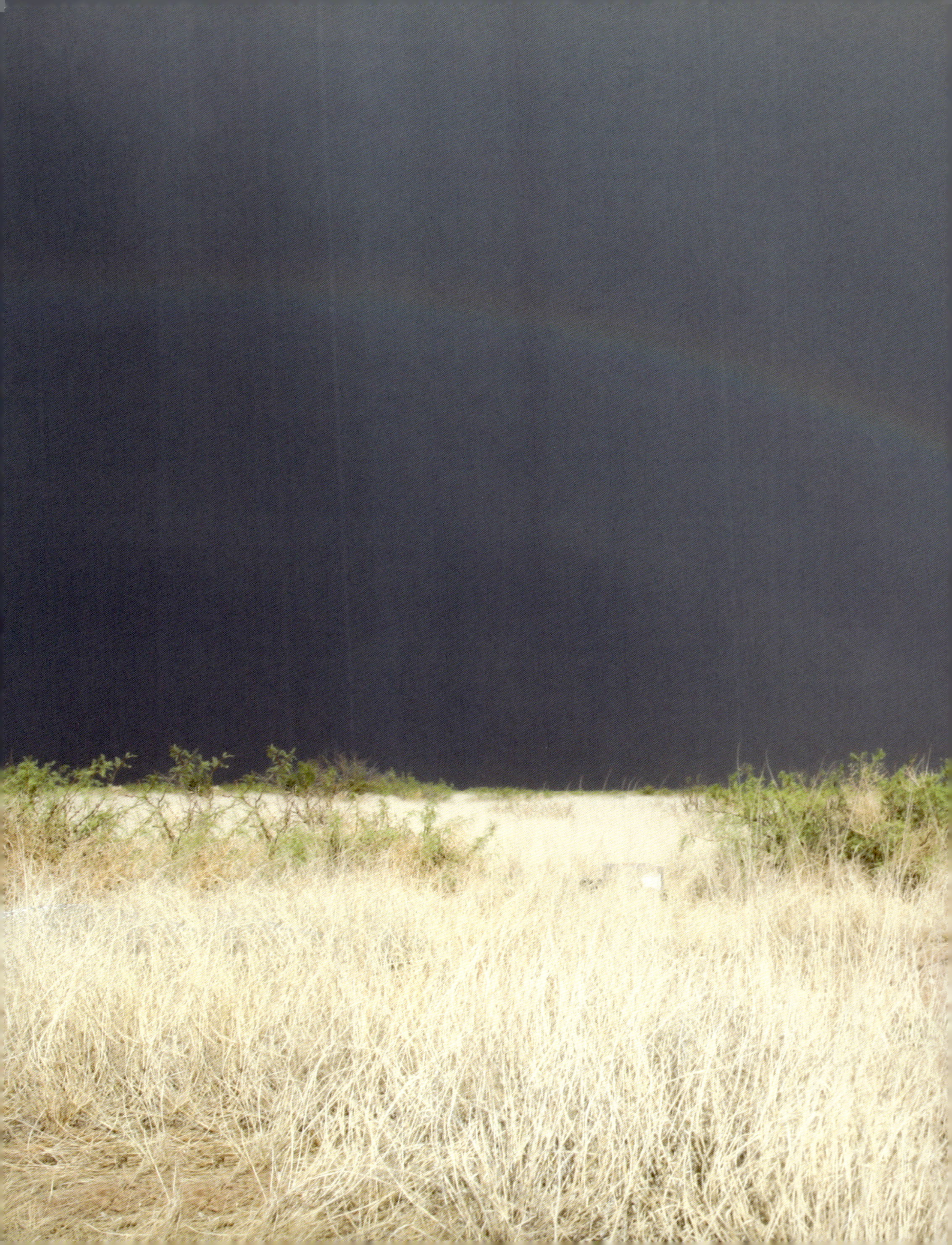

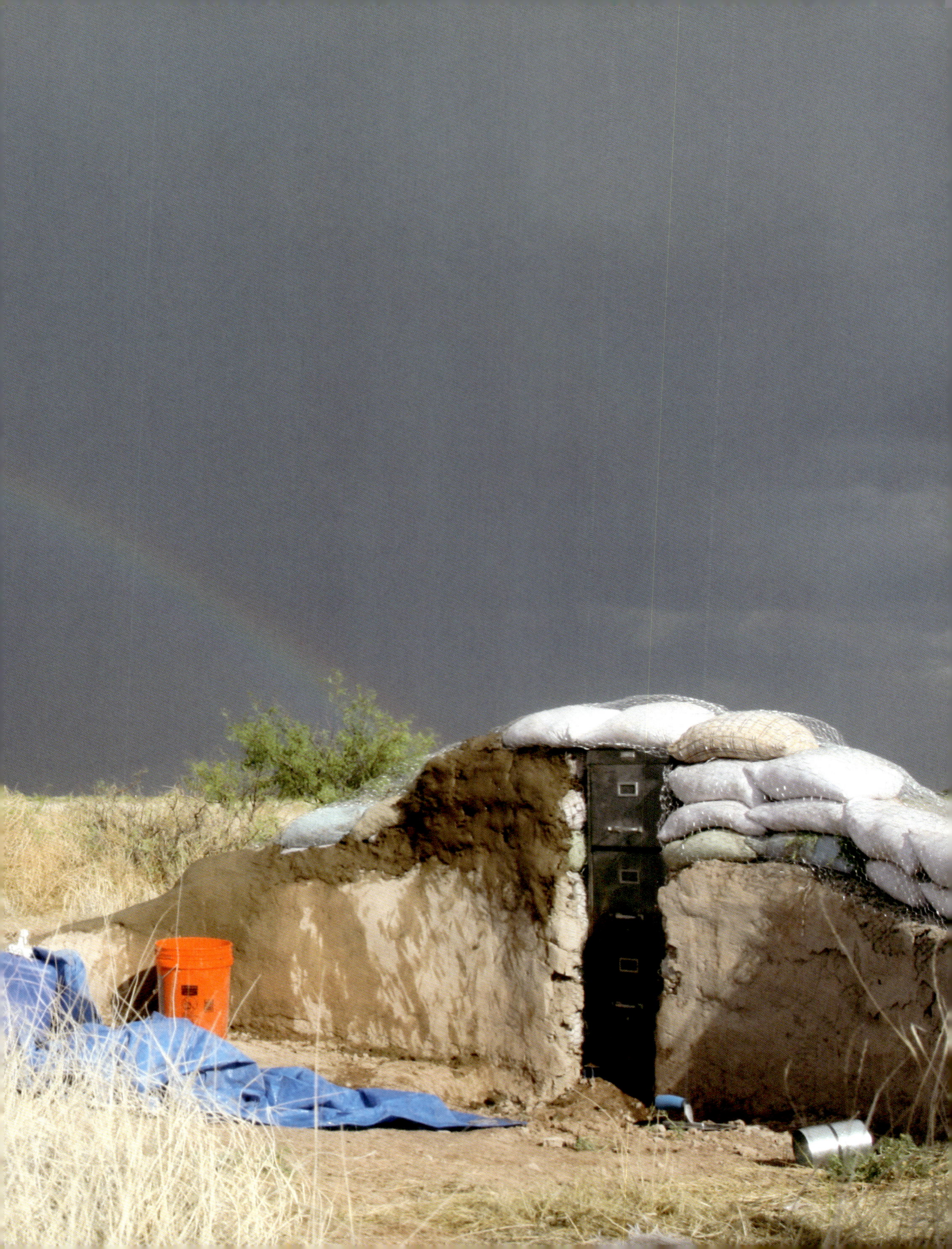

DUST

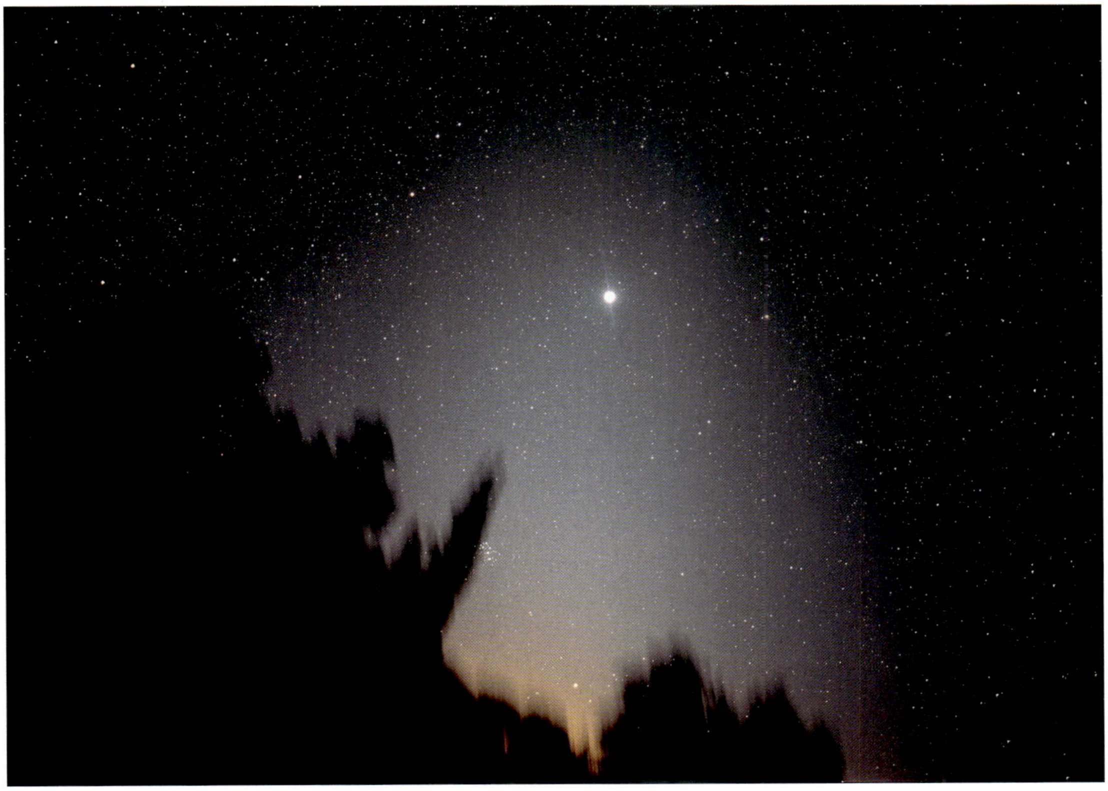

Zodiacal Light and Venus, Namibia, 2001. The Zodiacal Light is a hazy triangle that is the result of sunlight scattered by dust in the solar system's ecliptic plane; Venus is at the top of the triangle's cone. Courtesy Capella Observatory.

A DRY BLACK VEIL

BRIAN DILLON

By the last decades of the nineteenth century, an obscuring perplex of ideas regarding dust hung above the inhabitants of the European city like overlapping clouds, variously threatening or inspiring with the weight of knowledge, quantity of filth, or degree of infection they contained. London, especially—having only lately escaped a mid-century cholera season that had devastated parts of the inner city—seemed to exist in a miasmic haze of dirt, disease, and curiously aestheticized industrial pollution. As early as 1661, in the pages of his *Fumifugium: Or, The Inconvenience of the Aer and Smoake of London Dissipated*, the diarist and polymath John Evelyn had complained that citizens breathed "nothing but an impure and thick Mist, accompanied by a fuliginous and filthy vapour," which concoction scoured their lungs and disordered the entire body, so that coughs, catarrhs, and consumption raged more in London alone than in the whole of the rest of the world. The poison fug was partly attributable to domestic fires, but Evelyn blames brewers, dyers, lime-burners, and salt- and soap-boilers for the most noxious emanations:

> *Whilst these are belching forth from their sooty jaws, the City of* London *resembles the face rather of* Mount Aetna, *the* Court of Vulcan, Stromboli, *or the Suburbs of* Hell, *than an Assembly of Rational Creatures, and the imperial seat of our incomparable* Monarch. *For when in all other places the Aer is most Serene and Pure, it is here Ecclipsed with such a Cloud of Sulphure, as the Sun itself, which gives day to all the World besides, is hardly able to penetrate and impart it here; and the weary* Traveller, *at many Miles distance, sooner smells, than sees the City to which he repairs.*[1]

On arriving in London, avers Evelyn, the visitor in question would discover that a "sooty Crust or Fur" had settled on the city: a veil of dust that was at once obscure and "acrimonious," "superinduced" on all

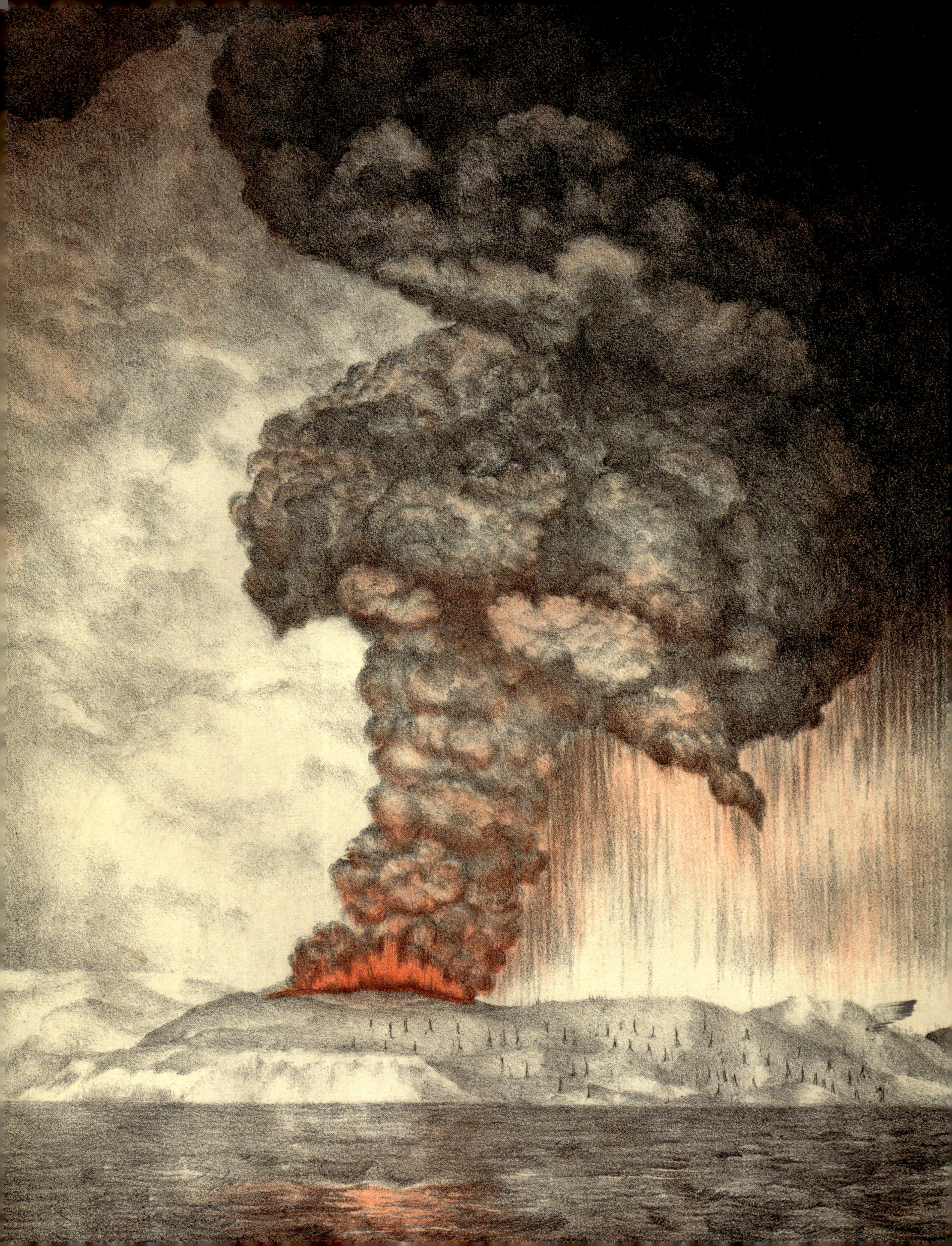

surfaces and viciously at work undermining the substance of iron, stone, and silver—even sullying the gleam of gold. In the centuries that followed, London became increasingly identified—to the point of a caricature that remained tenacious even after the implementation of the Clean Air Act of 1956—with the particulate soup that passed for a breathable medium among its encrusted streets and dust-heaped squares.

This was the city that the Victorians inherited: layered with the soot of countless coal fires, dusted with the deposits of industry, smeared everywhere with traces of the human and animal feces that fouled the air in dry weather and the feet of pedestrians in wet. (The diversion of this waste into the Thames early in the century was certainly an improvement on the piling up of ordure in streets or cellars, pending its removal by dustmen, but it had the unfortunate consequence of raising a fearsome stench along the river in mid-summer; the Great Stink of June 1858, which caused vomiting among railway passengers at London Bridge station, is just the most notorious instance.) Perhaps even more than the effects of breathing such an atmosphere in public, the Victorian bourgeoisie feared the insinuation of dust into the domestic interior, where it was transmuted from a threat to civic health into the marker of a household in disarray. This is among the more curious fates of dust in modernity: in the public sphere it signifies the depredations of industrial innovation or rising population on buildings and bodies, while in the private realm it continues to denote one's very lack of modernity, to point to an archaic or shameful inheritance, to signify lassitude or decay. The most vivid (if that is the word) example of the dust-laden domestic setting in the nineteenth century is the phantasmagoria of rot conjured by Charles Dickens in the eleventh chapter of *Great Expectations*. Entering for the first time the house of the decrepit and reclusive Miss Havisham, Pip eventually reaches her strangely frozen sanctum, a memorial chamber at the center of which sits a long-decayed wedding cake:

It was spacious, and I dare say has once been handsome, but every discernible thing in it was covered with dust and mould, and dropping to pieces. The most prominent object was a long table with a tablecloth spread on it, as if a feast had been in preparation when the house and the clocks all stopped together. An epergne or centre-piece of some kind was in the middle of this cloth; it was so heavily overburdened with cobwebs that its form was quite indistinguishable; and, as I looked along the yellow expanse out of which I remember its seeming to grow, like a fungus, I saw speckled-legged spiders with blotchy bodies running home to it, and running out from it, as if some circumstance of the greatest public importance had just transpired in the spider community.[2]

Dust is here expressly an adjunct to a certain domesticated Gothicism, but the passage can be read too as an example of the fate that might await any comfortable Victorian interior if it were allowed to languish undusted. This is the reading of the overstuffed and intricate nineteenth-century home advanced by Le Corbusier in 1923 in his *Vers une Architecture*; the comparative emptiness of the Modernist dwelling is designed to discourage the accumulation of dust, and among the architect's advice to readers concerning air, light, and vacant walls and floors is the instruction to "demand a vacuum cleaner."[3] For Modernism, to escape the nineteenth century is in part to escape the depredations of dust and the constant intimate attention that it demands to the surfaces and artifacts of the domestic sphere.

. . .

This vision of the recent past as already shrouded in dust acquires, in the works of a more dialectically or perversely inclined Modernism, the lineaments of the fantastic or of an oddly eroticized appreciation of decay. In the section of the *Arcades Project* entitled "Boredom, Eternal Return," Walter Benjamin briefly refers to the role of dust in the nineteenth-century interior, a substance at once magical and mundane: "Plush as dust collector. Mystery of dustmotes playing in the sunlight. Dust and the 'best room'.... Other arrangements to stir up dust: the trains of dresses."[4] In the decaying Paris arcades—the furred arteries of the modern city—dust both occludes and outlines the once-novel commodity and its slow desuetude. For Marcel Proust, too, dust was simultaneously to be feared (in the form of the lime-tree pollen that brought on his asthma, or the choking fumes of the coal fire in his bedroom) and welcomed for the physical and aesthetic veil it cast about him as he wrote; Proust lived his last decade in a cloud of medicinal powders, propped up among material remnants of his past—photographs, books, and furniture—that he refused to allow his servants to dust. And a few years after Proust's death, in the pages of his journal *Documents*, Georges Bataille pointed out that the dominion of dust in legend and reality had not yet been properly acknowledged:

---

opposite: Lithograph from *Royal Society Report on Krakatoa Eruption*, 1888. At the time, the dust from the eruption was believed to have affected sunrises and sunsets around the world.

The storytellers have not realised that the Sleeping Beauty would have awoken covered in a thick layer of dust; nor have they envisaged the sinister spiders' webs that would have been torn apart at the first movement of her red tresses. Meanwhile dismal sheets of dust constantly invade earthly habitations and uniformly defile them: as if it were a matter of making ready attics and old rooms for the imminent occupation of the obsessions, phantoms, spectres that the decayed odour of old dust nourishes and intoxicates. When plump young girls, "maids of all work," arm themselves each morning with a large feather-duster or even a vacuum-cleaner, they are perhaps not completely unaware that they are contributing every bit as much as the most positivist of scientists to dispelling the injurious phantoms that cleanliness and logic abhor.[5]

Dust, Bataille suggests, may one day gain the upper hand over domestic servants; he pictures a city in which dust has triumphed, "invading the immense ruins of abandoned buildings, deserted dockyards." In fact, Bataille hints in a fragment entitled "Débâcle," we may already be living in this grotesque and desiccated dustscape.

. . .

Against the deprecation of dust in the late nineteenth century and the early decades of the twentieth, an alternative body of scientific and aesthetic knowledge sought to convince of its potential for purity, beauty, and beneficence. In his 1898 essay "The Importance of Dust: A Source of Beauty," the British naturalist and explorer Alfred Russel Wallace deplored the disease-bearing dust produced by continued reliance on horses for transport and by the coal fires that were still burning at the end of the century, but celebrated for their beauty and utility the atmospheric phenomena that derived from dust:

We find that the much-abused and all-pervading dust, which, when too freely produced, deteriorates our climate and brings us dirt, discomfort, and even disease, is, nevertheless, under natural conditions, an essential portion of the economy of nature. It gives us much of the beauty of natural scenery as due to varying atmospheric effects of sky, and cloud, and sunset tints, and thus renders life more enjoyable; while, as an essential condition of diffused daylight and of moderate rainfalls combined with a dry atmosphere, it appears to be absolutely necessary for our existence upon the earth, perhaps even for the very development of terrestrial, as opposed to aquatic life.[6]

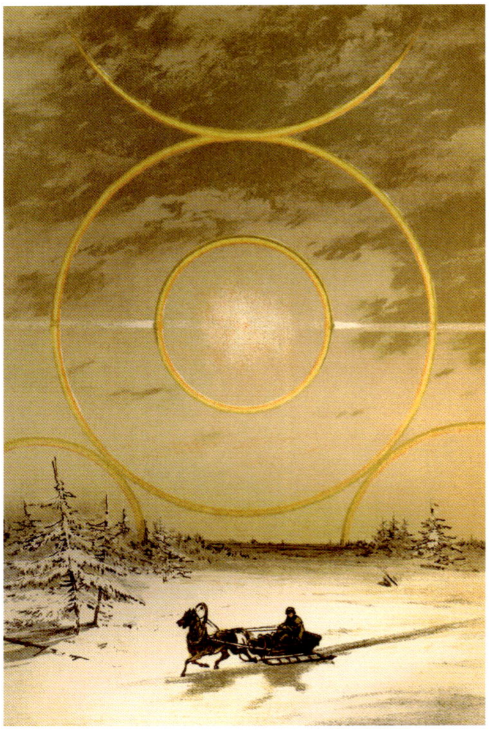

The refraction and reflection of light by tiny atmospheric ice crystals which form around dust particles produce solar halos. From Camille Flammarion, *L'Atmosphere*, 1872.

The 1883 eruption of Krakatoa produced such a volume of dust that dramatic and ravishing sunsets followed around the world for up to three years, noted Wallace, for whom the small and "despised" things had in the course of the century revealed themselves as essential adjuncts to the civilization in whose toxic and palling effects they also partake.

Wallace's scientific appreciation of the ambiguous utility of dust was mirrored in the aesthetic field by certain texts of John Ruskin, perhaps the nineteenth century's most refined (but also anxious) connoisseur of the cloudy, the gaseous, the particulate, and the friable. With respect to dust, a seam of conventional disparagement runs through Ruskin's massive oeuvre; in particular, the choking and tarnishing effects of industry and the railroads are frequent themes in his writings. But there are at least two other approaches to dust in Ruskin's work, both of them visionary, prophetic, attuned to the utopian and apocalyptic possibilities that inhere in earth and air. The first emerges in *The Ethics of the Dust*, published in 1866 and subtitled "Ten Lectures to Little Housewives on the Elements of Crystallization." The "housewives" were pupils at Winnington Hall, a girls' school in Cheshire where, Ruskin reports in his preface, he had actually supervised the lessons in crystallography that make up most of the book. (A good deal of this curious volume is devoted to the author's spreading of crystals on baize-covered tables and his whimsical efforts to get his prepubescent and teenage audience to form the shapes of various crystals with their own bodies on the grass of the school's playground.) As Ruskin's title suggests, the dialogues posit a morality born of the material and metaphorical potential of the earth itself, a deep tendency in the ground beneath our feet (however degraded) toward purity and integrity, and a parallel refinement, as of the crystallization of base matter, in the human heart. Regarding "the lowly framework of the dust," Ruskin writes:

There seems to be a continual effort to raise itself into a higher state; and a measured gain, through the fierce revulsion and slow renewal of the earth's frame, in beauty, and order, and permanence. The soft white sediments of the sea draw themselves, in process of time, into smoothed knots of sphered symmetry; burdened and strained under increase of pressure, they pass into a nascent marble. ... The dark drift of the inland river, or stagnant slime of inland pool and lake, divides, or resolves itself as it dries, into layers of its several elements; slowly purifying each by the patient withdrawal of it from the anarchy of the mass in which it was mingled.[7]

The morally inspiring process of crystallization may even occur, notes Ruskin, in "the mud or slime of a damp over-trodden path, in the outskirts of a manufacturing town." Clay, brick dust, soot, sand, and water: these substances contain the germs of precious stones, porcelain, and the elaborate integrity of snow and ice crystals. Under great pressure and over great tracts of time, they are transmuted into things of fantastic delicacy and strength—Ruskin's girlish audience is invited to emulate this exalting tendency of dust.

. . .

Ruskin had already revealed his ambiguous attitude to base particles in visible profusion in the pages of his *Modern Painters*, where he variously regrets a tendency towards cloudiness in modern landscape painting and approves indistinction as an aesthetic value: "EXCELLENCE OF THE HIGHEST KIND, WITHOUT OBSCURITY, CANNOT EXIST." But it was in his late

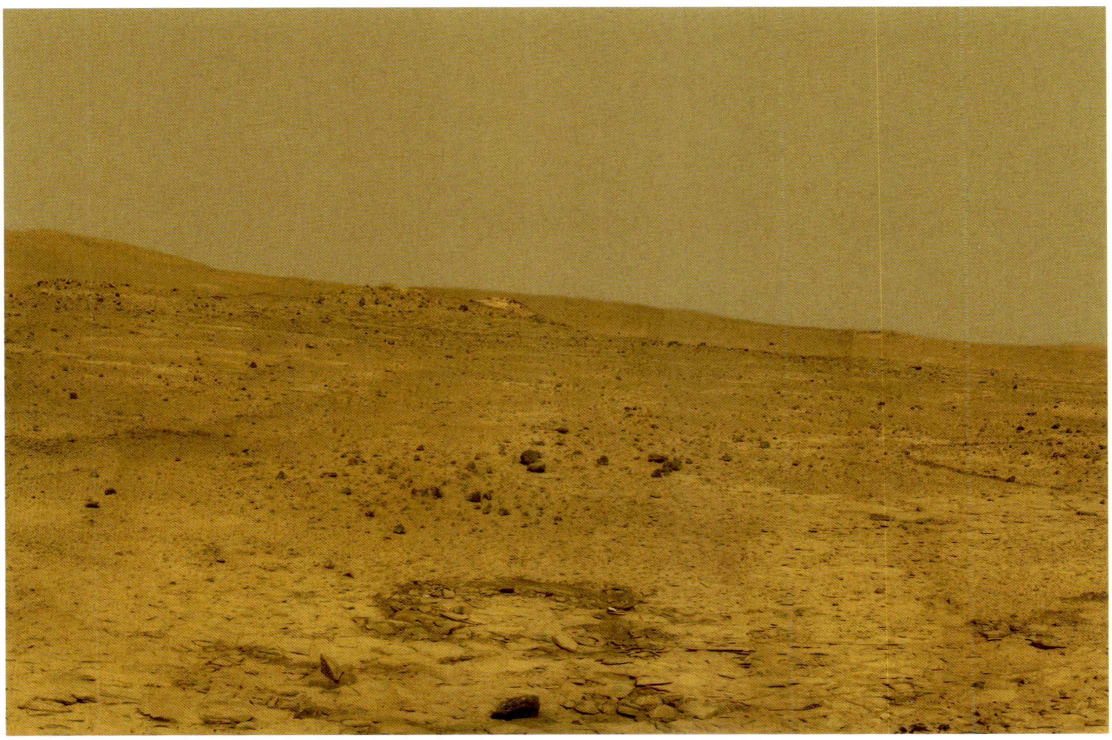

The characteristic "butterscotch" color of the Martian sky is caused by atmospheric dust containing magnetite. Photograph taken by the Mars Exploration Rover "Spirit" on 26 August 2008.

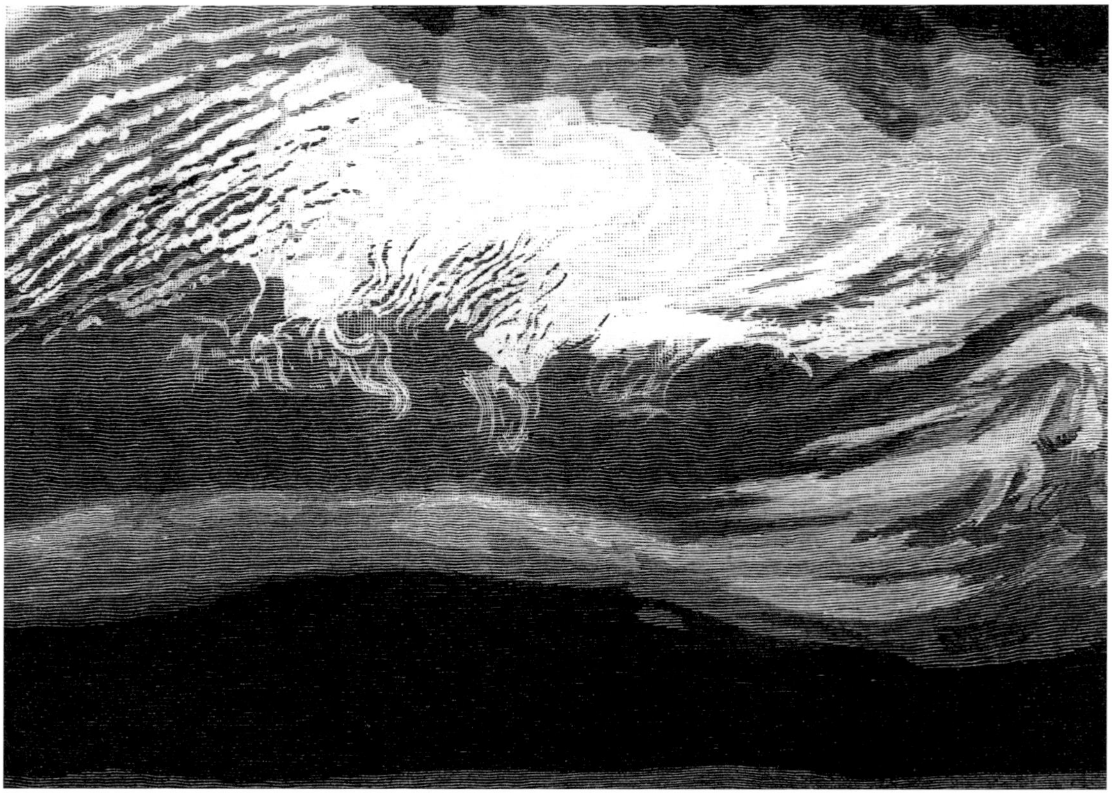

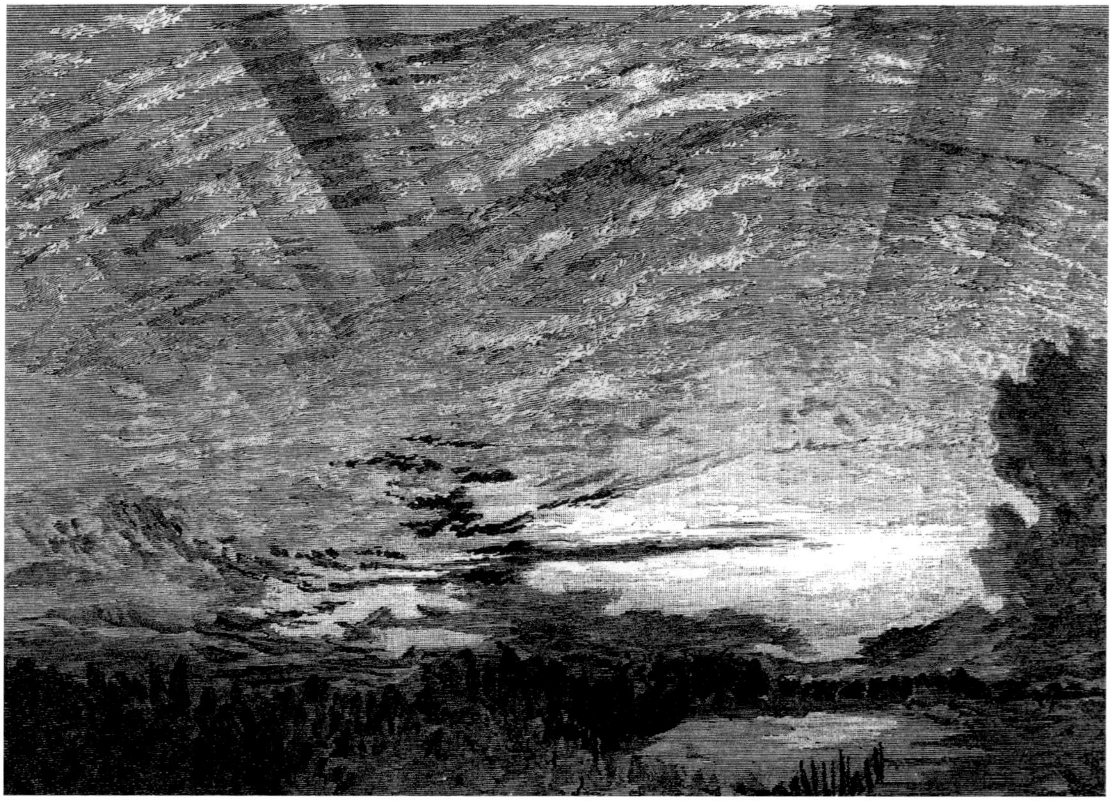

lectures on "The Storm-Cloud of the Nineteenth Century," delivered at the London Institution on the 4th and 11th of February 1884, that he finally tried to face down the modern demon of dust. The first lecture purports to provide its audience with what Ruskin calls an "absolutely true" account of a phenomenon he claims to have been observing for almost twenty years. Something has changed, he writes, in the weather of northern and Mediterranean Europe during that period. A new kind of cloud has appeared: a "plague-cloud," invariably heralded by a vicious, intermittent wind that seems to blow from all directions at once:

This wind is the plague-wind of the eighth decade of the nineteenth century; a period which will assuredly be recognized in future meteorological history as one of the phenomena hitherto unrecorded in the courses of nature, and characterized pre-eminently by the almost ceaseless action of this calamitous wind.[8]

Neither the cloud nor the ghastly wind that presages its arrival were formerly known to science or poetry; nowhere in the "traditions of air" do Shakespeare, Dante, or Wordsworth speak of the hovering horror that appears to have been recorded for the first time in Ruskin's own diary, where he kept a sedulous record of its brooding visitations. The cloud is "a dry black veil" that no ray of sunlight can pierce. Ruskin quotes a diary entry from the early 1870s:

[It] looks partly as if it were made of poisonous smoke; very possibly it may be: there are at least two hundred furnace chimneys in a square of two miles on either side of me. But mere smoke would not blow to and fro in that wild way. It looks more to me as if it were made of dead men's souls—such of them as are not yet gone where they have to go, and may be flitting hither and thither, doubting, themselves, of the fittest place for them. You know, if there are *such things as souls, and if ever any of them haunt places where they have been hurt, there must be many above us, just now, displeased enough!*[9]

This last fretful company of ghosts might be a remnant, Ruskin conjectures, of the dead of the Franco-Prussian war, their spirits adrift and troubling the skies from Sicily to the north of England. Its effect on the author himself is to render him also somewhat spectral, an anxious witness who watches the sky and subsequently feels himself dispersed among his own fragmentary diary entries.

This grotesque and opaque effluvium, Victorian successor to the miasma that appalled John Evelyn, is for Ruskin a real meteorological phenomenon; his second lecture is for the most part a defense of the first against the disbelieving and even mocking reactions of the press. But we ought surely to read too in Ruskin's anguished account of the way the cloud has overcome him in recent years an image of history that contends with Benjamin's more celebrated motif of the "angel of history." Like Benjamin, Ruskin sees the rubbish of the world accumulating about him; but where Benjamin's angel looks dolefully at its feet, the Victorian prophet looks to the sky, because he knows that the atmospheric and historical catastrophe will emerge, like a swirl of dust, out of the air itself.

1 John Evelyn, *Fumifugium: Or, the Inconvenience of the Aer and Smoake of London Dissipated* (London: National Society for Clean Air, 1961), p. 18.
2 Charles Dickens, *Great Expectations* (London: Penguin, 2003), p. 84.
3 Le Corbusier, *Towards a New Architecture*, trans. Frederick Etchells (New York: Dover, 1986), p. 123.
4 Walter Benjamin, *The Arcades Project*, trans. and ed. Howard Eiland and Kevin McLaughlin (Cambridge, MA.: Belknap Press, 1999), p. 103.
5 Georges Bataille, "Dust," in *Encyclopaedia Acephalica*, ed. Alastair Brotchie, trans. Iain White (London: Atlas Press, 1995), pp. 42–43.
6 Alfred Russel Wallace, *The Wonderful Century* (New York: Dodd, Mead & Company, 1899) p. 85.
7 John Ruskin, *The Ethics of the Dust* (London: George Allen & Unwin, 1916), p. 191.
8 John Ruskin, "The Storm-Cloud of the Nineteenth Century," in *Selected Writings* (Oxford: Oxford University Press, 2004). pp. 263–269.
9 Ibid., p. 270.

opposite: Ruskin's illustrations of English clouds before the advent of the "plague-cloud." ***An August Sky at Brantwood*, 1880 (top) and *A Sunset at Abbeville*, 1868 (bottom).**

SWEPT AWAY

SUSANNA WHATMAN

In the late eighteenth century, increased social mobility among the yeoman class—from which stratum domestic staff were most often hired by the aristocracy and merchant classes—led to a shortage of servants in England. The rate of staff turnover increased, and it was not unusual for an aristocratic or upper-middle-class woman to draw up a list of instructions, a plan of campaign in the war against dust and grime, that might be passed on by a housekeeper to her successor. One such text is *The Housekeeping Book of Susanna Whatman*, composed in the years following her marriage in 1776 to James Whatman, a prosperous paper-mill owner, and their setting up home at Turkey Court in the county of Kent.

In *Directions to Servants*, his satirical instruction manual of 1731, Jonathan Swift had suggested that a butler ought employ his sweaty palm to ensure an even surface to the salt cellar, and a footman should sneeze on a plate rather than spray his master's table. It is a good idea too, Swift writes, to fling several pounds of butter at the kitchen wall, and pluck it off as required. *Directions to Servants* is less an attack on slovenly staff than a scatological guide to enacting a filthy revenge on ingrate employers.

As the short extracts below may hint, Whatman's manuscript suggests, despite itself, a similarly rank and grubby revenge, and conjures the shades of exhausted bodies that move slowly and awkwardly, leaving decidedly unsettling traces behind them.

To use as little soap as possible (if any) in scowering rooms. Fuller's earth and fine sand preserves the colour of the boards, and does not leave a white appearance as soap does. All the rooms to be dry scrubbed with white sand.

To take the papers off the tops of the beds twice a year.

To whisk all the window curtains every Saturday. Shake mats, carpets, etc. every Saturday. To use a painter's brush to all the ledges, window frames and furniture, and then the duster. Never to use a hard brush to any mahogany carving that has been neglected and the dust suffered to settle in it.

To keep a small mop in the cupboard in the Water Closet, and use warm water every day to keep the inside clean. In frosty weather not to pour it too hot, only just warm. And it must be used in a mug, not in anything so wide as a bason, that it [do] not wet the sides of the pan.

To rise on Tuesday morning to wash her own things and the dusters, and help wash stockings. To iron her own things of an evening. To mend the towels and her Master's common stockings of an evening.

To take turns of going to Church every other Sunday with the Laundrymaid.

Never to dust the pictures, nor the frames of anything that has a gilt edge. Never to dust the black busts.

To force back all the window shutters: otherwise they get warped, and will not go into their place, which makes a room look very bad indeed. To sweep the steps in front of the house every morning when necessary.

When a floor cloth wants washing, not to use a brush or soapsuds, but a soft linen and some fresh milk and water. A steel should be used round the hearth and in all dirty corners.

[...]

All doors at places where the dust lodges should be attended to. Otherwise, if left too long, it takes a long time and much labour to get it off.

[...]

The sun comes into the Library very early. The window on that side of the bow must have the blind let down. ... The books are not to be meddled with, but they may be dusted as far as a wing of a goose will go. Nothing put behind the door besides the ladder. Tea leaves used on the carpet in this room, Drawingroom, and Eating Parlour, and Mrs Whatman's Dressingroom, no where else.

Drawingroom. The blinds always closed in the morning and window up. Kept dusted, and the chairs and sofas dusted occasionally, and the mahogany rubbed. The covers shook. The girandoles Mrs W always cleans herself. They should never be touched: nor the pictures. In damp weather a chafing dish with coals should be used, but something put under it to ketch any dirt that may fall. When the fire is light and the stove cleaned, something must be laid down to prevent the carpet from being dirtied, *as it is nailed down*. The other carpets are not.

[...]

Eating parlor. The sun never comes in. The chairs must be well dusted so that the mahogany should look bright. The carving on the mahogany sideboards should be kept free from dust with the painter['s] brush. No chair should be set in the corner near the door to the kitchen. The pianoforte and the harpsichord should not have anything struck against them.

Hall and Staircase. Swept and dusted every day, and the banister occasionally rubbed with a very little oil and every day with a dry cloth.

THE DUSTY, THE STICKY, AND THE GREASY

ADAM JASPER

Christian Enzensberger died this year at the age of seventy-eight. I never managed to speak to him, although I would have liked to. I wrote him a letter a few years ago, but it was returned to sender, unopened. Perhaps he was past getting fan mail. It was a belated thank you for a book that I had found years before. Fly-specked and yellowed, it was wedged into a shelf in a second-hand bookstore with flickering fluorescent lights—a place where the actively antisocial and the passively lonely spill coffee and dig through piles of paperbacks after the library has closed. The book, at first sight, resembled vintage pornography. The cover was stained and the pages were unevenly cut, the type cheaply set in a monospace font. It looked dog-eared, disreputable, attractive. The title of the book was *Smut: An Anatomy of Dirt*.

The dirty book turned out to be gripping, disturbing, articulate, and strange: a forgotten classic on the subject of filth, better than Dominique Laporte's excellent *History of Shit*, perhaps even better than Mary Douglas's *Purity and Danger*. Enzensberger's *Smut* was originally published in 1968 and was awarded the prestigious Bremer Prize for Literature in 1970. Enzensberger refused the award. He was the first and only person to have done so.

Enzensberger himself is an enigmatic figure. The two pictures of him from the *Smut* period (one published in *Der Spiegel* in 1969 and the other on the dust jacket of the 1972 edition) bear no physical resemblance to each other. The earlier one is of a thin, bespectacled young man with an eager air; the image from three years later is of a rather ugly bear-like figure with a Teutonic moustache and tousled hair. Each photo makes the other untrustworthy. The blurb tells me he was born in 1931 in Nuremberg. Wikipedia informs me that he is the "younger brother of the literary celebrity and political figure Hans Magnus Enzensberger." Christian is the other Enzensberger. There is virtually no more information available about him in English: a few marginal scholarly citations, but no monographs, no critical essays. A Java application on an internet bookseller's site automatically calculates that people likely to buy books by him are also likely to buy books by J. V. Eichendorff and Karl Phillip Morritz. On the same site, there is a one-line review of the book: "*Smut* is a rockin book." The author of the review is "Dude." Nothing more. No one is interested in Christian Enzensberger. So much the better. This leaves us only the book.

Smut is composed from paragraphs, shards of text that can be as long as three pages and as short as a line. The fragments range from description to monologues, from aphorisms to short excerpts from scientific monographs. The style is characterized by its lack of consistency. *Smut* shifts tenses and registers unpredictably, moves without cues. Moments from a formal lecture are interspersed with memories. The text is full of voices—from Beckett, Marx, and Mary Douglas to anonymous pronouns: *he*, *she*, *they*. And yet, arguably because there is no clear authorial voice or intent, Enzensberger is able to cover, mention, or point to every significant theme in the history of defilement.

Enzensberger starts with people as the originators of all filth when he states:

There are twenty-five forms of excretion known to man: each one a source of curiosity and pleasure. They are frequently preceded by a feeling of tense expectancy and followed inevitably by contentment. They appear as part of the individual, he welcomes them as his own. But this love is short-lived. Is it still me (their creator is soon asking himself) or is it not, is it still mine, or already an object like anything else? I am not sure, I don't like it, I want to disown it, it was never mine, away with all this horrid confusion! The fact is, man enjoys excreting.

I've tried to calculate the constituents of Enzensberger's twenty-five forms of excrement. I have no idea how he produces so many distinct types in his list. That the total is so much in excess of the number of orifices in the human body cannot be accidental. Enzensberger doesn't privilege any orifice. The implication must be that no complete list, no perfect categorization of filth, is possible, not even at its home on the margins of the human body. That is because anything that approaches or crosses these margins is dirt:

Dirt is anything which threatens the proper separateness of the individual, his anxiously guarded isolation; which is why he is unwilling to let anything approach him or escape from him. Apart from the dirt produced by contact and excretion, he also avoids anything that belongs to him only equivocally, and by analogy has a horror of intermingling.

Enzensberger's point is profound. This is the clearest single expression of the idea that anything that wishes to cross the skin of the human body is dirty. This is an obvious observation only after it has been made.

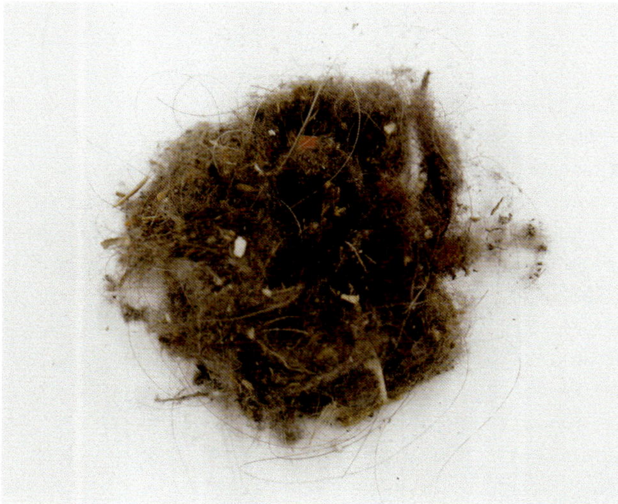

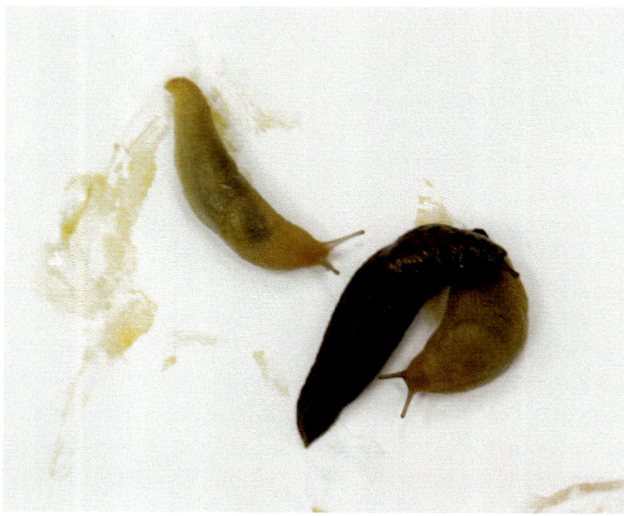

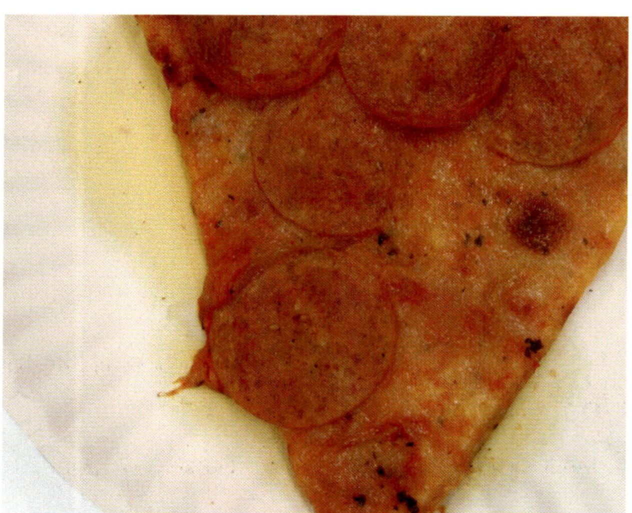

Let us return to Enzensberger, the genius of filth: "The fact is, man enjoys excreting. Then he rejects his own handiwork." And over on the next page: "Man's twenty-sixth excretion is himself." This terrifying statement is literally true. We are excretions of ourselves. The brain and the nervous system are, in terms of their fetal development, the excretions of the spinal chord. In our first weeks of development we are simple chordates. Evolutionary history is recapitulated in the development undergone by the fetus from flatworm through fish and pig to primate. People are their own excretions in that they consist of the leftovers of their own actions. In Enzensberger's ontology of filth, we are residue, the leftovers of all our previous hopes, ambitions, and projects, all of our actions, all our in-order-tos and for-the-sake-ofs.

Although dirt needs skin to become itself, dirt is still stuff with independent material qualities. It is clear that certain properties can make inanimate matter peculiarly threatening, particularly vile in the right context. These are all properties that enhance the ability of the substance to approach our margins, or worse still, cross them. Truly dirty substances seem animated by a desire to touch. Three great classes emerge immediately upon inspection—the dusty, the sticky, and the greasy. The dusty forms a category because dust covers and conceals:

Examples, by all means. Among dry things ashes and hair, the parings peelings shreds shivers from bottles shears skins, when mixed, as in garbage; also everything granular and crumbly, anything that crunches crushes splits splinters in a rotten spongy friable fibrous fashion, or like powder chalk soot drifts settles accumulates and sticks.

Dust indicates that something has remained unused or neglected for a long time, and when moved, dust forms clouds that choke. Furthermore, dust itself consists of objects that have long since lost their identity. Things that have dried out, decomposed, powdered, and shifted in a way that makes their true identities indiscernible. The dusty, however, is a minor category compared to the sticky and slimy:

Besides the countless nameless forms of slime from eggs snails mushrooms membranes jellyfish nodules mouths nostrils lips tubes stems glands fruits noses and together with them everything that gushes spurts oozes drivels drips trickles and drops. Right. Close to these come on the one hand things that stick cling make threads, honey cheese tar glue mucilage syrup pitch and varnish.

The sticky is a fluid animated by desire; it seems to want to hold on to the skin, to resist being removed. It clings, becomes entrenched, is difficult to eradicate. However its stickiness—its solidarity—is the one thing that allows it to be contained. A sticky substance can sometimes be removed simply by rolling it against itself. But the sticky pales in interest when compared with the virulence of grease:

Let us come back to grease. Grease also clings; not however by suction but as a film. Confronted with it, any surface, including the skin, succumbs to it; bloom down or velvet, it all turns into grease. Water runs off it, wiping only spreads it further, the thinnest coating will divide in two again, it increases as it pleases. Once I am greasy I am cut off, I cannot get along any more, I lose my footing, slip, cannot regain control. Because I no longer possess anything, everything is possessed by the grease, and each time in desperation I try to assure myself of my former possessions I merely put the seal of this new master upon them: I am lost.

The empire of grease is infinite. Grease is always happiest when spreading out in vast two-dimensional sheets. A thimble of grease dropped into a swimming pool will spread thin until the entire surface of the water is covered. Grease will, in fact, continue to spread until it is a film only one molecule thick. As such, it forms another membrane, another skin, sealing off its victim from the world. In contact with skin, grease curses us with a variation of the Midas touch. Everything we grasp becomes greasy. Everything we touch turns to shit.

We would prefer to leave Freud out of this, but we can't. Freud always equated gold with shit: "Feces—money—gift—baby—penis are treated [in the unconscious] as though they meant the same thing," he wrote in "Anxiety and Instinctual Life." And the Emperor Vespasian, on introducing a tax upon urine, encountered the objections of his son, Titus, who found the commerce in excrement disgusting. After a year, the Emperor held up a gold coin to his son's nose, and asked him what smelled, giving rise to the expression *pecunia non olet* ("money doesn't stink"). Is the story of Midas's touch the primal myth that connects the two? Midas is the Oedipus of the anus. There is a hidden promise of power in shit that the dictator Vespasian, the inheritor of the secret of the Midas myth, has learned to exploit.

opposite: Representatives of the three empires of filth.

Smut is, in the end, a book not so much about dirt as about politics. Enzensberger treats capitalism as having the same power as the dictator does in reducing his subjects to filth. The mechanism is dependent on the nature of the commodity. The perfect commodity is notable for "its sameness, its aseptic cleanness, its neat seductive packaging." One of the characteristics of this aseptic cleanness is that a perfect commodity has never been touched by human hands. Dirty finger marks are an indication that an object is second-hand. Customers in supermarkets reject the first containers of laundry soap, or milk, in a stack and reach back into the depths of shelves to take items that are less likely to have been prodded or stroked, objects that are somehow fresher. Ideally, consumer goods are protected by brightly colored boxes that are in turn shrink-wrapped, covered in protective plastic. Once the seals for our protection are broken, the plastic torn off, the box opened, we can no longer exchange the goods. It has been used up at the moment that it has been touched.

The agents of this touching are humans. We are the new filth. The logic of marginal violation is inexorable. That which desires to touch, which clings and makes its mark, is filth. The source of this filth is the abject. In a commodity economy, people are the new abjection.

The path of defense for the individual afraid of being marked out as filth is to attempt to imitate the commodity in every respect possible. We carry this out through an impeccable display of concern for our exterior appearance, and through conformity with our peers, whoever they might be. The apparent variety of subcultures and fashions might seem to argue against this, but then the same superficial variety is displayed in a supermarket aisle where a dozen separate brands of washing powder are for sale, all of them more or less identical in content. In the same way, we choose to conform as closely as possible to our individual, chosen subculture.

But then, he continued, the individual comes up against his non-commodity type limitations, and the most important of these is time. The commodity is not limited by time, it is neither the product nor the victim of it; always new, always glossy, always fresh, it lies there in the window, available at any moment and longing to be replaced by something even fresher. The commodity has no past, nothing but perpetual present and future, nothing will ever put an end to it. Because of its appointed dirt role it also knows nothing of decay, which of course requires time; on the other hand it uses every possible means to entice future contact—and ideally at the moment of touch explodes into nothing, a thing consumed. ... It is pathetic and horrible to see the individual vainly attempting to imitate the commodity even in this.

Contact with the object, once it is no longer a commodity but violated, is a form of contact with other people, and therefore defiles us. This pollution increases as the history of contact that the commodity has undergone becomes more difficult to trace. Once an object is in the household garbage, touching objects that have also been touched, it is dirtier than after it was opened. After this garbage is mixed with the trash of the city in the back of a garbage truck, our original object is more untouchable still. The only way of freeing ourselves of it is through burying it or burning it. Enormous cities of garbage stretch out in landfills outside our cities. The desperate drive for cleanliness, with the mass consumer engorgement that accompanies it, leaves us more polluted and defiled then ever before. Civilization is garbage. We are filth. Our commodities cry out to be rescued from us. What would their messiah look like?

Commodities, by transforming us into filth, by residing in timelessness, have turned us into corpses that rot while still alive. In so doing, they have fulfilled the old prophecy of an experience so nauseating that we can no longer thrust away the abject, but are ourselves expelled by it. We jump out of our skins.

PULVERULENCE

STEVEN CONNOR

Dust—a source of great contemporary fascination for artists, critics, and historians—is a powerful quasi-object, a magic substance, something to conjure with. Like anything magical, dust is ultimately a figuring not just of the possibility of magic, but also of the operations of magical thinking itself.

Much of the magical power of dust seems to come from the fact that it is reversible. Dust is simultaneously dispersive and concentrating: "to dust" means to cover with dust, or to make dusty, as when a cook dusts with flour or icing sugar, but it can also mean to clear of dust, a sense in use as early as 1587, when George Gascoigne refers to a youth who "curried was and dusted slicke and trimme."[1] This makes a quibble possible in the lament of Guidarius and Arviragus for Imogen in Shakespeare's *Cymbeline*: "Golden lads and girls all must, / As chimney-sweepers, come to dust"—in which the dusting can be both the relapse into and the clearing away of dust.[2]

Dust is, of course, the unmistakable emblem of death, decay, and dissolution, but it is also, under certain circumstances, powerfully generative. (A widespread belief among the upholders of spontaneous generation was that ticks, mites, fleas, and flies—all dust-like creatures—sprang up where drops of sweat fell on to dust.) An incident in the Finnish epic poem *Kalevala* shows the extra surge of transformative power than can be produced by grinding things down to their finest and most undifferentiated form. The wizard Lemminkainen, finding his way blocked by a fire-breathing eagle, reaches into his pockets for some chicken feathers he has previously gathered:

Searches in his pouch of leather,
Quickly takes the magic feathers,
Feathers from the hazel-chickens,
Rubs them into finest powder,
Rubs them with his magic fingers
Whence a flight of birds arises,
Hazel-chickens from the feathers,
Large the bevy of the young birds.
Quick the wizard, Lemminkainen,
Drives them to the eagle's fire-mouth,
Thus to satisfy his hunger.[3]

One would have thought that the feathers alone ought to have been enough for a competent wizard, but even wizards have to obey magical laws, and here in particular the law of the reversibility of extremes, according to which the possibility of a sudden change of form depends upon first grinding all recognizable form out of the magical residue.

Dust, in the form of pollen, for example, is also fertilizing. It may be that the idea of fairy dust derives from this association, via the close affinity (though it is quite recent, not going back very much earlier than the sixteenth century) between fairies and winged insects, especially bees, who are commonly laden with pollen, but more especially butterflies, the figure of the soul for the Greeks, for whom the word *psyche* meant soul as well as butterfly, which do not carry pollen, but whose talc-dusted wings may remind us of it.

Dust is amorphous, without form and almost void. But this very fact allows it to be thought of as metamorphic, with the same general capacity to assume any form as stem cells, the epithets of which—"pluripotent," and "totipotent"—seem to apply equally well to dust. The folk-atomism underlying this form of material imagination follows a magical or homeopathic logic of more-in-less, where the maximally comminuted form of the powder, in which all form is apparently decomposed, concentrates an elementary power of animation.

POWDER OF SYMPATHY

Dust can get everywhere, insinuating itself into every crevice. This makes it a medium of transformation and exchange. Almost without qualities itself, dust has the quality of qualitylessness, the virtual virtue of transmitting the virtues of other substances. It is both a terminal and a mediate matter, inert, but sometimes, for that very reason, omnivalent. In Hebrew magic, dust collected from an ant-heap and hung up inside a written charm in a workshop was believed to ensure the industry and prosperity of the business.[4] Basil Valentine recommended many forms of drying and powdering to extract and concentrate the virtue of medicinal substances, for example in this recipe for a powder to heal snakebite, formed on the principle of like curing like:

Take a living Toad, dry him first at the Sun, then in a covered Pot well luted, bring him to ashes, pound him, and lay the powder on venomous bitings, or such accidents, and you shall see one Venome attracting the other; and the reason is, because by burning or calcination, the vertue of the Toad is opened, and rendred effectually powerful to attract its like Poyson.[5]

The most extraordinary episode in the material imagination of particulates is the case of the "powder of sympathy," whose effects were enthusiastically brought

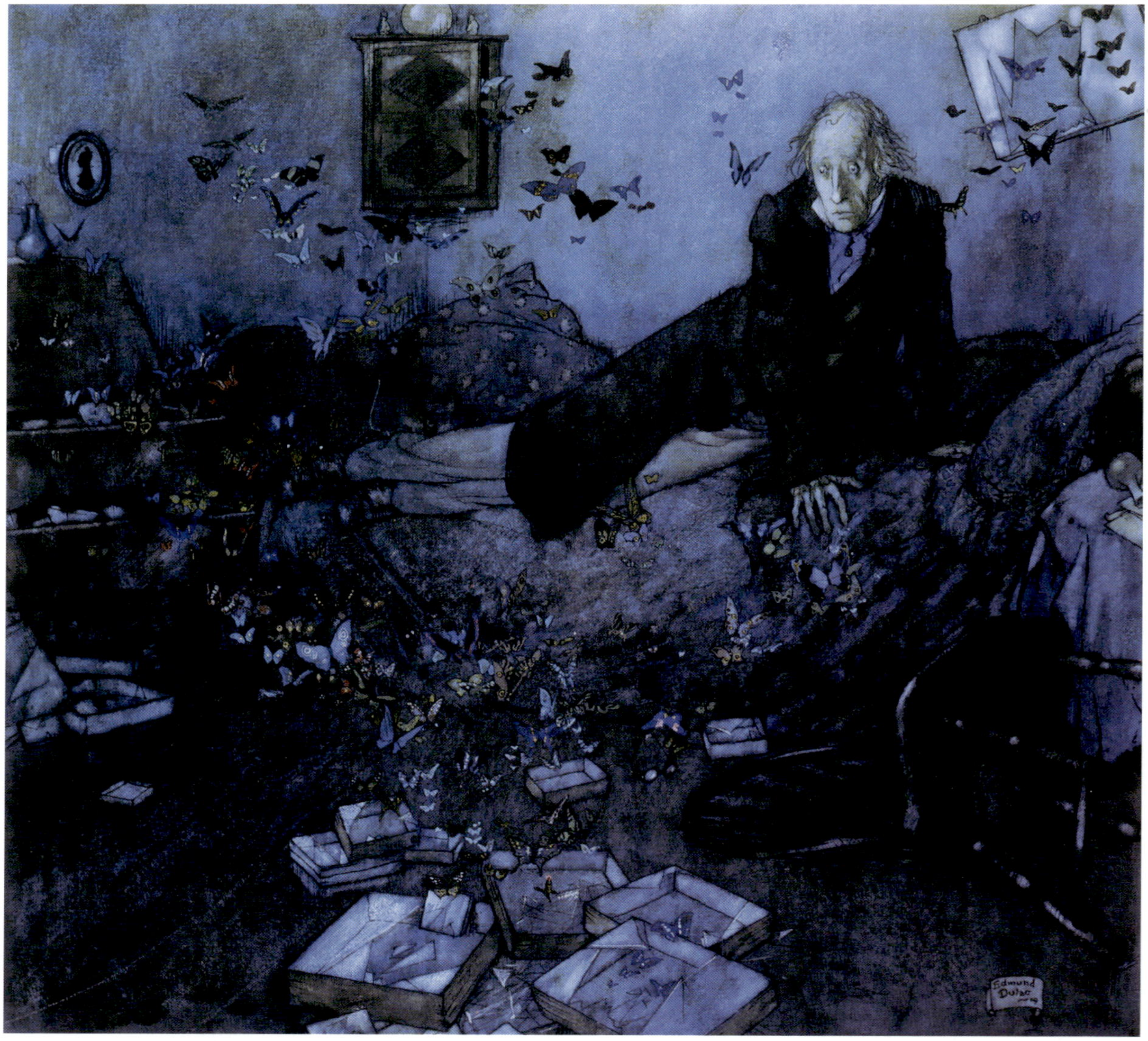

Edmund Dulac, *The Entomologist's Dream*, 1909.

to notice by Sir Kenelm Digby. Digby, whose father had been executed for his alleged part in the Gunpowder Plot, revived the idea of a magical cure for wounds that had first been proposed by Paracelsus. But where Paracelsus had prescribed an ointment, having as its principal active ingredient moss from the skull of a man who had died violently, plumped out with boar's and bear's fat, burnt worms, dried boar's brain, red sandal-wood, and mummy, Digby's remedy was a powder consisting essentially of "green vitriol," or ferrous sulfate. In a discourse before a learned assembly in Montpellier, Digby explained the process whereby the powder was applied, not to the wound, but to its efficient cause, or some associated property. He describes how he gave relief to the victim of a wound by dipping a bandage still impregnated with his blood into a basin in which the powder of sympathy had been dissolved. The magical logic seems to have been that the soothing and salutary effect on the bandage was conveyed by the powder to the wound. Just as dust and powder can transmit poison and contamination, so they can also convey care and cure.[6]

Digby's concoction recalls and is given credibility by alchemical beliefs about the "powder of projection," an alternative form of, or name for, the transmuting substance of the philosopher's stone. The Scottish alchemist Alexander Seton is reputed to have had a blackish powder which he used to turn other substances into gold, and to have bequeathed the residue of his supply to his assistant Sendivogus (whose career, however, ended in disgrace when, having run out of the sovereign substance, and not knowing the secret of its manufacture, he was driven to the expedient of gilding coins).[7]

The dust formed of previously hard substances is often believed to retain the force or properties of the originals, particularly in the case of stones and jewels. Albertus Magnus reported that the stone Mephis, "being broken into powder, and droonke with water, maketh insensibilitie of torture."[8] Its memory of hardness or sharpness means that dust can also be full of peril. In the case of diamond dust, the softness of the powder seems to preserve a memory of the hardness of its original, hence, perhaps, the many stories of its potency as a means of murder. There is a story that Paracelsus died of diamond dust poisoning, and Thomas Overbury was imprisoned in the Tower by the machinations of the Countess of Essex, who is said to have arranged for diamond dust to be added to his food.[9]

SUBTLE BODY

Much of the power of dust may derive from the fact that it is what might be called quasichoate. It instances the condition of the subtle body, a body that is as diffuse or scattered as it is possible to be while yet maintaining a minimal or even imaginary cohesion. Evacuated of the vital moisture, juice, or serum that Aristotle and many others believed to be necessary for a being's coherence to be maintained, the parched dust seems to thirst after being, to be stirred and charged by a straining after contour and concretion. Dust, in all its allotropes—powder, sand, grit—rarely appears as pure, or uniform dissolution, but borrows the suggestion of form, gathering into clumps or clouds.

Dust may be thought of not just as primary matter, but also as a kind of anti-matter, the matrix or negative of form. Dust is in one sense evacuated of air, the gaps between the particles reduced to their minimum—hence its muffling, choking effects. At the same time, dust is characterized by a maximum of what might be called internal exposure, in which the ratio of the surface area of particles to their internal mass is extremely high. The availability of such a large surface area for chemical reactions accounts for the effectiveness of powders in forming solutions and suspensions. And, because they have no inside, because they are all a kind of internal exposure, dust-like substances can give contours or clarifying outlines to other things. Thus, dust, itself formless and edgeless, can both dissolve form and disclose it, like the snow that, in the right amount, can give to things a magical new clarity of outline, but passing beyond that point erases every landmark beneath its featureless drifts and dunes.

Dust is attracted to other objects by static electricity, but is also itself a kind of strange attractor, which reveals forms in movements of eddy and turbulence. Dusting for fingerprints reveals the otherwise invisible traces of human presence and action. The prospector's sluice riddles out the gold-dust from the silt in which it is suspended, and the Hoover uses filters to separate the dust from the air in which it is inmixed. But dust itself can also be a kind of riddle or filter, which simplifies and separates out forms through its selective attentions. The Italian artist Claudio Parmiggiani, whose work has been evocatively discussed by Georges Didi-Huberman, fills sealed rooms with smoke, allows the soot to settle in sheets and films, and then removes the fittings and furniture, leaving behind their sculpted outlines. We strive with dustpan and vacuum cleaner to separate ourselves from our dust, but here the dust is a way of separating objects from their silhouettes, just as the incandescent cinders turned the bodies of the Pompeians into their own inverted images or moulds. The soot effects a fall-out photography, a soft, spectral frottage, or finger-painting of the space.

The disclosive power of dust has connections with divinatory practices that employ apparently chaotic or quasichoate forms to lift the veil of time—reading the future in dispositions of sand, cinders, moles and freckles, tea leaves, and flocks of birds. Supernatural beings are also often picked out from backgrounds of swirl and drift, of temporarily massed and rippling multiplicities. Fairies and other elemental entities are thought to inhabit the next-to-nothing bodies of wind, blizzard, or storm. We might think of the vortical bodies of dust-devils, the Italian witches who were known as "knots of wind," and the Irish Sidhe who are said to become visible in the gyrations of leaves. Divinity has the physiology of air and of the pulveriform or particulate matter that cousins it. Zeus appears to Danae in the form of a shower of gold; Dracula transports himself in the form of a mist, a power he shares with Satan; foam-formed Aphrodite's name announces her as an emanation of spray and spindrift. And the sky is strewn with the pointillist body-abstracts of mythical gods, heroes, and heroines—Orion, Andromeda, Perseus.

DREAM DUST

Dust is the occasion or receptacle of magical fantasy. But, in a telling inversion, it can also be the cause of it, for dusts and powders have a particular prominence in the history of opiates and intoxicants. The sleeping draughts of Victorian melodrama and sensation novels and the Mickey Finn of the gangster thriller alike are normally represented not as a liquid, or as a capsule, but rather as a finely ground powder that is then poured into a drink to form a potion.

The idea of magic or pixie dust probably cooperates closely with the idea that sleep is heralded by the smarting or itching eyes caused by the sandman, who brings sleep by flinging or blowing sand into the eyes, like Ole Lukøje ("Ollie Shuteye") in Denmark; indeed, an alternative name for the sandman was the "dustman."[10] The gritty residue around the eyes on waking that is commonly called "sleep" is also sometimes thought of as the evidence of the sandman's attentions.[11] Since dust can block or modify vision, magic dust is sometimes used to confer invisibility, or to cloak one's appearance, as at the beginning of Milton's *Comus*, where the woodland wizard uses magic dust to transform his appearance when he hears the approach of a luckless virgin: "When once her eye/Hath met the virtue of this magic dust/I shall appear some harmless villager."[12]

Dust is the bearer of sleep, vision, and intoxication, a notion which hangs around some of the contemporary street and slang names of opiates and other drugs, like the "magic dust," "angel dust," and "monkey dust" that are all names for the hallucinogen PCP. Dust is a magical mixture of lightness and weight: though it will eventually settle, it seems to do so tardily and reluctantly, as though possessed of an indwelling, Aristotelian quality of positive or intrinsic levity. Like the flying ointment of seventeenth-century belief, there is something intrinsically airborne about magical dusts and powders, which therefore seem capable of lifting the spirit into the mid-air or suspensive time-out-of-time of dream and delusion. The principal function of the fairy dust that Tinkerbell scatters in *Peter Pan* is to allow the children to shed their mortal gravity and give them the power of flight.

In its first appearances, *stardust* originally referred to the dust-like appearance of crowds of stars that are so minute as not to be distinguishable by the most powerful telescopes, the first usage in this sense being recorded in 1843: "In their faintest aspect they dwindle to points so minute as appropriately to be denominated star-dust. Beyond this, no stars are distinctly visible, but only streaks or patches of milky light," wrote one popular astronomer.[13] But then the metaphor is transferred to the idea that there might be a dust that comes from the stars, and to the recognition that all of our constituent matter has ultimately derived from such cosmic matter. From here in turn comes the idea of a special, powerful stuff of illusion, often associated with the glamour of show business. This is evident in the phrase "to have stardust in one's eyes," which does not seem to appear in English until the 1920s, although there is a reference in 1872—the proof of God's existence is not "made of metaphysic star-dust, like the solar system of nebulae, but inborn," writes C. A. Bartol—that suggests a movement towards this idea of ideality in the word *stardust*.[14] When Joni Mitchell sings, "We are star-dust, we are golden, and we've got to get ourselves back to the garden," she convokes the cosmic, the primal, and the visionary.

All of these associations make dust a riddling kind of "thinking thing," an image of imagination itself, a magical precipitate of the act of magical thought.[15] It is not surprising that it should resemble the forms of "lyric substance" that Daniel Tiffany has analyzed in the shifting meteorologies of haze, hail, sleet, and blizzard in which the mind may glimpse or figure itself. In a critical review of the arguments for "panpsychism"—the idea that, if it is impossible to say at what point in the plenum of things mind supervenes upon matter, or diminishes to nothing in it, then the whole of matter must be in some sense possessed of mind, or even in fact formed of it—William James reasons that the primary state of

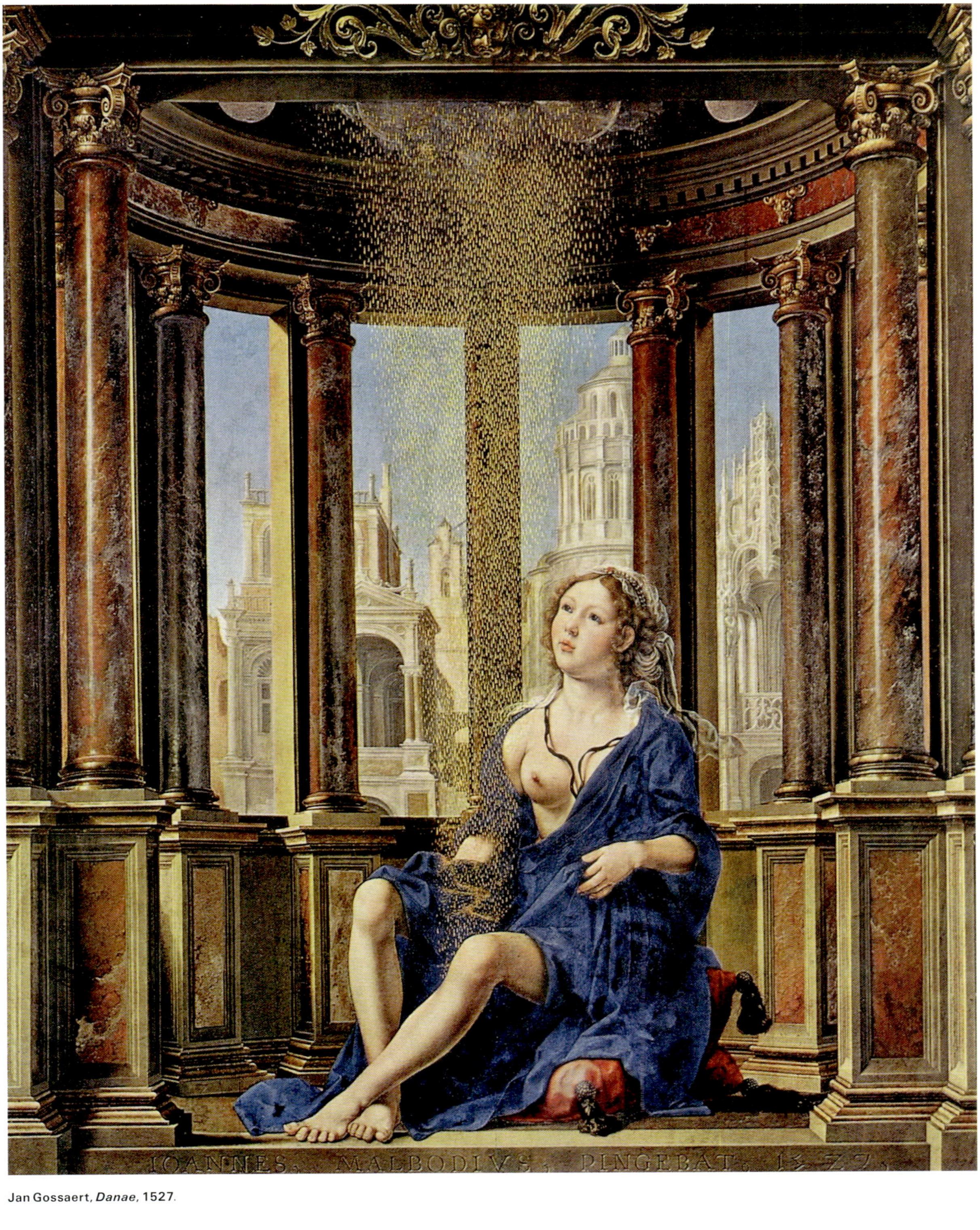

Jan Gossaert, *Danae*, 1527.

mind must in fact be identical with the most elementary state of matter:

If evolution is to work smoothly, consciousness in some shape must have been present at the very origin of things. Accordingly we find that the more clear-sighted evolutionary philosophers are beginning to posit it there. Each atom of the nebula, they suppose, must have had an aboriginal atom of consciousness linked with it; and, just as the material atoms have formed bodies and brains by massing themselves together, so the mental atoms, by an analogous process of aggregation, have fused into those larger consciousnesses which we know in ourselves and suppose to exist in our fellow-animals.[16]

For James, there was only one way in which to conceive the essential form of the mind-stuff of which the cosmos would be composed—namely, as "mind-dust." Perhaps all dust harbors the intimation of this minimal condition of mind.

1 George Gascoigne, *The Whole woorkes of George Gascoigne* (London: Abel Jeffes, 1587), p. 180.
2 William Shakespeare, *Cymbeline*, ed. J. M. Nosworthy (London: Arden, 2002), p. 133.
3 Anonymous, *The Kalevala: The Epic Poem of Finland*, trans. John Martin Crawford (New York: G. Alden / London: G. P. Putnam's Sons, 1889), p. 428.
4 Reginald Campbell Thompson, *Semitic Magic: Its Origins and Development* (London: Luzac, 1908), p. 33.
5 Basil Valentine, *The Triumphant Chariot of Antimony Being a Conscientious Discovery of the Many Reall Transcendent Excellencies Included in That Minerall*, trans. "J.H."(Oxford: A. Litchfield, 1660), p. 48.
6 Kenelm Digby, *A Late Discourse Made in a Solemne Assembly of Nobles and Learned Men at Montpellier in France Touching the Cure of Wounds by the Powder of Sympathy* (London: R. Lownes and T. Davies, 1658).
7 Lewis Spence, *Encyclopedia of Occultism* (New York: Dodd, Mead & Co., 1920), pp. 322–323.
8 Reginald Scot, *The Discoverie of Witchcraft* (London: William Brome Tennant, 1584), p. 295.
9 George Frederick Kunz, *Curious Lore of Precious Stones* (Philadelphia: J.B. Lippincott, 1913), pp. 154–156.
10 Carol Rose, *Spirits, Fairies, Gnomes, and Goblins: An Encyclopedia of the Little People* (Santa Barbara and Oxford: ABC-CLIO, 1996), p. 93.
11 Walter Avis and Thomas Pyles, "Miscellany," in *American Speech* (Spring 1981), vol. 56, no. 1, p. 80.
12 John Milton, *The Complete Poems*, ed. John Leonard (London: Penguin, 1998), p. 51.
13 Denison Olmsted, *Letters on Astronomy* (New York: Harper and Brothers, 1853), p. 377.
14 C.A. Bartol, *Radical Problems* (Boston: Roberts Brothers, 1872), pp. 357–358.
15 Steven Connor, "Thinking Things" (2008), available online at <www.stevenconnor.com/thinkingthings>. Accessed 30 August 2009.
16 William James, *The Principles of Psychology*, 2 vols. (New York: Henry Holt, 1890), vol. 1, p. 149.

---

opposite: A dust devil in the desert near Eloy, Arizona. Photo NASA.

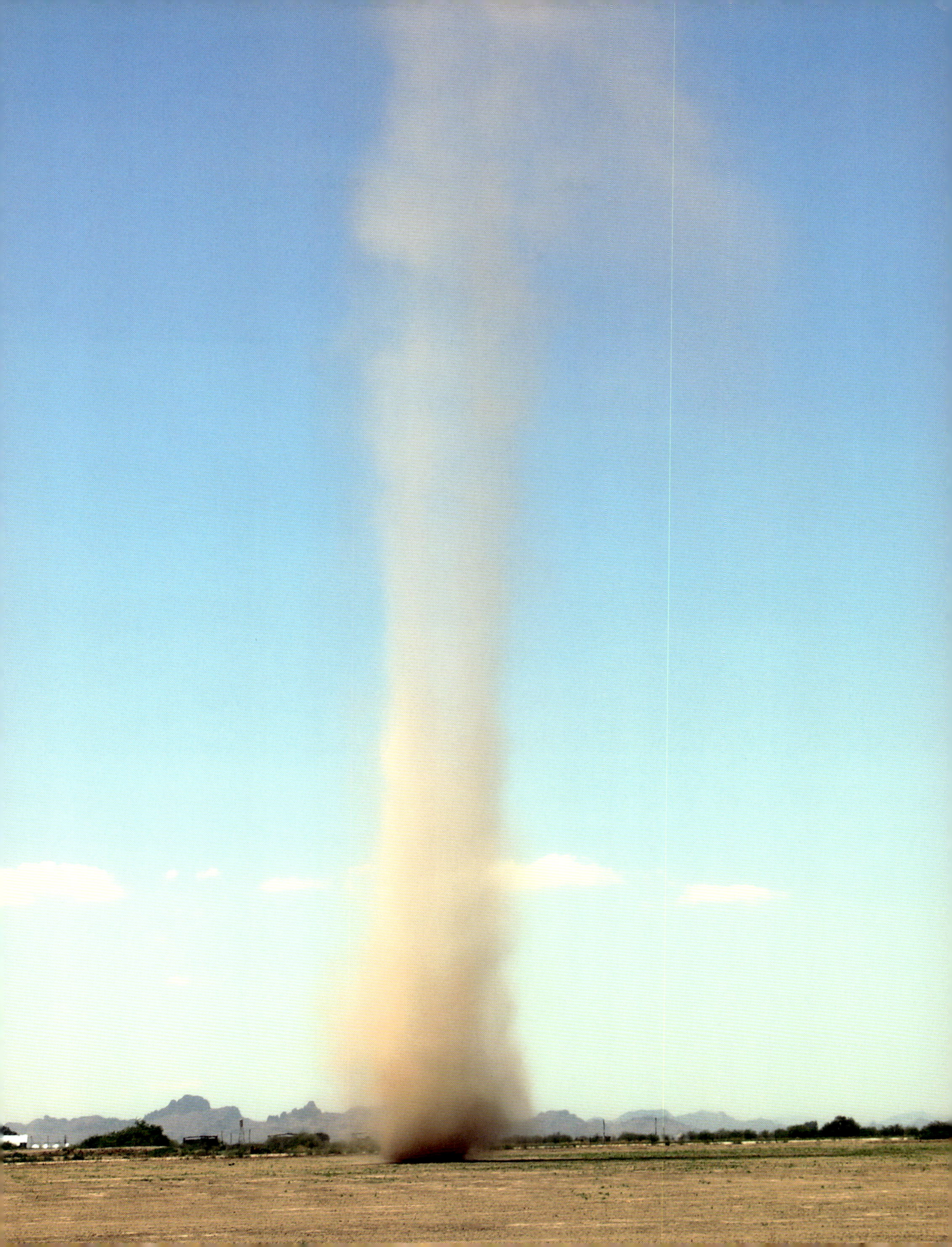

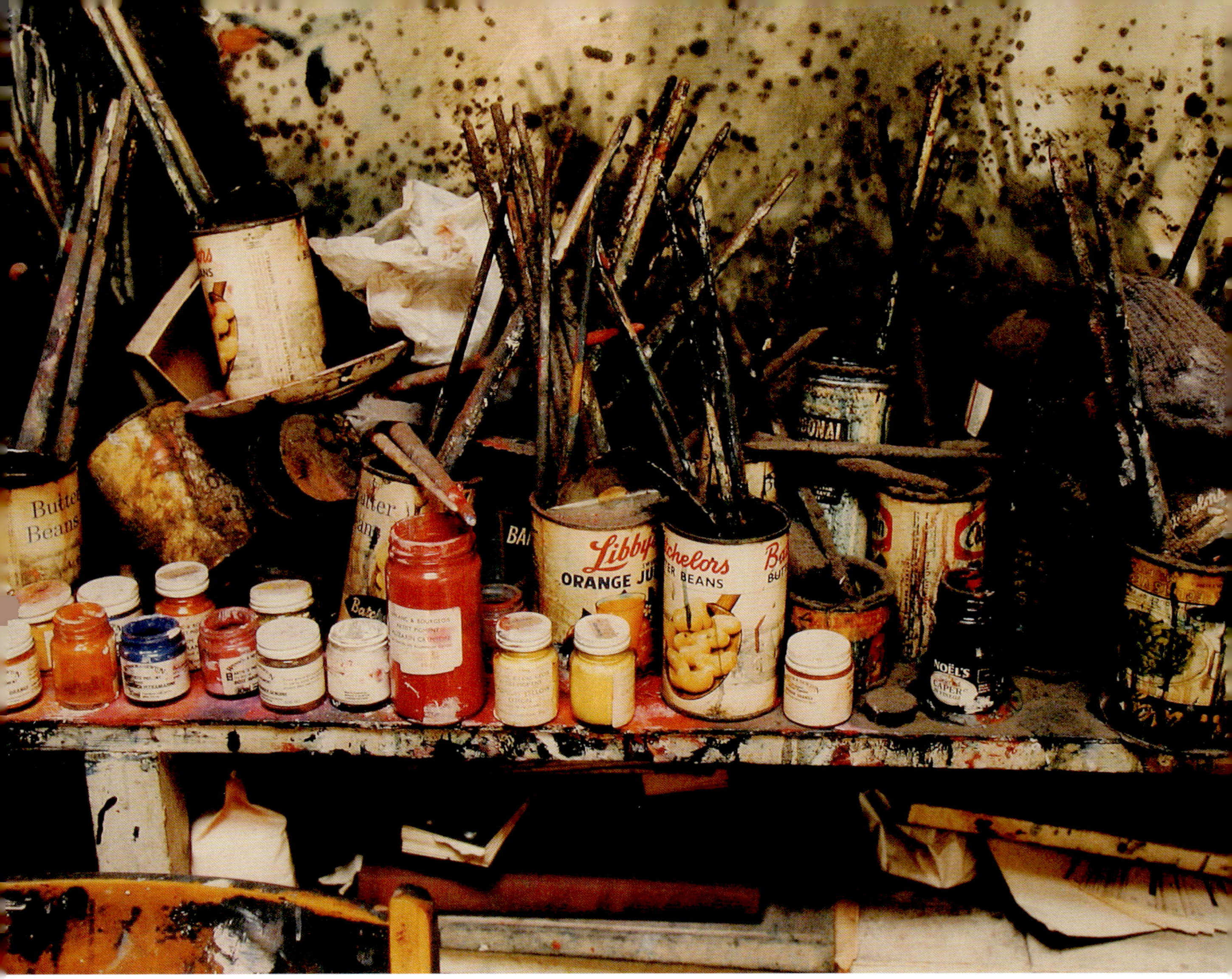

Francis Bacon's studio, which the artist did not allow his cleaning lady Jean Ward to tidy up. All photos Perry Ogden. Courtesy Dublin City Gallery, The Estate of Francis Bacon/DACS.

BACON DUST

CHRISTOPHER TURNER

Art washes away from the soul the dust of everyday life.
—Pablo Picasso

Several years ago, I met Francis Bacon's cleaning lady. Bacon's amanuensis, the art critic David Sylvester, referred me to her, as he had her to Bacon. Jean Ward, who had her grey hair swept back into a thin ponytail like a pirate's, welcomed me to her flat on a housing estate in Tooting Beck, South London. In a raspy voice she told me about her decade working for the painter whose legendarily messy studio—layer upon layer of dust, paint, discarded imagery, champagne bottles, and other detritus—would not have provided her much of a recommendation for future jobs.

"I wasn't daunted," she said when recalling her first visit to 7 Reece Mews in the early 1980s, "because I had read certain things about how some artists have tidy studios and some don't—so I wasn't really shocked. I just looked at the nice colors on the door that he used to try out paint on." (Bacon referred to these giant palettes as his "only abstract paintings.") Traditionally, it was the sculptor who was necessarily slovenly for, as Leonardo da Vinci wrote in his *Treatise on Painting*, "his face is smeared and dusted all over with marble powder so that he looks like a baker, and he is completely covered with little chips of marble, so that he seems as if his back has been snowed on; and his house is full of splinters of stone and dust." The painter, in contrast, "sits in front of his work in perfect comfort. He is well-dressed and handles the lightest of brushes which he dips in pleasant colours. He wears the clothes he likes; and his house is full of delightful paintings and is spotlessly clean."[1]

"I live in squalor," Bacon once boasted of his own practice, "the woman who cleans is not allowed to touch the studio. Besides, I like the dust—I set it like pastel." Bacon's biographer Daniel Farson reported that the artist "never had the studio in the Mews cottage cleaned because it helped him to lift up dust from the floor and apply it to the canvas when painting his sand dunes; he also rubbed his fingers along the dust and then on to the wet paint." Bacon did this in his portrait of his patron and lover, Eric Hall: "Actually there is no paint at all on the suit apart from a very thin grey wash on which I put dust from the floor," Bacon said of *Figure in a Landscape* (1945). "I thought: well, how can I make that slightly furry quality of a flannel suit? And then I suddenly thought: well, I'll get some dust. And you can see how near it is to a decent flannel suit."

"He definitely didn't like anyone going into his studio, that was his domain," Ward confirmed. "I was never allowed to clean it. Occasionally, he and John [Edwards, Bacon's companion for the last sixteen years of his life] would get together and clean out some of the clutter;[2] otherwise it would get so high that you'd have to clamber over, and he did like to stand back and look at his paintings. .. All that clutter, sometimes I would expect it to start moving with cockroaches!" Bacon was proud of his disorderly studio, which was a kind of metaphor for the creative act: "I feel at home in this chaos," he said of his workspace, "because chaos suggests images to me. ... I think it may be a spur to create order." On another occasion he explained, "I like to live among the memories and the damage."

When Ward first met Bacon, he had no cleaning equipment, apart from the odd can of Ajax, a domestic bleach he sometimes used to powder his face. He took Ward to Harrods department store so that she could help him choose his first vacuum cleaner. To use it in the South Kensington mews garret where the artist lived and worked, Ward often had to step over a drunk Bacon when she arrived in the morning (now and again, to celebrate a particularly successful night at one of Soho's casinos, her employer would give her a generous wad of cash). The flat, up a steep flight of stairs from the street, had an eccentric arrangement. In addition to the studio, there were two other rooms—a kitchen which also held the bath, and a small bedroom that doubled as a living room. In Perry Ogden's photographs of Reece Mews, taken after the artist's death, you can see that these domestic spaces, unlike the studio, were modest, simply decorated, and, thanks to Ward, spick-and-span. "The dust wasn't good for him," Ward told me, "sometimes he could hardly breathe. I kept it down as best I could and when he went off on trips, then I would really go to town." Ward likes to think her cleaning "helped him to stay alive a bit longer and do more work."

The dust that he sometimes applied to his canvases was particularly dangerous to Bacon, who suffered from asthma so badly that he was declared unfit for military service during World War II. He volunteered for civil defense instead, working for Air Raid Precautions, but the fine dust of the London Blitz aggravated his asthma and he was discharged on medical grounds. He and Eric Hall rented a cottage in Hampshire where they sat out the war. "If I hadn't been asthmatic," the artist once commented dryly, "I might never have gone on painting at all."

Dust for Bacon, therefore, contained a particularly poignant existential message. "The world is just a dung

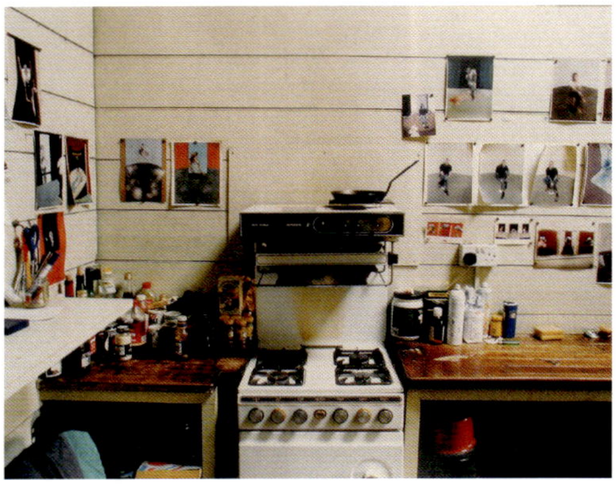

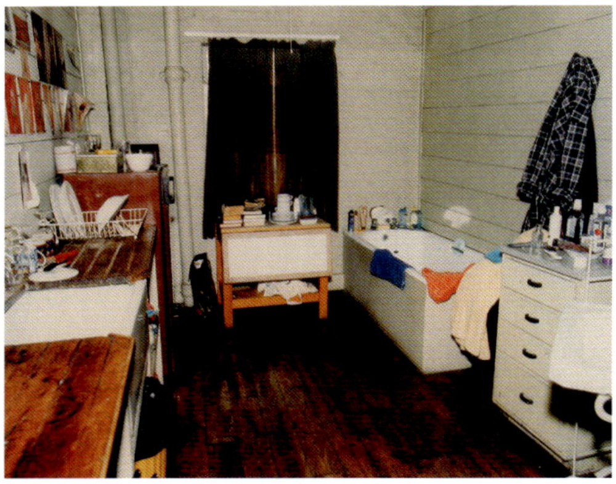

Bacon's kitchen, kept spick-and-span thanks to Ward.

heap," Bacon told Joshua Gilder in 1980, when he was seventy-one. "It's made up of compost of the millions and millions who have died and are blowing about. The dead are blowing in your nostrils every hour, every second you breathe in. It's a macabre way of putting it, perhaps; but anything that's at all accurate about life is always macabre. After all, you're born, you die."

Bacon was an interior decorator and furniture designer before becoming an artist. His showroom at 17 Queensberry Mews West, also in South Kensington, was photographed for an article in *The Studio* magazine titled "The 1930 Look in British Decoration." It is spotless, decorated with tubular steel furniture and Modernist rugs of his design. Only the circular mirror, which later had a prominent place in the painter's studio, provides any sense of continuity with Reece Mews. An early pen-and-wash drawing known as *Corner of the Studio* (1934) depicts Queensberry Mews, making it one of Bacon's first subjects, and it was here that he held the first exhibition of his paintings. Bacon thought that his previous career as a designer-decorator detracted from his prestige as a painter; his later messy workspace might be seen as an attempt to escape this past, even though the disarray itself can be understood as a form of décor.

It was while viewing an exhibition of Picasso's paintings in Paris in the late 1920s that Bacon decided he too would paint. Picasso was often photographed in his studio for publicity purposes, and Bacon, who also liked to pose amid his own debris, might have self-consciously imitated Picasso's bohemian clutter. In 1932, Brassaï met Picasso at 23 rue La Boétie in Paris. "I was expecting an artist's studio," Brassaï wrote in *Conversations with Picasso*, "but it was an apartment turned pigsty ... filled with piles of pictures, reams of paper, stacks of books, packages, wrapped models for sculptures, all lying helter-skelter on the floor, everything covered with a thick coating of dust. ... Except for a few friends, Picasso allowed no one in. The dust could fall and settle wherever it liked, without fear of some cleaning woman's feather duster." Picasso lived in the apartment below, which was very much his wife Olga's domain, "no clutter, not a speck of dust."

Picasso, whom Jean Cocteau called "the king of rag-pickers" because he never threw anything away, told Brassaï that his favorite outfit had been a grey suit because it best matched the dust (perhaps Bacon had this in mind when he painted Eric Hall). "I always forbade anyone to clean my studio," Picasso said, "because I used to rely on dust for my protection ... Dust was my ally. When I noticed that here and there the dust had disappeared, I would know at once that someone had been meddling with my things."

Jean Ward was cleaning Reece Mews on 28 April 1992 when Bacon died of a heart attack in Madrid, age eighty-two. "I didn't often switch the radio on but I did that morning. ... It came over that he had passed away. I was half way through and I thought, well what do I do now? I was really upset, but I thought I'd better finish what I was doing." After that, the studio sat empty, a shrine to its former occupant. "I kept on cleaning for a couple of years, once a month, after John inherited it. What used to worry me was that a few mice found their way into the studio. I had to inform them to watch that, because if they were hoping to keep anything, the mice would soon eat their way through and there'd be nothing left."

In 1998, 7 Reece Mews, where Bacon had worked for thirty-one years, was dismantled by a team of archaeologists and transported in its entirety to Dublin, the city where Bacon was born but which he left at the age of seventeen, never to return. This was somewhat ironic given Bacon's ambivalent relationship to Ireland: his

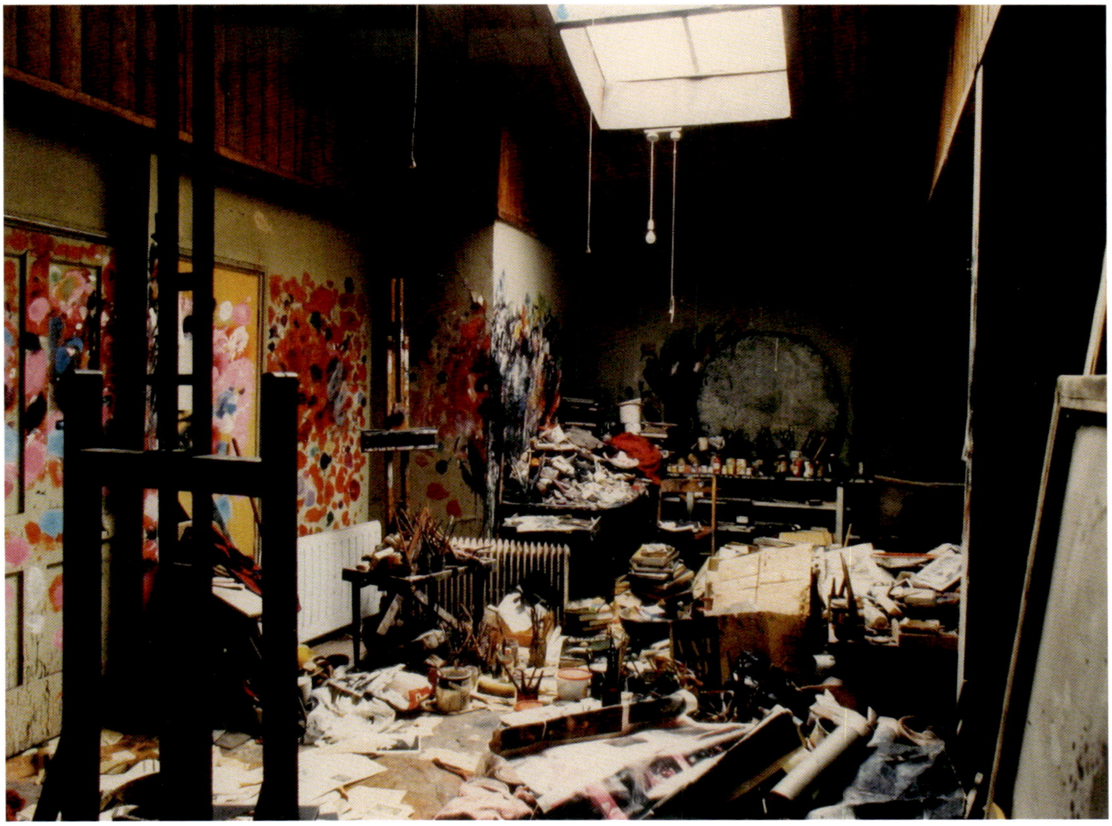

Bacon's studio in all its chaotic glory.

friend, Lady Caroline Blackwood, who was married to Lucian Freud, once said that Bacon "developed a neurotic attack of asthma on the plane whenever he tried to get there." Every time she tried to broach the subject of his traumatic childhood "he became agitated ... he started to tug at the collar of his shirt as if he were trying to loosen some kind of noose which he found asphyxiating; for a moment he resembled the agonized figures in his paintings whose faces turn a truly dangerous shade of indigo purple." In Dublin, the studio was reassembled as a permanent installation in the city's Hugh Lane Gallery. Everything appears exactly as Bacon left it, including the dust.

Blaze O'Connor, one of the archaeologists who painstakingly reconstructed the studio (repositioning every scrap of paper, paint-smeared cashmere jumper, dog-eared book, and discarded tube of paint and brush), recalled: "The films of dust that lay upon the surfaces of the long shelves at the back of the studio were carefully curated. These ephemeral contexts had been lovingly but scientifically bagged, their precise provenance labeled, and archived along with all the thousands of other physical remnants." These samples—"dust, fluff, minute and unidentifiable fragments"—were then painstakingly returned to their correct respective shelves.

After the London studio had been carefully emptied and its contents packed for shipping, the archaeologists had swept up all the remaining dust from the floor and put it in a bag that was simply labeled "Bacon dust." The bag—which, like one of Ward's Hoover bags, must have included Bacon's own sloughed skin—was scattered like ashes over the final installation.

1 Cited in Sigmund Freud, *Leonard da Vinci and a Memory of His Childhood* (New York: W.W. Norton & Co., 1990), p. 10.

2 In 1978, Barry Joule—Bacon's handyman, chauffeur, and drinking partner—rescued three sacks of studio trash including unfinished canvases, diaries, and imagery culled from newspapers, books, and magazines that had been over-painted in ink and crayon. The so-called Barry Joule Archive is now in the Tate's collection.

KISS OF LIFE

RAIFORD GUINS

The games all work great but haven't been played in years so may be a little dusty to a lot dusty.

—eBay description for lot of thirty-two Nintendo NES Games

Lips pursed: blow. Warm air rushes across metal connector pins, along the exposed edge of the thin printed circuit board (PCB) peering out of its protective plastic case. The game cartridge's metal contacts are dirty, littered with the debris of both late twentieth-century and early twenty-first century life. In symphony, the television screen flashes blue and the Nintendo Entertainment System's (NES) power button blinks red as my game cartridge struggles in vain to offer its 8-bit ROM program to the console's 72-pin connector. Despite being fortressed within a recess of durable ABS plastic, the cartridge's little metal contacts are not immune to it: dust.

This is not the first time that I've kissed a game cartridge. After a lifetime of playing video games, and now, more recently, having been happily tasked with constructing a university archive of such games, I am called upon with increasing frequency to perform this wanton act. I am not alone; many gamers blow. We must regularly exorcise dust from game cartridge pins as a result of the NES's front-loading cartridge socket design flaw. The insertion of cartridges into the NES puts pressure on the connector pins, wearing them out and rendering them incredibly sensitive to the cling of dust and grime. NES mouth-to-mouth resuscitation is hardly an ideal solution. It is, nonetheless, a requisite practice for gamers and archivists who lovingly revive antiquated cartridge-based games. The preferred method for restoring life (or, more precisely, "memory," as PCBs contain a game's ROM) is coaxing a cotton swab dipped in isopropyl rubbing alcohol along the cartridge's contacts until it is primed for play.

This isn't the image of video games that springs to mind when we clutch next-generation controllers to work inches off our waistline with Wii *Fit*. Dust, which renders a game cartridge inaccessible, signals a relationship, though admittedly strange (and intimate), that we endure as artifacts from game history relish a vivacious life beyond obsolescence. They seduce us into habitually breathing new life into their dated bodies. Since cartridges are incredibly durable, simply removing dust revives a game that, in the case of the NES, is a quarter of a century old.

Dust is peculiar. For Celeste Olalquiaga, the presence of dust on the surface of things re-awakens a longing for the "lost splendor" of an object; it serves as an ephemeral "signature of lost time."[1] But game dust is not entirely about the "lost time"or "lost splendor" of retrospection, about today's retro-culture of aging gamers attempting to return to the "old school" or "classics" of their past. Surprisingly, it reveals something other than loss. Carolyn Steedman deems dust a perpetual marker of presence rather than loss. Dust, she writes, is about "circularity, the impossibility of things disappearing, or going away, or being gone."[2] It marks the state of "not-going-away-ness"[3]— a condition often borne out by research on game artifacts, history, cultural memory, and preservation. (Recently, I spent a week cleaning hundreds and hundreds of game cartridges for the Intellivision, Colecovision, NES, SuperNES, N64, Sega Genesis, and Atari 2600, 5200, and 7800 game consoles. Tired, grimy, beaten down by piles of plastic that needed cleaning, cataloging, and transporting across campus to special collections, the scene evoked less an uncovering of "lost splendor" than a banal encounter with *things that remain.*)

Old games appear as if by spontaneous generation. They are far from lost. Universities dedicate archive space to them. Specialist collector shops such as Video Games New York on the city's Lower East Side literally have walls of game cartridges encasing their claustrophobic interiors. Classic gaming expos are held annually the world over. On eBay, the epicenter of abundance for game history, sellers scoff at obsolescence with the torrential outpouring of game stuff from attics, garages, basements, and closets. Given new life, new splendor, they are shipped out to new lives and experiences. Dust sticks to the objects across these spaces. As my epigraph warns, dust is part of the bidding price—the highest bidder also wins the dust of other people's things, of the people themselves. More than a peripheral phenomenon, blowing is part of playing, as dust is never still.

1 Celeste Olalquiaga, *The Artificial Kingdom: A Treasury of the Kitsch Experience* (New York: Pantheon Books, 1998), pp. 94–95.

2 Carolyn Steedman, *Dust: The Archive and Cultural History* (New Brunswick: Rutgers University Press, 2001), p. 164.

3 Ibid., p. 165.

opposite: Old Nintendo games waiting to be cleaned. Photo Ryo Manabe.

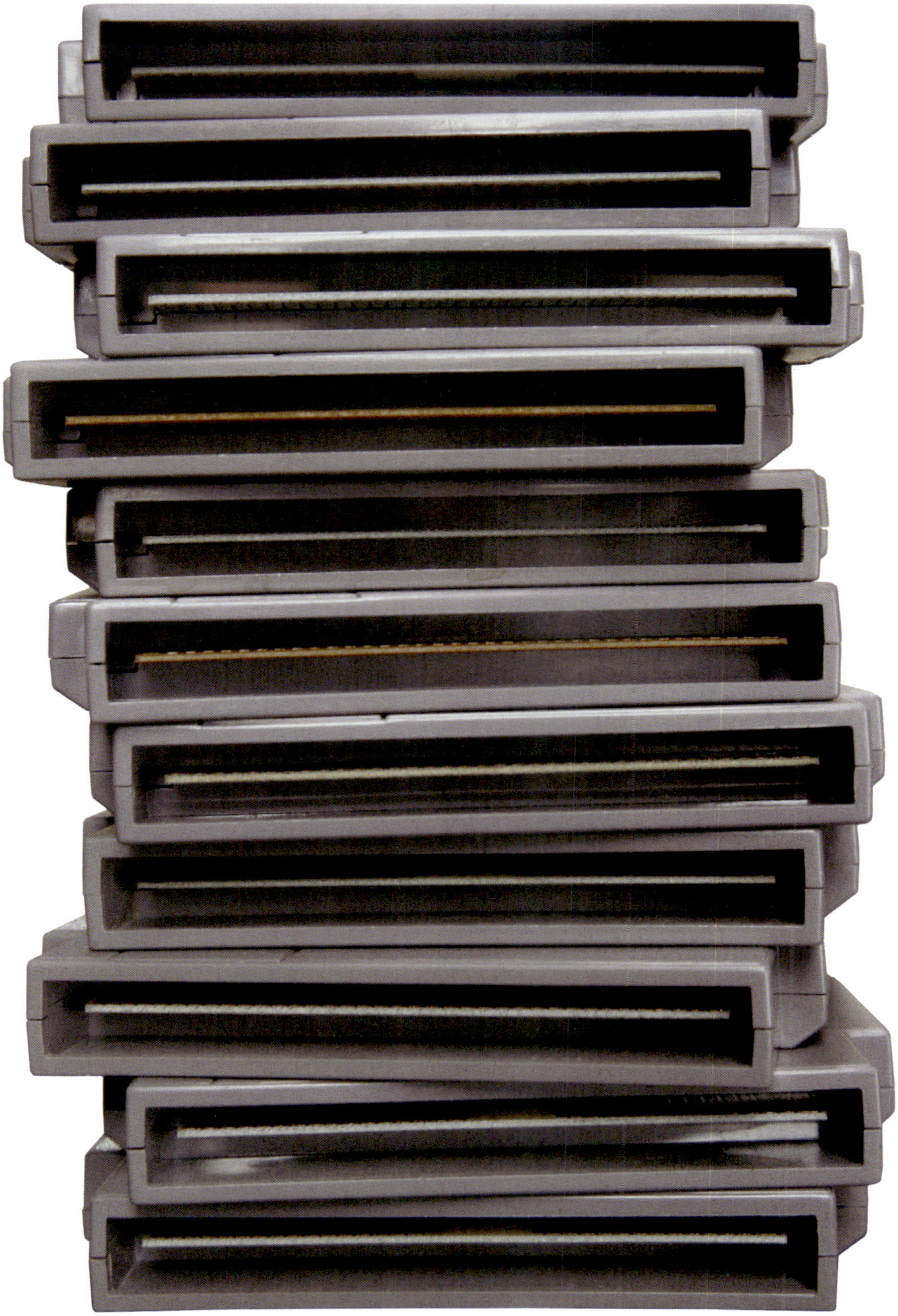

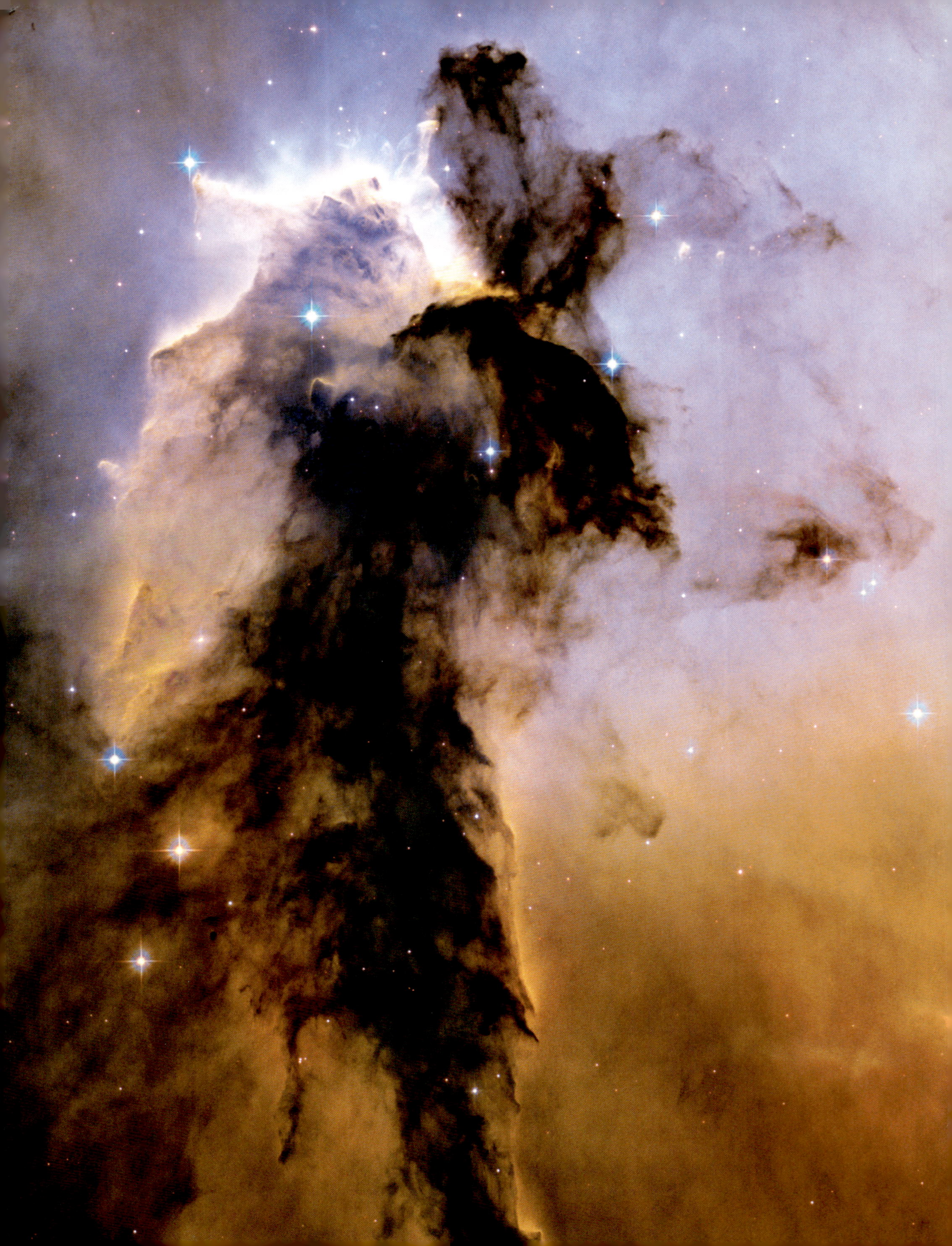

SILENT WITNESS: AN INTERVIEW WITH JEAN DUPRAT

BRIAN DILLON

Approximately 30,000 tons of cosmic dust enter our atmosphere annually. The micrometeorites of which it is comprised arrive either in the form of irregularly shaped particles or cosmic spherules that have partially melted and lost much of their mass before reaching the surface of the earth as tiny rounded objects. Except at the most remote regions, the study of such particles is considerably hampered by the profusion of other kinds of dust raised on the planet's great landmasses. Consequently, interplanetary dust has been most readily retrieved from the deep oceans and the South Pole.

Jean Duprat is a nuclear physicist and leader of the Solid Astrophysics team at the Centre de la Recherche Scientifique (CSNSM-CNRS) in Orsay, University of Paris XI. In 2000, Duprat and his team, in conjunction with the French polar institute IPEV and its Italian counterpart PNRA, began collecting micrometeorites at the Antarctic site known as Dome C. Duprat spoke to Brian Dillon by phone from France in August 2009.

Can you first of all explain why it's important to study micrometeorites or cosmic dust?

There are many reasons to study dust. If you want to study the primitive solar system, you absolutely have to examine small bodies, because larger bodies only yield answers about their own history—only by studying dust can you determine the primitive component. Everywhere you look, you will find dust, even in the most remote places in the universe. It tells you things about its birth and where it traveled. It records a history. In that sense, it's really a witness, because it can record, for example, the irradiation in different environments—interplanetary or interstellar. It's a very silent witness: it penetrates but doesn't disturb.

Would you call all the particles you study "dust"? And if so, how is that defined? Is it purely a matter of size?

Below a centimeter in diameter we always speak in terms of dust, whether it's dust that enters the atmosphere, dust that collects on the earth's surface, or even dust within the interplanetary medium. In terms of composition, the major difference between rocks and dust (except for size, of course) is that the composition of rocks varies a lot, since they have different geological histories, whereas, when you look at dust within the solar system, it's clear that it is really rather uniform in terms of composition. It's quite homogeneous, in fact. And this tells us something quite profound about the solar system itself; it means that below a certain size, the solar system is very well mixed. This is not obvious; theoretically, we could have expected something else. The composition of these dust particles is the composition of the sun, except for the volatile parts—the gases, I mean. If you take away the gas, the pattern of the elements in extraterrestrial dust mimics the element pattern of the sun extremely well. That is because the sun itself is made of this dust. The two share the same pattern; even the trace elements are in more or less the same ratios. That makes sense once you know it, but it's still a rather impressive thing, because the dust is so tiny and the sun is so big!

And the precise composition of the particles...

The major elements are oxygen, silicon, magnesium, and the characteristic of extraterrestrial dust is that it's more enriched in iron and nickel, or, to be more precise, it's the earth that is depleted in iron and nickel. The reason for that is quite simple: because the earth is rather large, it has melted and differentiated—it has a core, a mantle, and a crust. Originally, the composition of the earth was very much like that of the sun or of the dust; but most of our iron and nickel went into the core when the earth melted, so if you take an earth rock—an average crystal rock—it will be depleted of iron and nickel, and this is a very straightforward way to see whether a rock is of extraterrestrial origin or not.

What are the special conditions that make Antarctic dust preferable to study? Is it entirely a matter of the relative absence of contamination?

That's the key. There are several things to say; the first is that there is a difference between the North Pole and the South Pole. Antarctica is better for our purposes because the southern hemisphere is dominated by oceans, whereas in the north you have a lot of land. The north produces quite a lot of terrestrial dust, which can reach areas as remote as the center of Greenland, whereas in the south there are oceans that do not produce dust and right in the middle, lost and very far from anything, is Antarctica. We went to the center of Antarctica, where there are three kilometers of ice on

opposite: Hubble Space Telescope photograph of the Eagle Nebula, showing pillars of star-forming gas and dust, 7 July 2006.

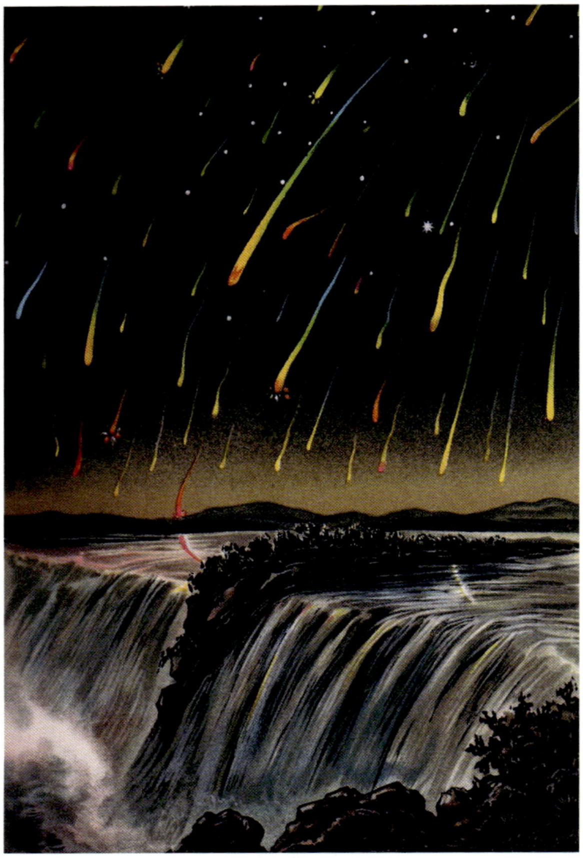

Leonid meteor shower over North America the night of 12 November 1833, considered the most spectacular ever. The light of the showers is produced by the comet Tempel-Tuttle, whose trail of dust-sized particles collides with air molecules, which combine and give off photons. From E. Weiss, *Bilderatlas der Sternenwelt*, 1888.

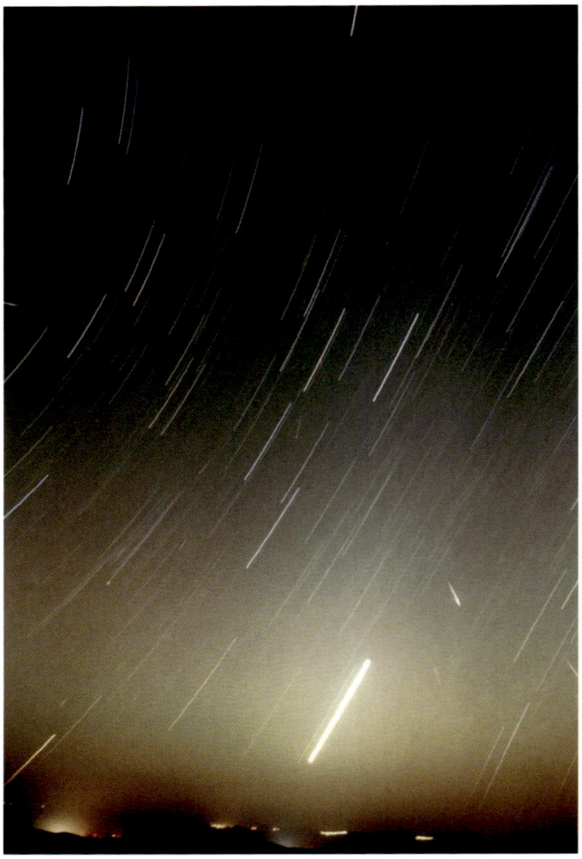

Leonid shower, 17 November 1999. Photo Ofer Gabzo.

the land. The wind constantly blows from the center of the continent to the coast and produces a natural clean room, and in fact, the only terrestrial dust that can reach central Antarctica is dust that's below a few microns—whereas we are searching for dust that is above thirty microns and typically around a hundred. So it's tiny, but it's something like two orders of magnitude larger. And within that range what we've proven is that most of the dust in the Antarctic snow is of extraterrestrial origin, except the dust we brought with us.

Are the particles uncovered in the Antarctic different or more numerous than those at other remote parts of the earth: the deep ocean beds, for example?

In deep sea collections, you essentially find cosmic spherules; these are micrometeorites that have been altered on atmospheric entry—essentially they have completely melted into round spherules, sometimes losing more than eighty or ninety percent of their mass. They were first recorded in the deep sea by the *Challenger* expedition in the 1870s. That expedition performed a collection in the middle of the Pacific, which is in fact a sort of desert because there isn't a lot of terrestrial dust, so they were able to find extraterrestrial particles. The particles fall everywhere, but you will only be able to find them in regions where you have very low contamination of terrestrial particles. In Antarctica, it is possible to find much more fragile interplanetary particles that have endured a minimal terrestrial alteration during their stay in the snow.

How old are the micrometeorites that are found at the Antarctic? When did they arrive on earth and how deep are they submerged?

You can define different ages. The first would be when the particles formed. All the particles formed, more or less, 4.5 billion years ago, which is the time when the solar system formed. All this dust condensed within a few million years. The second age would be the time when the dust arrived on the earth—this is the age of the snow where we collected it. And there it's very precise—it's within the last century, and it's more precisely between the 1950s and the 1970s, because we dug trenches that were about five meters deep, and this more or less corresponds to that period. What you've got to realize here is that central Antarctica is of course very remote and cold, but it has another characteristic: it's extremely dry, with an average precipitation of about 3.5 cm per year, which is essentially nothing. Of course it never rains: the temperature range is between −30°C and −80°C . It can snow, but in fact it never really snows as such; there are little particles of snow in the air, but at the end of a year it makes between three and four centimeters of water, which is about ten centimeters of snow. So if you dig about four meters, you will be more or less in the 1970s.

Why was it important to dig to that particular depth, or to that date?

Because we were searching for something, but we failed. In 1966, there was a shooting-star storm. The cosmic spherules are residues of shooting stars. When they enter the atmosphere, they heat up very quickly and they ionize. You don't see the particle itself of course—that's something like three millimeters across—but what you see is a tube of atmospheric gas that is ionized by friction. It's very similar to a neon light; it's the same phenomenon. Now, in 1966 the earth's trajectory around the sun crossed the tail of a comet that had been around a few centuries ago and left behind a trail of dust. The storm is a regular occurrence: it's called the Leonids—it occurs in November. The 1966 storm was quite heavy, and so we hoped to find the residual dust. As it turned out, we didn't find any, that is, we couldn't identify any difference, in terms of the concentration or composition of particles, between the snow layer corresponding to the 1966 Leonids and other snow layers. The other reason for digging so deep was that we wanted to reach layers of snow that pre-dated any exploration; the first trip to that zone was in the 1990s, and so digging between the 1950s and 1970s was very safe for us, because that stratum had seen no pollution at all.

How are the particles extracted, observed, and stored?

The collection took place on the central Antarctic plateau in the vicinity of the Concordia Research Station located at Dome C (73°S, 123°E), about twelve hundred kilometers from the coasts of Adélie Land. This is a permanent inland scientific station that was built by IPEV and PNRA, the French and Italian polar institutes. Thanks to their logistical help, we were able to go and work there. We dug huge trenches—they're about forty meters long, eight meters wide, and five meters deep—and then manually cleaned them by excavating the snow. We had to avoid any sort of smoke. Within one cubic meter, you'll find perhaps twenty or thirty particles, which means you've got to be extremely clean and rather strict about pollution. Once you've dug this large trench, you remove the first ten centimeters of the flank and then you begin digging in the flank of the trench. You take the snow and put it into very clean cans and

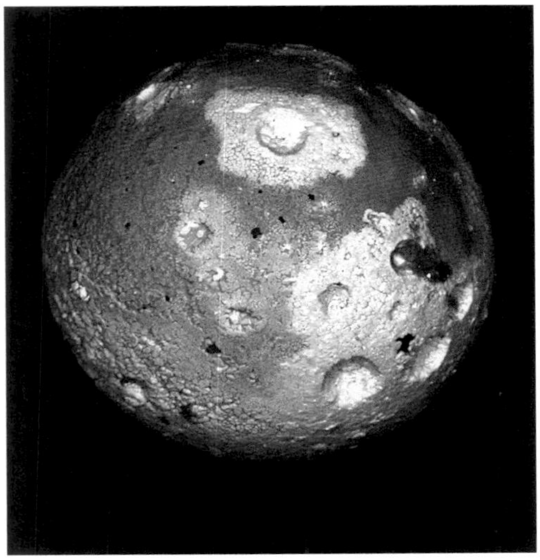

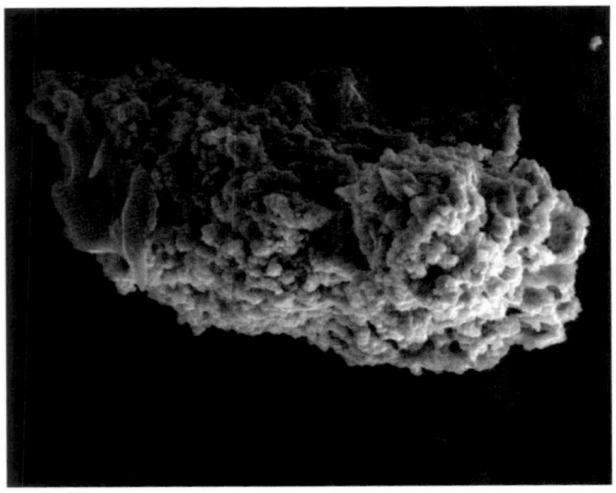

Cosmic spherule and fluffy, fine-grained micrometeorite, both collected in the Antarctic in the vicinity of the Concordia Research Station in January 2006. Photos courtesy Duprat/Engrand CSNSM-CNRS.

bring them back to the station to melt them very gently in a dedicated smelter. You melt a few cubic meters per day, and filter that water; if you've got the correct protocol and you're very cautious about pollution, you end up with something that is essentially extraterrestrial. This was really a surprise for us—we knew we'd find something, but we never realized that once we'd figured out how to get rid of the pollution we'd end up with essentially one particle out of two which is extraterrestrial, which is unique. It's the cleanest collection ever performed.

Once we've melted the snow, we check the filters to ensure there's no contamination and we make a vacuum to get rid of the remaining water; we are left with the particles, which we store in dry nitrogen gas to avoid any rust. Once we're back in the lab in France, we open the filters and extract the particles; we fragment them and we mount one fragment of each particle for analysis. With these grains, with the external aspect, and the bulk composition, you can rather easily find out what is extraterrestrial and what is not.

Does the rate of dust fall vary historically, and does it now vary over the course of a year?

Yes, it does; it's very clear on radar, where you can see the dust entering the atmosphere—you can see, for instance, that in August there are more shooting stars than the rest of the year, and this corresponds to the earth's trajectory across an old cometary tail that creates this phenomenon, the Perseids. The interplanetary medium is not homogeneous in terms of dust; there are regions where there is more dust, due to comets, and there are regions where there is only what we call the sporadic flux. If you want to picture it: the dust is more or less located, like the planets, within the ecliptic plane, which is the plane of the rotation of the earth.

How much of the dust is from asteroids, how much from comets, and what are the differences?

This is the big question at the moment. Of course, there's a difference between asteroids and comets: asteroids are large rocks from the hot inner solar system that are in orbit between Mars and Jupiter. They're our close neighbors, whereas comets come from a very remote place beyond the orbit of Pluto. There are two reservoirs of comets: the Kuiper Belt, which is just at Pluto's orbit, and the Oort Cloud, which is at the border of the solar system. Comets are records of what happened early in the solar system in the very coldest place, where there was ice. Comets are icy objects. From that point of view, you would expect asteroids and comets to be very different from each other.

What we realize now, however, is that quite surprisingly, the dust or the rocky parts of comets look amazingly like the most ancient and most primitive asteroid matter that we know, which is called the carbonaceous chondrites. This has a profound implication: it means that very early in the solar system there was a radial mixing: dust from the inner part of the solar system was thrown to the outer part of the solar system. We know this because there is dust in comets that has obviously been processed much closer to the sun than the point at which the comets themselves were formed. This was the main result of NASA's Stardust mission.

The actual question of the proportion of cometary and asteroid dust in the interplanetary particles is a difficult one: it's not fully answered yet. What we can say is that we do find dust that is probably from the two parent bodies and, more precisely, I think we have found cometary dust in the collection we performed in central Antarctica. We've got dust that is extremely rich in organic matter—though not the kind that has anything to do with terrestrial life: it's in the form of the long carbonaceous chains that are present in comets.

What does the dust tell us about the universe? About the solar system? About the earth?

Here we need a brief history of matter! If you look at the nuclei out of which the solar system is formed—leaving aside hydrogen and helium, which were made during the Big Bang—but if you look at the heavier elements, then everything on earth, including us, is stardust. There is no way to synthesize nuclei—at least in an efficient way—within the solar system itself; you can have a few nuclear reactions, but it's nothing in terms of production of matter. All the matter has been synthesized in the very heart of stars before our solar system formed. Once this matter is formed into stars and ejected into the interstellar medium, it forms very tiny dust particles which are about a micron in size. In regions where it's cold enough and dense enough—they're called molecular clouds—you can have a proto-star that collapses in on itself to form a star like the sun. It's at that very period that the dust begins to form the particles that we find.

opposite: Fine dust in the Witch Head Nebula, associated with the bright star Rigel in the constellation Orion, reflects the light. The blue color is caused in part by Rigel's blue color and in part because the dust grains reflect blue light more efficiently than red. The same physical process causes Earth's daytime sky to appear blue.

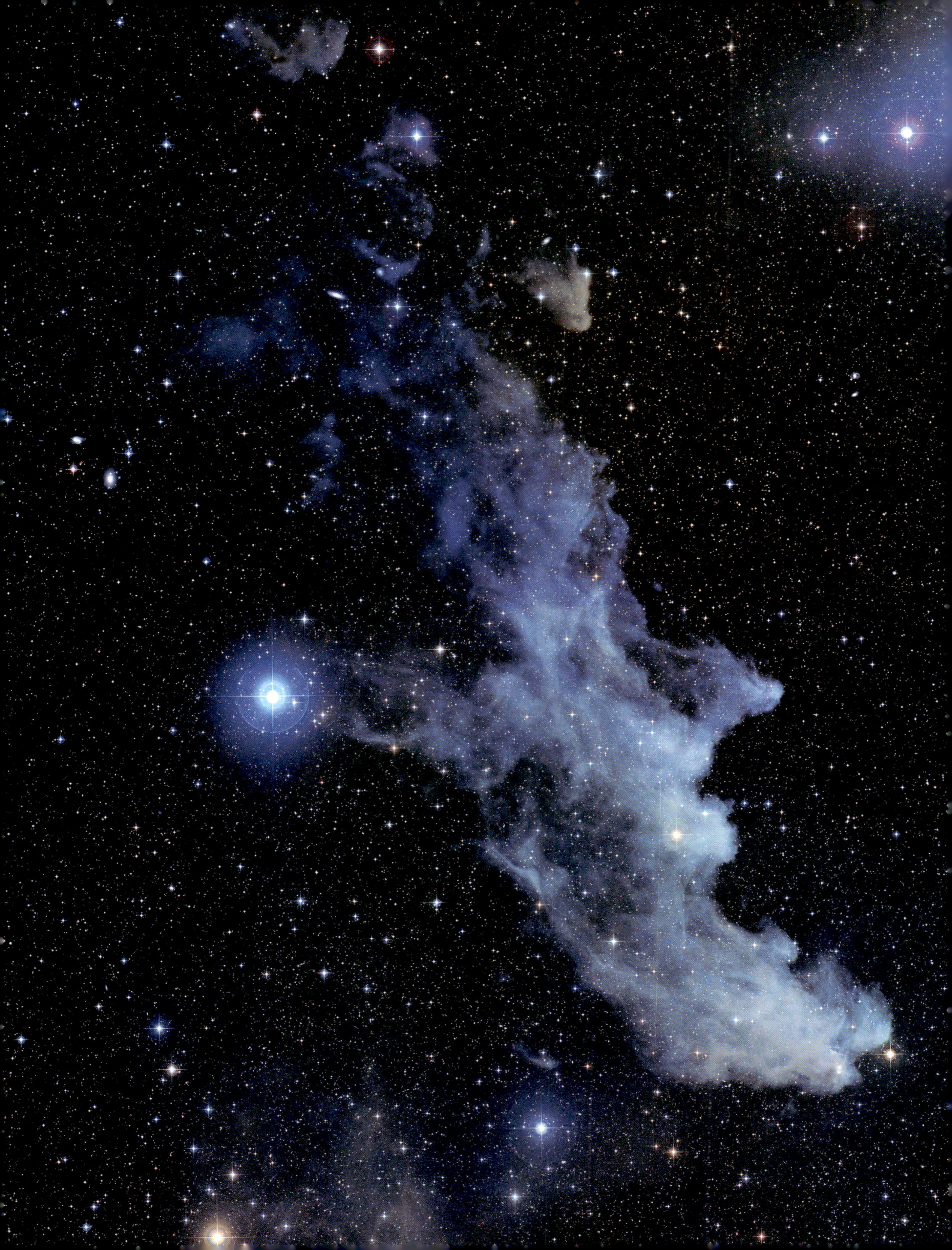

So, the particles tell us things about the first million years—when the solar system formed and how it formed. But if you look carefully at that dust, you can find tiny mineral phases that condensed within the envelopes of the previous stars, and these are called presolar grains. These allow us to glimpse a more ancient history, from before the birth of our solar system. You can also find some dust that belongs to large bodies such as asteroids or maybe planets—this tells us about a much more recent history; the history of the moon, for example, or the history of Mars. But this is very rare. So basically the answer is that most of what we find and study has to do with the birth of the solar system.

Have you found any dust that can't be identified in terms of its substance?

Well, maybe, but it's hard for me to tell you about something I don't yet understand at all. ... There might be a surprise in store because we analyze everything, and it's the first time we've been able to do that. So we end up with particles that we're absolutely not used to and we don't understand what they are, and they might be extraterrestrial but they might as easily be terrestrial; we don't know. Let me put it this way: in previous collections we were obliged to do a pre-sorting, so we only analyzed dust that was close to what we believed to be extraterrestrial. And with central Antarctica, the major change is that we're able to analyze everything, because there are so few particles. And of course when you analyze everything, you sometimes end up with something that is completely weird. So that's more or less where we find ourselves.

SOMETHING IN THE AIR

COLBY CHAMBERLAIN

It was Marcel Duchamp who brought dust into the museum. In 1920, he took the pane of glass on which he had begun to create *The Bride Stripped Bare by Her Bachelors, Even* (also known as the *Large Glass*) and placed it on sawhorses by an open window in his New York studio, exposing it to the grit of the street below. According to his friend Henri-Pierre Roché, Duchamp hung a sign nearby to prevent cleaning attempts by well-meaning visitors: "Dust breeding," it read. "To be respected." When the artist Man Ray photographed the glass later that year, a thick film of dust had settled on the surface. Duchamp eventually wiped most of the dust clean, but left untouched a few select patches as an unorthodox means of coloring his composition. He had made work of doing nothing: dust, typically the trace of neglect, was instead the product of purposeful inactivity. The *Large Glass* now stands in the Philadelphia Museum of Art, a smudge on a pristine setting. That said, Duchamp's dust is safely quarantined, sandwiched between panes of glass. (Man Ray later observed that the *Large Glass* was sufficiently sealed to be washable in the shower.) Though Duchamp called for dust to be respected, museums' campaigns against it persist unabated—much to the chagrin of Anthony McCall.

In 1973, McCall, an artist and graphic designer from England, was aboard a ship bound for New York when he came up with an idea for a new film, *Line Describing a Cone*. Looking at the film reel itself, the piece is extremely simple: a white dot appears on a black background and, over the course of thirty minutes' worth of celluloid, that single dot grows into the outline of a circle. Now imagine that film projected across an empty room to a bare wall forty or so feet away. That single dot shoots out a narrow beam of light and, as the dot extends and curves, that initial beam becomes a veil. Three or four minutes pass, and the light begins to suggest the sloping surface of a cone, with the projector's lens as its tip and the circle appearing on the opposite wall as its base. At the close of thirty minutes, the

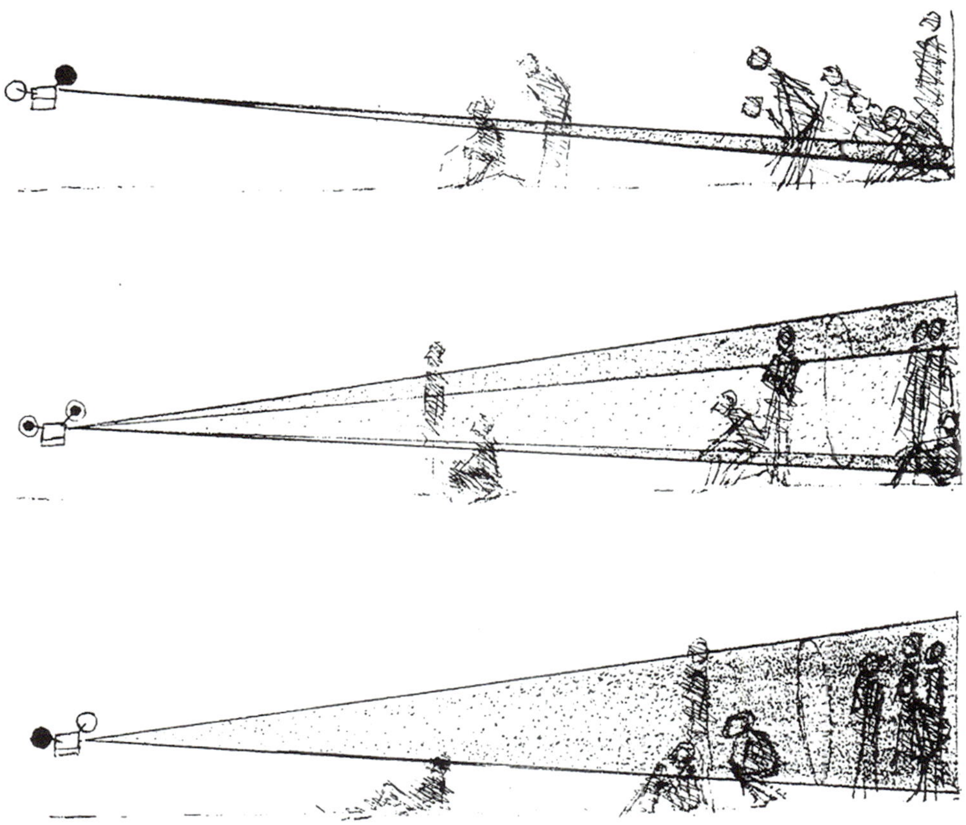

Anthony McCall, *Line Describing a Cone*, 1973, sequential drawing.

completed cone sits between projector and wall like a phantom megaphone, apparent enough that some viewers walk circumspectly around it, but so impalpable that others cross straight through. McCall dubbed it a "solid light" film.

Line Describing a Cone, as well as several subsequent variations, utilized the barest elements of film—celluloid and projected light—but it clearly needed to be experienced as a three-dimensional object, like a sculpture. The film's straddling of two mediums accounts for its varied exhibition history: in New York alone, *Line Describing a Cone* was alternately screened at avant-garde cinemas, like Millennium Film Workshop, and downtown galleries, like Artists Space and the Clocktower. Neither setting was ideal, so each screening required advance preparation, such as removing chairs (in film theaters) or blacking out windows (in galleries). As it turned out, the formerly industrial trappings of these alternative venues provided McCall's films with a crucial additional element: *dust*. If Duchamp's dust settled over glass in a thick *film*, then floating dust functioned for McCall as a sort of diffuse *screen* that allowed his veils of light to be seen across space.

McCall emphasized the importance of air quality in a set of projection instructions he wrote in 1974: "The light of the beam is visible through contact with particles in the air, be they from dust, humidity or cigarette smoke. Smoking should not be prohibited." But when McCall had the opportunity to exhibit outside of low-budget avant-garde enclaves, he found these stipulations more difficult to fulfill. Other venues were too tidy. During a 1975 screening of *Line Describing a Cone* at Malmö Konsthall in Sweden, he watched in horror as the usual veil of light simply failed to appear. He described his reaction in a 2007 interview with Mark Godfrey:

I raced out of the Konsthall, and across the road to a tobacconist, and hurried back into the projection space with three, lit, Swedish cigarettes in my mouth. I blew smoke into the air near the beams in an attempt to make them visible. This did help. However at that moment I was tapped on the shoulder. I turned round to find an angry-looking guard who confiscated the cigarettes and ordered me out of the room. So for the next fifteen minutes, an art audience drawn from the city of Malmö politely watched a three-dimensional projection that was absolutely invisible. If they were bored or disappointed, they didn't show it.

The challenge of rendering his work visible in museum contexts was a significant factor in McCall's decision to abandon his solid light films for over twenty years. More recently, a renewed interest in his work, along with the invention of sophisticated fog machines called hazers, has brought McCall back into the studio. But his earlier encounter with museums' war on dust remains a cautionary tale of the often irreconcilable differences between the rough spaces where art is typically made and the pristine institutions that frequently present it. As much as nature abhors a vacuum, culture disdains cleanliness.

---

opposite: *Line Describing a Cone* being projected at Artists Space, New York, in 1974. Photo Peter Moore.

JACKET REQUIRED

ALEXANDRA CARDIA

Defined by the Oxford English Dictionary as referring to "a protective (and usually decorative) paper cover placed around a bound book, usually with the title and author's name printed on it," the phrase "dust cover" or "dust jacket" was first used in the late nineteenth century. The earliest dust jackets, dating to the 1830s, encased the entire book. Their primary function was as protective wrapping, which means that many nineteenth-century dust jackets were disposed of or lost after being removed from their books. The standard library practice of unsheathing books before cataloging them for circulation has also contributed to the rarity of surviving early dust jackets.

In April 2009, for example, one of the earliest-known dust jackets was found at Oxford University's Bodleian Library. Hidden in an assortment of book-trade ephemera purchased in the 1890s and never fully catalogued, the worn and faded piece of paper imprinted with black ink had long been separated from the volume it encased, an 1830 gift book entitled *Friendship's Offering*. Gift books, or literary annuals—popular collections of essays, short fiction, and poetry based upon late eighteenth-century French and German illuminated almanacs—were richly decorated volumes, bound in silk, leather, or glazed paper, and designed to be given away, particularly around the Christmas and New Year holidays. Dust jackets, such as the one at the Bodleian, ensured that the gift reached its recipient in perfect condition. Clive Hurst, the head of rare books and printed ephemera at the Bodleian, believes that such a dust jacket is more accurately described as a wrapper, "protecting the book from handling damage (which could include dust)." In fact, the creases where the paper had been folded around the volume, as well as remnants of wax where it had been sealed, are still visible on the jacket.

Toward the end of the nineteenth century, as publishers began to employ more durable bookbinding materials, the need for strictly protective wrappings diminished. The sober, utilitarian cover gave way to the dust jacket as advertising vehicle, culminating in the vivid graphics, stylized fonts, and "special effects" such as embossing and metallic inks that today scream from bookstore shelves everywhere.

---

opposite: An 1830 dustjacket, one of the oldest to have survived. Courtesy Bodleian Library, Oxford University.

FRIENDSHIP'S OFFERING.

1830.

"This is Affection's Tribute,—Friendship's Offering;
Whose silent eloquence, more rich than words,
Tells of the Giver's faith and truth in absence,
And says—Forget me not!"

PRICE TWELVE SHILLINGS, ELEGANTLY BOUND.

FRIENDSHIP'S OFFERING.

1830.

PROOFS OF THE ENGRAVINGS IN A PORTFOLIO.

		£	s.	d.
India before the Writing	Price	£1	11	6
Ditto after the Writing	,,	1	1	[illegible]
French Proofs Ditto	,,	0	15	0

*** A very limited number of the Plates for 1828 and 1829 may still be had on the above Terms.

A few sets of *Friendship's Offering*, from its commencement in 1824, have just been completed, Price £3 12s. per Set of Six Vols. uniformly done up in the improved binding.

STARDUST MEMORIES

DORION SAGAN

The true harvest of my daily life is somewhat as intangible and indescribable as the tints of morning or evening. It is a little star-dust caught, a segment of the rainbow which I have clutched.

—Henry David Thoreau

Quantitatively, dust refers to solid particles with diameters of less than 500 micrometers. A micrometer, also known as a micron, is a millionth of a meter, or 0.000039 of an inch. The eye of a needle is 750 microns wide, enough to get some camel dust through. The diameter of the period that ends this sentence is about 450 microns—it would make a nice little piece of dust if it could be liberated from the prison of this page.

But despite its physical insignificance, dust has outsized negative connotations. It is an avatar of the unclean. It is the ensign of entropy, of buildings destroyed or neglected, matter without purpose. Dust is what gathers on books that are not read, on cabinets and shelves. It is the figure of the fragment, of division and disintegration, of the unswept, the unloved, the overlooked, and discarded. It is what Tad Allagash snorts in his comical attempt to hoover any remaining traces of "Bolivian marching powder"—cocaine—in Jay McInerney's 1980s novel, *Bright Lights, Big City*. To be clear, a Buddhist saying goes, you must wipe the dust from the mirror of your mind.

Much of household dust is keratin, the main protein of skin. Human skin sheds continuously. You lose about 1.5 grams of it per day. The detritus does not go entirely to waste. First, it is decomposed by fungi, who like it moist. Human flakes predigested by fungi are a staple for *Dermatophagoides farinae*, *Dermatophagoides pteronyssinus*, and *Euroglyphus maynei*. These mite species excrete protease enzymes that linger in mattresses and furniture—until the comparatively colossal rear end of a person sits down, at which time they are released in sometimes invisible puffs. The allergenic dust is a main reason for indoor sneezing, itching, and irritated eyes.

But dust ain't all bad. Illuminated by slanting rays, it becomes pixie dust. Like a wink of the Lucretian real behind all mythology, it becomes a princess kissed by the sun. Thus, this same humble substance that builds on bookshelves, that darkens corners and lies flat on surfaces in an apparent effort to disguise its pitiable dishevelment (and why shouldn't it, after all, for what is dust but a debased form of dirt?), this asthmatic antithesis of the grandeur of existence, this figure of

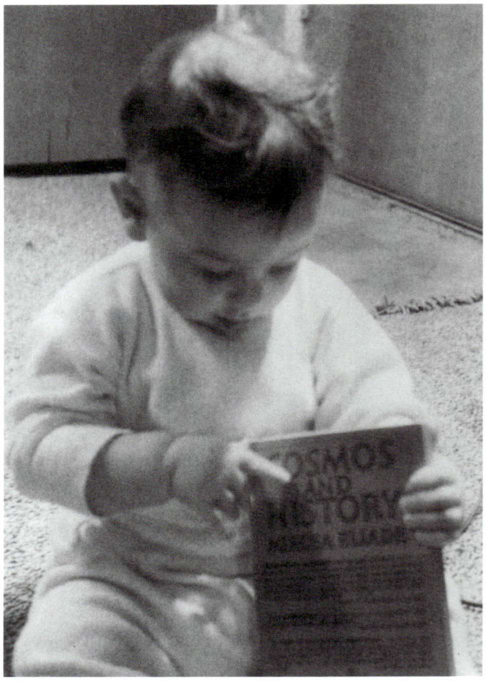

Dorion Sagan trying to grapple with Mircea Eliade's *Cosmos and History*, 1959.

the unwanted so unremarkable it often escapes even negative attention, this forerunner of filth on the clichéd white glove of the fastidious housecleaner, this accoutrement of the homeless, this essence of crumbling, sometimes swirls and reflects, like glitter happy to be free of the mirror of our minds.

A dust grain can be a world. In Dr. Seuss's *Horton Hears a Who!*, a perspicacious elephant listens to a talking speck which turns out to be a tiny world on a grain of dust, one city of which, Whoville, contains a bustling community of humanoid Whos. I read the Seuss book to my son. It was a crash course in imaginary microbiology and crypto-anthropology; its lesson was that within what we overlook are sometimes rich and unsuspected worlds.

. . .

When I was eighteen, in 1978, I would sometimes smoke angel dust in the bleachers with the black kids at lunch. This was in LA. My fellow students bought it sprinkled on parsley. This is a dangerous drug that can cause very bad reactions. I was lucky that, for me, it just led to pleasant numb feelings under the California sun.

My father Carl was filming the *Cosmos* series for television at the time and I was living with him and his second wife, sharing a room with their son, my seven-year-old half-brother Nick, now a successful science fiction writer. It was the first time I had lived with my father since my parents divorced when I was five. My dad let me hang out in his trailer, which had belonged to Marlon Brando, on the lot at KCET in LA, where I would listen to punk rock on FM radio. I was from the east coast, out of place, and had no friends to speak of. There was one girl I had my eye on, but that was about it. Blair High School was ethnically partitioned, one-quarter Hispanic kids, one-quarter black kids, one-quarter Asian kids who gravitated towards studies and chess club, and one-quarter spoiled white kids. In gym, I had the chance to take modern jazz dance. There was only one other boy in the class. He was tall and effeminate, and got in a fight with a very dark girl half his size but twice as fast. She whipped off her two earrings, he whipped off his one, and they started flailing away at each other. This led to him getting kicked out. The white teacher asked me to stay after and asked me what I thought of the situation. I asked her if she was asking me because I was the only guy, and she said yes. "But you're the only white girl in the class," I said.

The next day after class, I was jumped by several boys on the steps of the little building past the pool. Phyllis, one of the black girls who knew me from the bleachers, was by the tennis courts and yelled, "Just run, White Boy, as fast as you can to the Principal's office. Don't look back." I did and identified the kids. For a few days, I stayed away from school, accepting my stepmother's painkillers, which she had for her back pain and which allowed me to forget about the fact that I'd have to return to school once the bruises and swelling on my face died down. When I returned to school, my tough black friend "Blue" informed me the kids I'd identified got kicked out and that there was a contract out on me. I did not take this seriously, considering it movie bluster inspired by *The Godfather*.

Aside from Blue, my only other friend at the time was Tim, a white boy who was gay and had an older boyfriend who was a professional therapist. One day, Tim and I were in my room listening to my David Bowie albums, whose songs like "Starman" and "Life on Mars" I half-hoped to share with my dad (not so much "Space Oddity," I explained, which was too popular). My half-brother, Nick, was playing superhero and jumped from the arm of the couch toward Tim, who stepped away. When he hit the floor, my stepmother had enough. She insisted my father speak with me. Soon thereafter, to my smug amusement, he lectured me, giving a rationalist discourse on natural selection as the basis for a normal heterosexual relationship. He underscored the evolutionary uselessness of Eros diverted from its natural goal. Instead of the Old Testament, he was appealing to Darwin to make the same point.

I was glad he was paying attention to me, even if it was negative attention. The stories of neutron stars a spoonful of which weighed tons, of black hole portals to different places and times, and of higher-dimension objects moving through lower-dimension worlds that he'd told me as a boy he was now sharing with the nameless masses. Why, my unconscious must have wondered, was he spreading his message about contacting life in outer space to millions when I, his first-born, had been neglected? Was I mere human dust, disposable detritus taken root in the fertile medium of my microbiologist mother, only to be forever after confined to the plutonic outskirts of his emotional universe? At least in Adriatic Italian dialect, as I would learn two years later from my college girlfriend, whose own undivorced parents were bhang-smoking partiers on Cape Cod who welcomed me into their home, there was a name for the dust you swept up—*mundessa*. Ah, to be embraced, named, recognized, even if only momentarily, on the way to the eternal dustbin.

. . .

Dust's relegation to a trope of dirt and insignificance, entropy and loss, is belied by its astronomical grandeur. And few, if any, have been more eloquent on this grandeur than my father, whose own bones now gather the stuff in sites next to his parents, moved from Florida to accompany him in Lakeview Cemetery in Ithaca, New York. From Martian dust storms as part of the genesis of his thoughts on how dust and smoke could affect life on Earth, to his study of Triton's streaks as windblown dust, to his "pale blue dot" speech, perhaps his most beautiful, in which he calls Earth seen from space "a mote of dust," my father took dust deadly seriously. And he led others to do so. He drew the world's attention to the role of particulate matter in blocking out light. Extrapolating from Martian dust storms, he tirelessly warned of a nuclear winter, the unsuspected result of smoke and dust rising in the aftermath of a superpower confrontation. The darkening blanket would, he suggested, shut down agriculture on a global scale. His advocacy and interaction with Soviet scientists played a role in ending the Cold War—which, ironically, was inaugurated by the Soviet launch of the Sputnik satellite that set off the space race and the attendant massive funding that made his spectacular career in space science possible.

My father was deeply moved by the tiny blue speck the Earth became when NASA, partly due to his

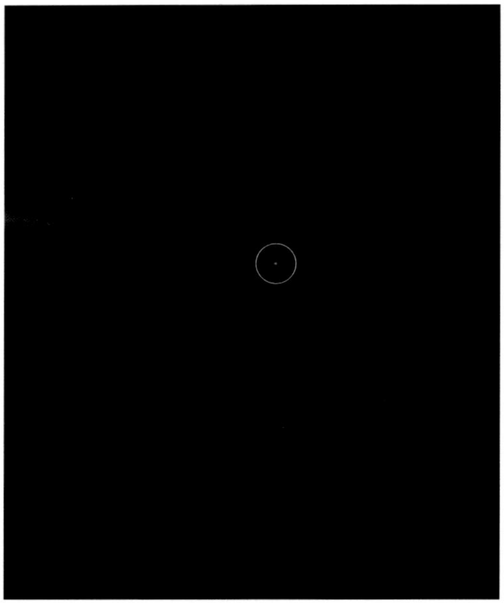

Photograph taken in 1990 by Voyager 1 of a barely visible Earth against the vastness of space. The idea that Voyager 1 turn in space and take the photo was Sagan's, as was the name by which the image is now known—the "Pale Blue Dot." In his book of the same name, Sagan wrote: "Look again at that dot. That's here. That's home. That's us. On it everyone you love, everyone you know, everyone you ever heard of, every human being who ever was, lived out their lives. The aggregate of our joy and suffering, thousands of confident religions, ideologies, and economic doctrines, every hunter and forager, every hero and coward, every creator and destroyer of civilization, every king and peasant, every young couple in love, every mother and father, hopeful child, inventor and explorer, every teacher of morals, every corrupt politician, every 'superstar,' every 'supreme leader,' every saint and sinner in the history of our species lived there—on a mote of dust suspended in a sunbeam."

advocacy, directed Voyager 1 to turn back in 1990 and photograph our planet. At the edge of our solar system, Voyager 1 relayed an image in which Earth was less than a single pixel (0.12 pixel) in size. That was us—a speck. My father's point was that every historical event, every sinner and saint, every loved person—and Voyager started relaying images on Valentine's Day—lived out their lives on this turquoise dot. Some 3.7 billion miles from its source, our planet looks like "a mote of dust suspended in a sunbeam."

Although he died in 1996, my father would also have liked another image, taken 8 May 2003 by the Mars Orbiter Camera of the Mars Global Surveyor, when Earth and Jupiter were aligned with Mars. Earth was about 86 million miles away and Jupiter almost 600 million miles away. Because Earth is closer to the sun than Mars, Earth appears half-illuminated, exhibiting a phase, like the moon: a crescent Earth. Blown up, the image shows our moon, as well as Callisto, Ganymede, and Europa, three of the moons of Jupiter and the inspiration for characters in serial adventure stories my father used to tell me, my brother Jeremy, and our friend David Grinspoon (now a professional astronomer) when we were children.

When my father was a child, his mother took him to the Brooklyn Public Library and introduced him to the librarian so he could get an answer to his question, "What are the stars?" After struggling with a boyhood facial tic, he overcame his shyness to ask the question and a few moments later the librarian, saying she had just the thing, came back with a book on movie stars. Later, he became a television star. In *Cosmos*, he liked to talk about how we are "star-stuff."

. . .

We are not exactly star*dust*. The scientific definition of dust does not distinguish between mite droppings and pulverized diamonds streaming outside a cosmically careening spaceship. But dust must be solid, and stars are gas. Our Milky Way galaxy, with some four hundred billion stars, has a lot of dust. There is cosmic dust—space particles which may be only a few molecules in size—which takes different names depending on its location: intergalactic dust exists between the galaxies; circumplanetary dust around planets, such as in the icy rings of Jupiter and Saturn; interplanetary dust between planets; and interstellar dust between the stars themselves. Solid dust only forms about 1% of the interstellar medium, with hydrogen and helium gas forming most of the rest of it. Hydrogen, as H_2O, is the most common element in our bodies, as well as in stars, which turn it into helium in their core.

We are star-stuff also in the sense that not only hydrogen gas but other elements that come into being inside stars are distributed when they explode. A normal-sized star produces pressures and temperatures that turn hydrogen into heavier helium, but a supernova with twenty to one hundred times the mass of our sun transmutes elements in layers like an onion via nuclear reactions in a natural alchemical process called nucleosynthesis. These elements are recycled when new stars, and planets, form. Our earth formed with the other planets and the sun from a rotating disk of ice, gas, and dust. Near the center of the protosolar nebula, intense pressures and temperatures vaporized debris, sending lighter materials away from the aggregating center and leaving

opposite: A photograph that Carl Sagan would have liked. Image taken by the Mars Global Surveyor on 8 May 2003 when Earth and Jupiter were aligned with Mars. Courtesy NASA/JPL/Malin Space Science Systems.

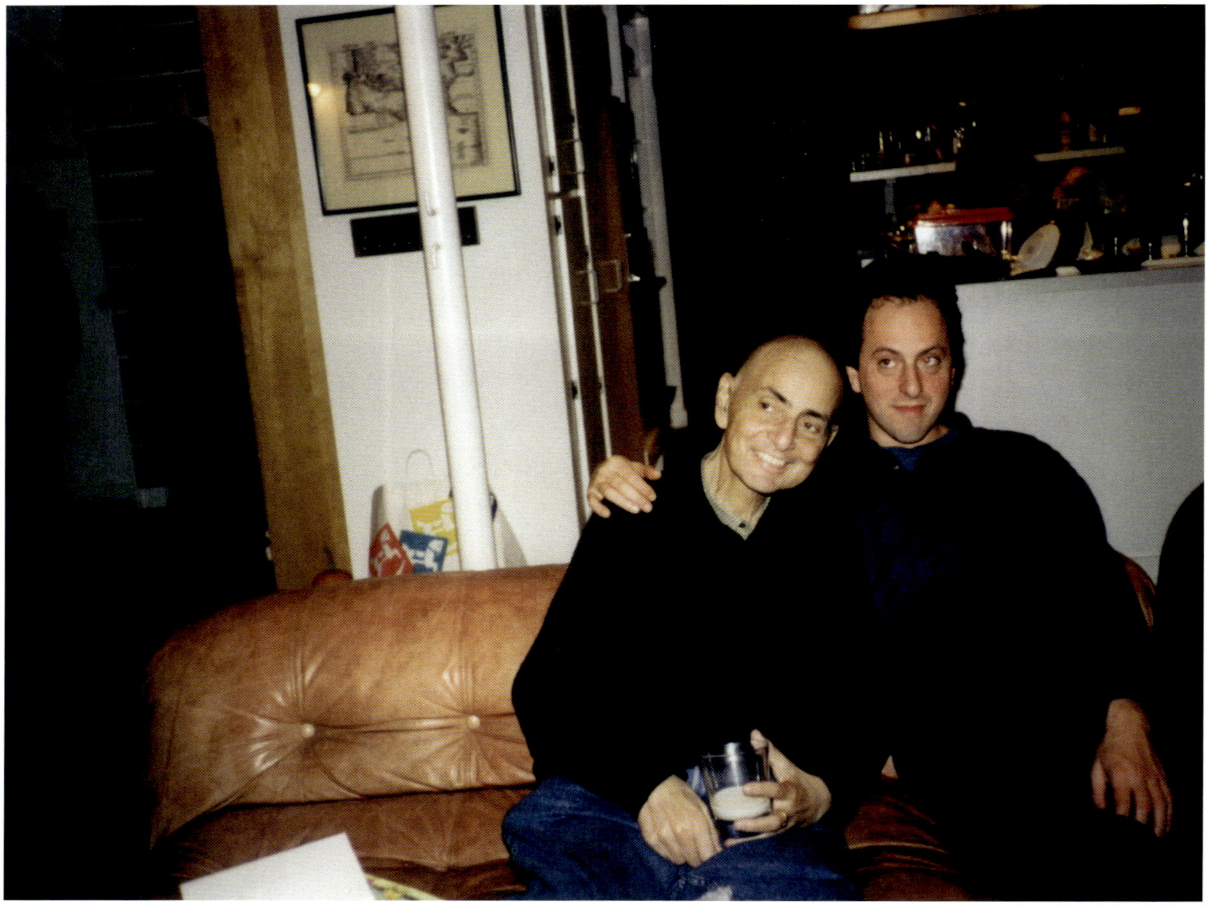

Dorion and Carl Sagan in 1996, shortly before the scientist died of cancer.

grains of rock and dust consisting of heavier elements such as iron, silicon, and carbon to form the inner planets Mercury, Earth, Venus, and Mars, as well as their moons. Sly and the Family Stone were on the same cosmic track as my father when they sang, "Everybody Is a Star."

It would be interesting to deconstruct dust, but dust, as the fragmentary end state of solid matter, is already deconstructed. After the recently contested Iranian elections, in which the Interior Ministry declared Mahmoud Ahmadinejad winner by a "landslide," he tagged protesters as "dust and pebbles" who within "the transparent river of the Iranian nation" would find no place to "shine." The Bible, presciently anticipating modern knowledge of ecological recycling, advises us not to set store on things of this world with its tantalizingly transient treasures, as the matter of our bodies moves from earth to earth, ashes to ashes, dust to dust. But dust deserves its reconstructive due. Here astrobiology helps. It's possible that some dust in space harbors life. Life, as bacteria, can be extremely hardy. Bacteria live in solid rock on this planet a mile beneath Earth's crust. Bacterial spores are resistant to desiccation and radiation, and bacteria show far more metabolic diversity than all animals and plants combined. It is also possible that solar winds can distribute *Horton-Hears-a Who*-sized dust grains containing bacteria across the universe, although they might not survive the cosmic rays. The Greek sage Anaxagoras gave this idea of a cosmos sprinkled with universe-traversing life its name, *panspermia*, from the Greek for "all seeds." Swedish naturalist Svante Arrhenius liked the idea. So did Francis Crick, co-discoverer in 1953 of the structure of the DNA molecule (which discovery, it has recently been reported, was accompanied by the ingestion of low levels of LSD). When my father positively reviewed Crick's version of panspermia, which he detailed in his book *Life Itself*, I protested, "How does moving the problem of life's origin into outer space explain anything? It just transports the location of the problem." He conceded I might be right, but his heart didn't seem in it. In any case, Earth itself is in space, so even if life evolved here, it evolved in space.

Panspermia has the power to reinvigorate our notion of dust from a figure of neglect and unimportance to one of essential substance. Working with Sir Fred Hoyle (who coined the term "Big Bang"), the astronomer Chandra Wickramasinghe found decades ago that the infrared signatures of dust seen in all directions by peering astronomers matches the wavelengths of dried bacteria, suggesting that the cosmos might be full of bacterial dust. More recently, with his colleagues at the Cardiff Centre for Astrobiology, Wickramasinghe calculated that radioactive material such as aluminium-26, injected into our solar system during its formation from shock waves emanating from a nearby supernova explosion, heated the frozen centers of comets to produce subsurface oceans. Provided a liquid medium, bacterial dust may thus have come to life inside these hurling comets. Rocky on the outside, watery on the inside, they invert the composition of playground bullies' rock-filled snowballs. These astral bodies may be legion among the hundreds of billions of comets flying about just in our own solar system. Photos such as those of comet Tempel 1 taken by the Deep Impact probe in 2005 show evidence of ice core melting, which might happen as comets approach stars or burn through atmospheres. So maybe bacterial dust can stow away, sometimes coming to life inside spherical lakes, where they live in the dark inside whizzing comets for perhaps millions of years. And if one of the comets hits—*voilà*! They have light and the opportunity to evolve photosynthesis. Within a starry firmament filled with particles, a cosmos of violence and transformation, everything, even germs careening through space, may someday get the opportunity to shine.

THE MAGIC LAKE

VALERIE SMITH

In the long American tradition of itinerant tradesmen, entertainers, and teachers who made their living traveling across the country, one of the more intriguing figures was that of the wandering artist and instructor. Among the unusual skills in which a nineteenth-century enthusiast could be tutored was the art of drawing on marble dust. A discipline that lay somewhere between novelty, craft, and draftsmanship, these artworks—"monochromatic paintings," as they were later called—were done on various-sized paperboards of relatively thick ply to which a thin white wash of a glue adhesive was applied. Just before the wash dried, a thin layer of marble dust would be evenly sifted over the surface, where it adhered. When the dust had set in the wash, a drawing, usually in charcoal or black crayon, was added.

Known mistakenly today as "sandpaper drawings" for the sparkle and texture the marble dust imparted to their surfaces, these works first began appearing in the US in the mid-1830s, after a book describing the technique—B. F. Gandee's *The Artist, or Young Ladies' Instructor in Ornamental Painting, Drawing, &c.*—was published in London and New York.[1] These drawings seem to have been produced widely, but particularly in the Northeast, and although men also practiced the medium—including famous figures such as Albert Bierstadt—the majority of signed pictures reveal a woman's name. Indeed, draftsmanship was an essential element of every young woman's education, and instruction books such as Gandee's were found in the library of every young lady of breeding—even the Brönte sisters had one. Since there were few women's academies and seminaries at the time, it is probable that the itinerant instructors earned their keep through individual instruction, as well as teaching groups in town halls (which served cultural as well as civic purposes) and the drawing rooms or back parlors of larger private homes.

The motifs of marble dust drawings vary greatly. The predominant sources were penny prints, engraved images featuring landscapes or touristic scenes already found on the walls of many middle-class homes. Sources also included publications such as *Barlett's Classic Illustrations of America: All 121 Engravings from American Scenery*, of 1840, or the inexpensive and popular pictures of New York City printers Currier and Ives.

Of all the subjects marble dust artists drew, the "Magic Lake" is one of the most mysterious. Like many of the artform's themes, this one derived from a print. It was in this way that artists such as Marion Wheelock, a middle-aged woman bed-ridden with tuberculosis, came to draw *The Magic Lake* in the winter of 1853. Her interpretation is faithful to the original source, a print published in the April 1852 issue of *Sartain's Union Magazine of Literature and Art*.[2] The print was designed by James Hamilton and translated into a mezzotint by Sartain himself to illustrate Henry Beck Hirst's poem *The Pilgrim of Love*.

Hirst's verse poem tells the story of Brunhilda, who dreams of a handsome king. In her quest to find her love, she embarks on a journey and meets a hermit who mysteriously knows of her quest. He invites her to rest in his cave and in the morning informs her that the king is in fact a spirit that he can summon. The hermit instructs her to travel to a ruined abbey and throw herself into an open tomb in order to leave the mortal world behind and enter paradise, where her lover awaits.

The Pilgrim of Love—with its "wehr wolves," witches, castles, and kings mixed in with sacred and profane love—satisfied because it was an amalgam of Dante, Wagner, Shakespeare and lesser-known writers such as the Englishman John Graham, whose 1836 poem *Geoffrey Rudel: or The Pilgrim of Love* recounts a Christian crusade in which a love story ends in death. Hirst's tale, with its promise of fulfillment in the afterlife, would obviously have been alluring to the dying Wheelock. But there were many such visions on offer in the former colonies at that time. An enormous groundswell of religious feeling took hold in America during the wave of mid-nineteenth-century "Great Awakenings," in which the question of one's personal faith merged with sociopolitical and pedagogic concerns into a kind of national ethics. Between the third (1830) and the fourth (1857) Great Awakening, Thomas Cole produced his "Voyage of Life" paintings (1840), which were translated into engravings by James Smillie after the artist's death in 1848 and widely distributed in the US. The engravings spread the Christian message of the paintings: God is in nature and it will deliver you. Like Cole's angel, who safely navigates the four stages of Man through the turbulence of life, the spiritual leader in Wheelock's rendering, also drawn between these periods of religious fervor, leads his charge from the darkness to the light of the magic lake and its promised paradise.

1 As a reviewer of Gandee's new technique pointed out, the method had already been identified by William Kingston as "Grecian Painting" in his *The Kingstonian System of Painting in Dry Colors, After the Ancient Grecian Method*. See *The Literary Gazette and Journal of Belles Lettres, Arts, Sciences, &c.*, 7 March 1835, p. 157.

2 Shelley R. Langdale, "The Enchantment of the Magic Lake: The Origin and Iconography of a Nineteenth-Century Sandpaper Drawing," in *Folk Art*, Winter 1998/1999, pp. 52–62.

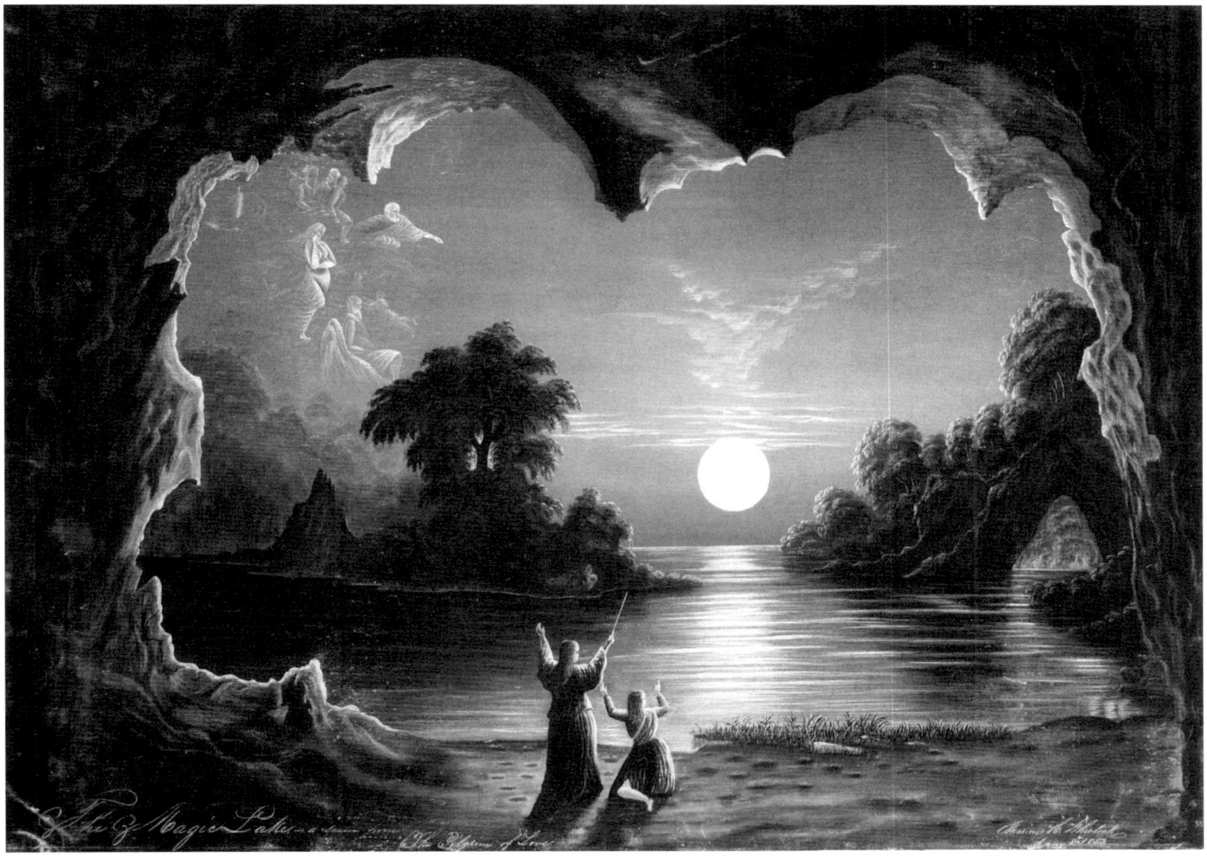

Marion Wheelock, *The Magic Lake*, 1853. All photos Matt Mullican.

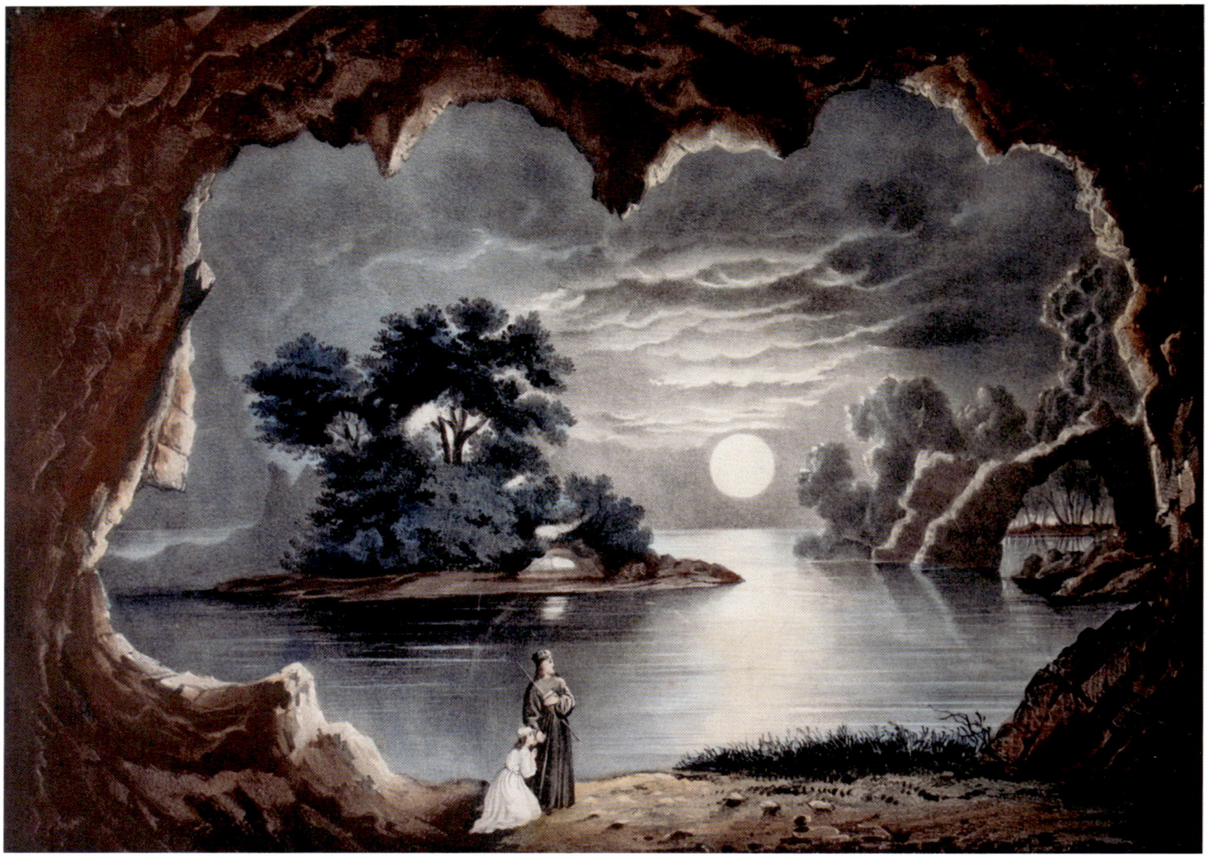

Currier and Ives print featuring the Magic Lake motif, between 1857 and 1872.

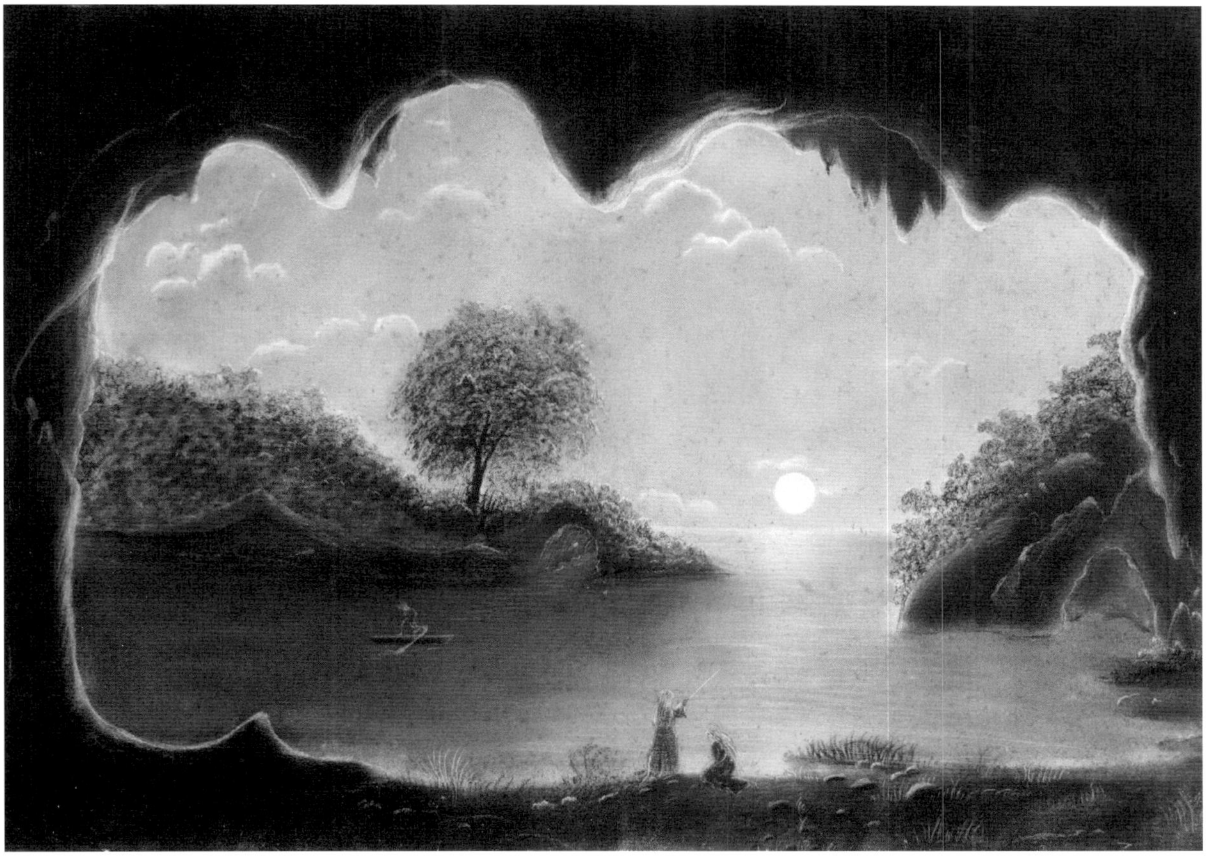

Another variation on the Magic Lake by an anonymous artist, undated.

CABINET BACK ISSUES

Available back issues (pictured below) are $10 each plus postage. Postage rates: US $2.75 per issue; Canada & Mexico $10.40 for 1, 2, or 3 issues; Elsewhere $12.30 for 1, 2, or 3 issues.

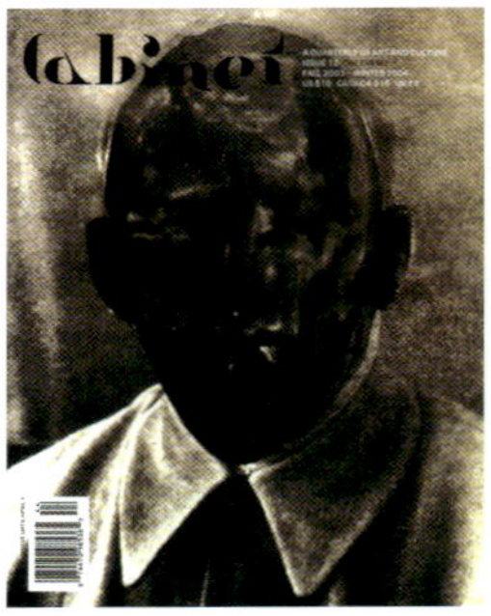

Issue 12 / **The Enemy**

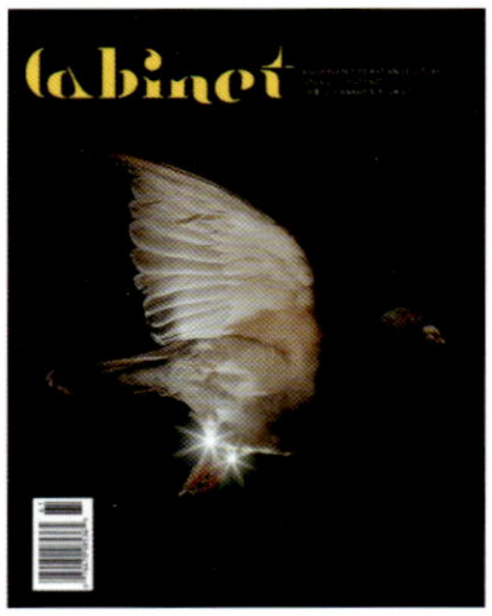

Issue 21 / **Electricity**

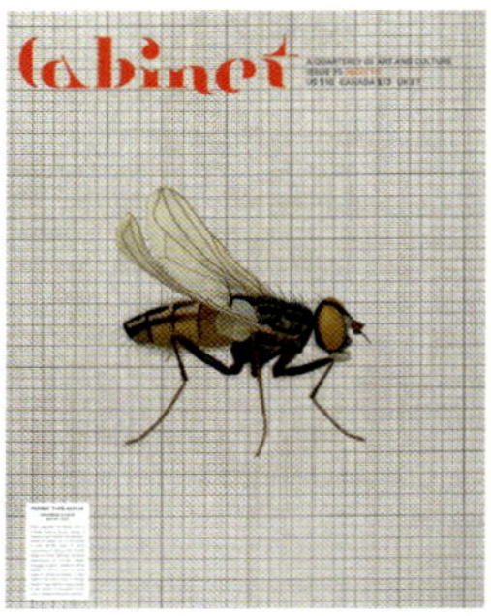

Issue 25 / **Insects**

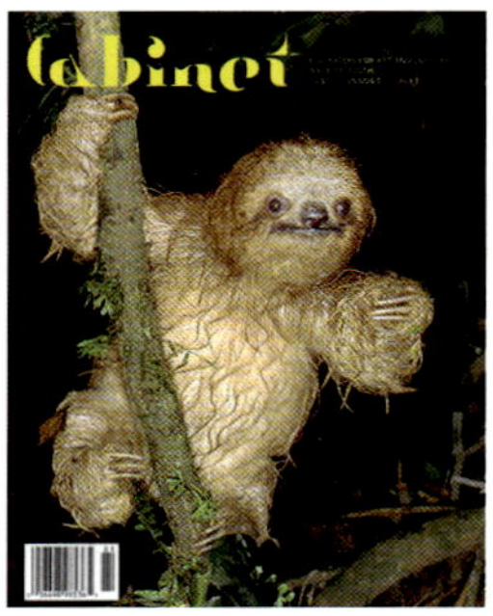

Issue 29 / **Sloth**

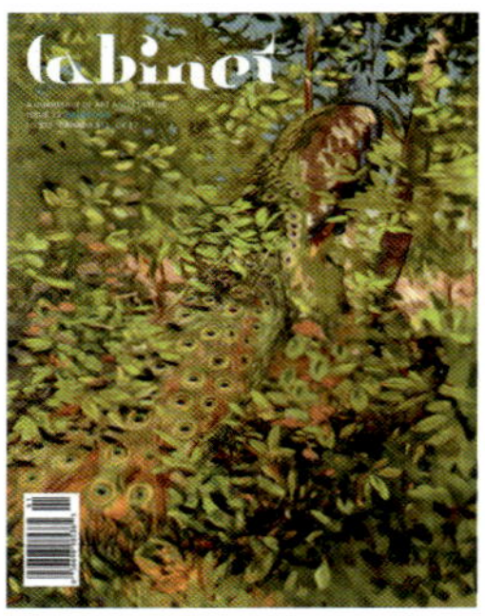

Issue 33 / **Deception**

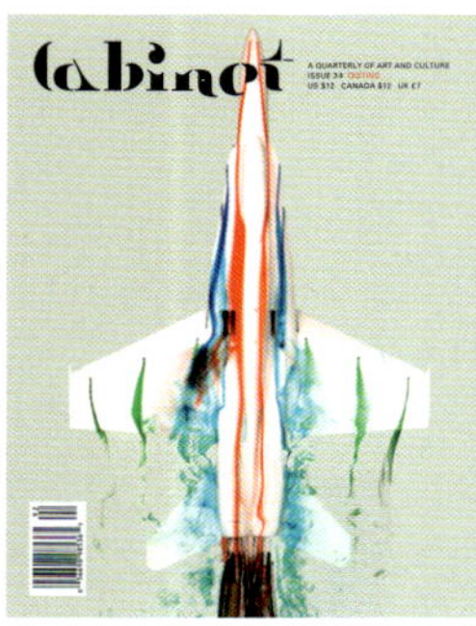

Issue 34 / **Testing**

CABINET BOOKS

Prices in USD including postage.
Current subscribers: Take $5 off prices below.

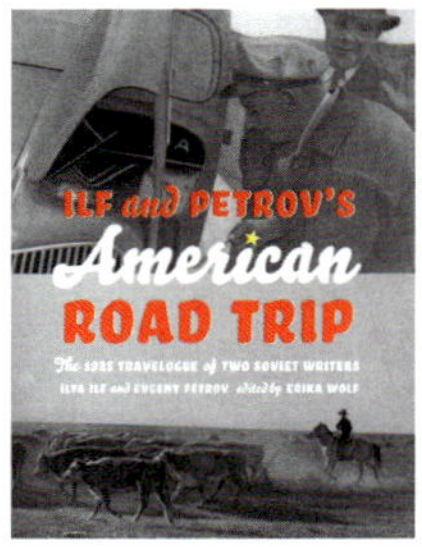

Ilf and Petrov's American Road Trip
The 1935 travelogue of two Soviet writers

US $18; Canada & Mexico $25; Elsewhere $27

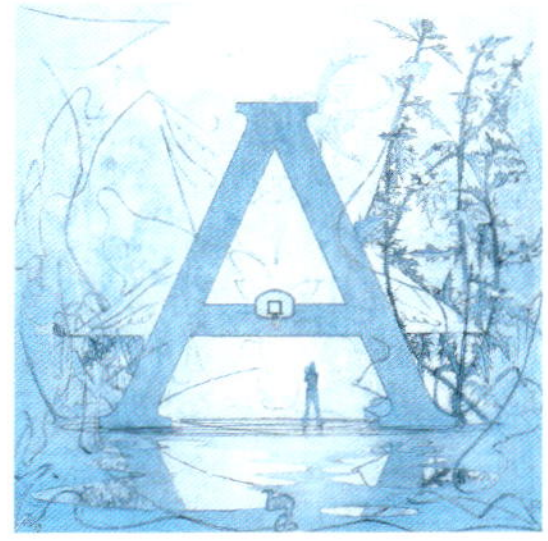

Letters from Mayhem
A board book in the form of an ABC. Illustrations by Roger Andersson; text by Albert Mobilio

US $27; Canada $40; Mexico $45; Elsewhere $50

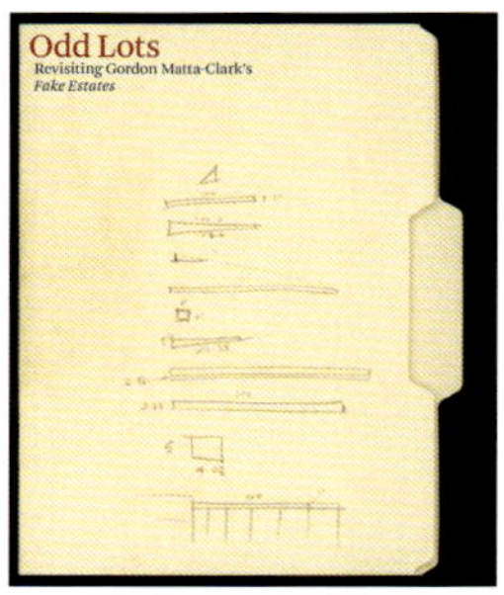

Odd Lots: Revisiting Gordon Matta Clark's "Fake Estates"
Essays and artist projects responding to Matta-Clark's seminal project

US $18; Canada & Mexico $22; Elsewhere $25

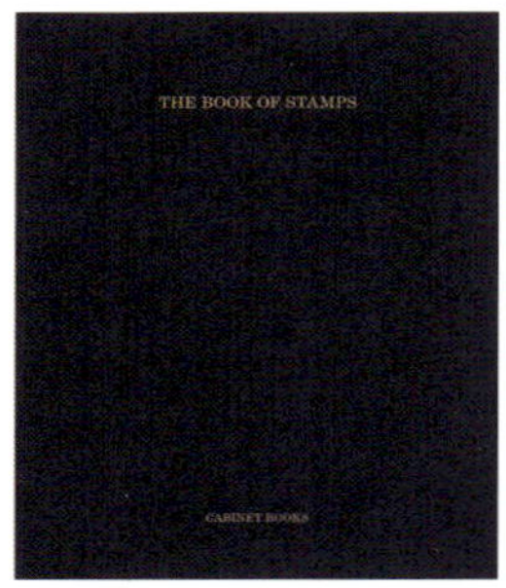

The Book of Stamps
15 detachable sheets of limited edition artist-designed stamps

US $23; Canada & Mexico $30; Elsewhere $33

HOW TO ORDER

1. Mail a check to Cabinet, 181 Wyckoff Street, Brooklyn, NY 11217 USA
2. Shop online at cabinetmagazine.org/shop
3. Fax +1 718 222 3700.
4. Call +1 718 222 8434.

Checks, made out to Cabinet, must be in USD and drawn on a US bank. We also accept Visa, MC, AmEx, Discover, and Paypal (paypal@cabinetmagazine.org) Prices and availability valid through 1 January 2010.

Visit cabinetmagazine.org to view our limited and unlimited editions, posters, and other tchotchkes.